AFTER THE CRASH

ASSESSMENT AND TREATMENT OF
MOTOR VEHICLE ACCIDENT SURVIVORS

AFTER THE CRASH

ASSESSMENT AND TREATMENT OF
MOTOR VEHICLE ACCIDENT SURVIVORS

EDWARD B. BLANCHARD, PhD
EDWARD J. HICKLING, PsyD

AMERICAN PSYCHOLOGICAL ASSOCIATION
WASHINGTON, DC

First printing July 1996
Second printing November 1997

Published by the
American Psychological Association
750 First Street, NE
Washington, DC 20002

Copies may be ordered from
APA Order Department
P.O. Box 92984
Washington, DC 20090-2984

In the United Kingdom and Europe, copies may be ordered from
American Psychological Association
3 Henrietta Street
Covent Garden, London
WC2E 8LU England

Typeset in Palatino by Typo·Graphics, Orlando, FL

Printer: United Book Press, Baltimore, MD
Cover designer: Minker Design, Bethesda, MD
Technical/Production editor: Tanya Y. Alexander

Library of Congress Cataloging-in-Publication Data
Blanchard, Edward B.
    After the crash : assessment and treatment of motor vehicle
accident survivors / Edward B. Blanchard and Edward J. Hickling.
        p.   cm.
    Includes bibliographical references and index.
    ISBN 1-55798-424-7 (acid-free paper)
        1.Traffic accident victims.   2.Traffic accidents—Psychological aspects.
3.Post-traumatic stress disorder.   I. Hickling, Edward J.   II. Title.
RC1045.P78B56   1997
616.85'21—dc21   97-5336
                                                                                   CIP

British Library Cataloguing in Publication Data
A CIP record is available from the British Library.

Printed in the United States of America

To John, my favorite MVA survivor.
EBB

To Linda, Matthew, and Michael for being
there and being you.
EJH

Contents

Section Three: Treatment for Survivors

Acknowledgments

There are many people who have helped make this book a reality. First of all, we would like to acknowledge Grants MH-48476 and MH-55478 from the National Institute of Mental Health (NIMH), which underwrote most of this research. In addition, we would like to acknowledge the assistance and support of three of the staff of the Violence and Traumatic Stress Branch of NIMH: Dr. Ellen Gerrity, Dr. Susan Solomon, and Ms. Phyllis Gordon.

Next, we would like to thank the various University at Albany graduate students who worked on this project: Alisa Vollmer, Shannon Turner, Catherine Forneris, Kristine Barton, Jackie Jones-Alexander, and Janine Walsh. Two graduate students were especially helpful as the book was being prepared by running analysis after analysis and finding interesting details. Our special thanks to Ann Taylor and to Todd Buckley. We also thank Dr. Warren Loos and Dr. Rob Gerardi for assessing part of the participants in this project.

Finally, we would like to acknowledge and thank Ms. Sandy Agosto, who typed numerous drafts of chapters and who served a central coordinating role throughout the project.

Prologue: The Case of Mary J.

Moments before her fateful crash, Mary signaled for a left turn and moved into the left lane. She pressed her foot on the brake, waiting for oncoming traffic to clear, and was pleased to see very few cars in the parking lot. "I should be in and out in 10 minutes," she said to herself.

Suddenly, Mary saw headlights in her rearview mirror. The next thing she felt was a tremendous blow to the rear of her car. She felt her neck snap back and then her body lurch forward against the shoulder belt. She also saw out of the corner of her eye a large oncoming car bearing down on her.

"No!" she remembers screaming just before the other car struck her right front fender. At that moment she was afraid she'd be killed. She also saw the other driver's look of surprise and horror just before they hit.

Another crash, the sound of crunching metal, violent jerking from side to side, and then the tinkling of glass as it fell to the pavement. Mary was thrown against the seatbelt and then against the post supporting the roof.

She immediately became aware of pain in her neck and shoulders and on the side of her head. Next, she realized that her right ankle hurt and that she couldn't get her right foot loose.

She thought, "My beautiful car is smashed; it's ruined." Mary really loved the car. Her parents had made the down payment as a graduation present, and she had paid it off in 3 years. She had been pleased to have no monthly car payment.

Only a few minutes earlier, at 4:30 p.m. on Friday, Mary had closed up her desk, shut off her computer, and put on her boots and heavy coat. As she was leaving, she saw her supervisor, Karen, and said, "Remember that I am taking the day off on Monday and won't be in."

All case examples in this book have been modified to prevent ready identification of the participant; however, important facts are accurate. At times the case material represents a composite of cases to illustrate a point in the text.

"Oh yes, have a good trip. It looks like you'll have fresh snow on the mountain."

"Thanks."

Mary walked across the employee's parking lot to her car, unlocked the driver's door to her white Escort, and got in. It started on the first try; "Good car," she thought. She picked up the snow brush and got out to clear her windows. She brushed the 2 inches of new snow off her front and back windows and then cleared the side windows.

"There," she said to herself, "at least I can see." It was snowing fairly heavily and was already dark. She gave the driver's window one more brush, got in, and buckled her seatbelt.

She left the parking lot and headed up Manning Boulevard to cut over to Washington Avenue. Traffic was moving steadily as she made the left turn onto Washington Avenue. She did notice a little skidding as she made the turn.

Traffic was moving at a moderate pace on Washington Avenue; the cars seemed to be turning the snow to slush. She thought again how much she liked her car: The heater worked very well, the windshield wipers were doing their job, and WQBK came in clear on the stereo speakers.

After passing the university, traffic began to thin out and speed up. Mary thought, "this isn't as bad as I thought it would be."

On impulse she decided to stop for Chinese take-out at Lee's. That would save time when she got home. Besides, there wasn't much in the refrigerator.

Just as the weather forecast had predicted, it had started to snow in the middle of the afternoon on Friday. Mary heard about the snow from a co-worker. Although she had spent 27 winters in Albany, and did not look forward to driving home in the snow, she considered herself a good winter weather driver.

"It will take me an hour to get home," she thought, "and then I'll be behind." She reviewed her plans for leaving town Saturday morning for a long weekend of skiing at Sugarbush. "I have to get home, do my laundry and my grocery shopping tonight, and then pack for the trip."

"Oh, well, I'll just stay up until midnight so everything will be ready when Tim, Bob, and Judy come by at 6:00 a.m. to get me."

Then in her usual optimistic way she said to herself, "At least there will be fresh powder on the slopes."

After the crash, Mary's thoughts of her ski trip were replaced by a growing awareness of her pain. As Mary was fighting the pain, she noticed someone at her car window. She rolled down the window part way. "Are you all right? Are you all right?" the man yelled. As she struggled to gain composure she grew more aware of the pain in her ankle, neck, and shoulders.

Through the partially opened window she said, "I can't get my foot loose, and my ankle hurts." Then she added, "and my neck hurts too."

The stranger told her, "See if you can open your door and I'll help you get out."

Mary tried the door handle, but nothing happened. The door was jammed! She felt a bit panicky and trapped.

The stranger said, "Just try to sit still. We've called the police and an ambulance."

Mary then noticed the large blue Buick that had hit her on the right side, and she could see people standing around that vehicle.

The stranger said, "My name's Ed; just try to stay still and help will be here in a minute. Can I call anyone for you?"

Mary's thoughts were racing. "I'm still alive." "How can I reach Tim and get him to help?" "Oh shit, my vacation is ruined." "Oh no, my beautiful car." "God, my ankle and neck are really hurting."

Finally, the stranger's questions penetrated. "Can I call anyone?" she heard.

She stammered, "call Tim B. at 534-2407," and then she said, "call my mother, Ellen J., at 439-6189," and she began to tear up and cry.

Ed asked, "Are you all right?"

Mary replied, "Nooo! My ankle hurts and my car is ruined," and then the tears came.

Ed was replaced by another stranger, a woman. She said, "Don't cry, honey. Help is on the way."

Next, Mary heard a siren in the distance. The rescue squad arrived first, followed by the police.

A woman in a fireman's suit and hat came to the window. She said, "My name is Betty. What is your name?"

"Mary J."

"How are you, Mary? Are you hurt?"

"Yes, my foot is trapped, and my right ankle hurts and so does my neck and shoulders—and my head hurts."

Betty said, "I want you to sit very still. I'm going to reach in and roll the window down. Then I'm going to put this collar around your neck to stabilize your head. Okay? Then we are going to get you out of the car, okay? Things will be all right, but I want to stabilize your head and neck first."

Mary felt a bit reassured by Betty's calm manner and mumbled, "Okay." Then Betty reached through the window and put the collar carefully in place, all the time reassuring Mary.

Next, Betty tried to open the car door by reaching inside. It was stuck.

Betty called to another fireman, "Fred, we're going to need the Jaws of Life to get this door open. It's stuck."

"Okay," yelled Fred.

Betty began to take down information, name: Mary J.; age: 27; address: 12 Pinedale Court West. "Who should we call?"

"My mother, Ellen J., at 439-6189. I asked the other fellow to call her."

Betty reassured Mary, "I'm going to stay here with you until we can get you out and into the ambulance."

Fred and another fireman brought over a large tool. Betty explained, "We are going to have to pry the door loose from the frame. It will sound awful, but it won't hurt you."

The door was forced open with a terrible screech of metal. Betty reached in to check on Mary's foot, and freed it.

Then Betty and Fred carefully removed Mary from the wrecked car and put Mary on a backboard. Her head was stabilized, and the strap was tightened around her forehead. Her lower right leg was also stabilized in an air cast. Out of the corner of her eye Mary saw the mangled wreck that had been her car, and she sobbed again.

Her mother arrived, looking fearful. "Are you all right?" She exclaimed.

"No," Mary said, "my ankle and neck hurt," and with a sob, "my car is ruined."

At 6:35, almost two hours after she had left, Mary was at St. Peter's Hospital, arriving by ambulance at the emergency room.

X-rays revealed a broken right ankle, which was put in a cast, but no structural damage to her neck and upper back. She was given a set of crutches, a soft collar, a 3-day prescription for Tylenol with codeine, and a follow-up appointment with the orthopedist and told to rest in bed as much as she could. After a brief debate, she agreed to go home with her mother rather than to her own apartment.

With this accident, Mary J. joined the more than 3 million Americans who in 1993 were involved in a personal injury motor vehicle accident. She joined our study two months later and was found to meet the criteria for posttraumatic stress disorder (PTSD). Her symptoms that were consistent with PTSD included intrusive memories of the accident, frequent and severe distress at reminders of the accident, some mild flashbacks, and frequent distressing dreams about the accident that awoken her. She also was exerting moderate effort to avoid thoughts about the accident; she avoided driving except when absolutely necessary and did not drive at all if the weather was threatening; she had diminished interest in activities she had previously enjoyed; she felt estranged from her friends and family to some degree; and she had a restricted range of affect in that she no longer felt the warmth and affection she had previously felt for most people. In addition, she was having almost nightly sleep disturbance, noticeable irritability, and hypervigilance on a daily basis; she had difficulty concentrating and had become easily startled and jumpy. Finally, she reported feeling her heart pound and her palms become sweaty when in a car that was in close traffic. She had a Clinician Administered Post-Traumatic Stress Disorder Scale (CAPS)[1] score of 86. She had not been able to return to work, although she was back in her own apartment. She still wore an elastic brace on her ankle for support. Her whiplash injury was still extremely bothersome and prevented her from

---

[1] The CAPS is a structured interview for assessing PTSD. It is described in detail in chapter 4.

returning to work (she had tried to go into work twice, 2 weeks before calling us, and could not last the day because of the pain). She had not returned to driving because she had no vehicle, and she was anxious when riding with others.

At the 6-month follow-up Mary J. still met the full criteria for PTSD, with a CAPS score of 65. She had not been able to return to work and was becoming desperate financially. She was driving an older, used car her parents had helped her buy. She was very fearful of losing her apartment, as her savings were almost depleted. At this point she also met the criteria for a major depressive episode.

At the 12-month follow-up, Mary J.'s appearance and overall manner of presentation had improved; the depression had lifted. She was back to work. Her CAPS score was 14, and she no longer met the criteria for PTSD, despite testing positive for distress when exposed to events that reminded her of the accident, avoidance of thoughts related to the accident, some sleep difficulty, and some continued exaggerated startle response.

This case typifies the motor vehicle accident (MVA) survivors we have studied. The chapters that follow will flesh out the psychological assessment and treatment work on this large, but under-studied, population.

Section One

Quantifying the Problem

1

Introduction and Overview

Involvement in motor vehicle accidents (MVAs) is a wide-spread experience for Americans. As chapter 2 details, each year over 1% (3,386,000 in 1995) of the American population is involved in a serious (personal injury) MVA. Moreover, a large-scale survey has shown (Kessler, Sonnega, Bromet, Hughes, & Nelson, 1995) that MVAs are the most frequent trauma for American males (25% lifetime) and second most frequent trauma for American females (13.8%). Moreover, Norris (1992), in another large-scale survey, found that MVAs were the single leading cause of PTSD in the general population.

Despite the prevalence of MVA-associated trauma, the psychological assessment and treatment of the road crash survivor has been little studied in America. Interestingly, there has been fairly widespread study of the MVA survivor in other countries over the past 10 years. There are active research groups in Norway, The Netherlands, the United Kingdom (at least three groups), Australia (two groups), and Canada (two groups).

This book describes the details of a 5-year study of MVA survivors in the Albany, New York, area and thus fills a gap in the knowledge base of this common phenomenon. Moreover, we have tried to summarize and integrate the results from this worldwide array of research groups with our own findings to present a comprehensive view of what is known about the survivors of serious MVAs.

PTSD and MVA Survivors

PTSD has been much studied since it was introduced in the *Diagnostic and Statistical Manual of Mental Disorders* (*DSM–III*; American Psychiatric Association [APA], 1980) with numerous books appearing on the broad topic and on special segments of the PTSD population. Four primary populations of trauma victims have been studied for PTSD: combat veterans, particularly veterans of the Vietnam war (these individuals are mostly male and were typically studied 10 to 25 years post-trauma; sexual-assault victims (these are almost exclusively female and were studied within either days or weeks of the trauma or more than 5 years post-trauma—for treatment); survivors of natural disasters (these are approximately equally representative of both genders and have been studied acutely and over long-term follow-up); and adult survivors of child sexual and physical abuse.

MVA survivors present a different population in many ways: (a) Males are typically as frequently represented as females so that potential gender differences in response to trauma and response to treatment for PTSD can be studied. Historically, there are few data on the treatment of males with PTSD of relatively short (months) duration. (b) Frequently, there are lingering physical injuries in this population, which offers an opportunity to study what role (potentially negative) physical injury plays in treatment and recovery. (c) The MVA survivor with PTSD is frequently involved in litigation so that studying this population can enable us to learn, in part, what role litigation plays (see chapter 10) in recovery. (d) Finally, as Norris (1992) has documented, MVA survivors with PTSD constitute a large population, and their similarities and differences with other PTSD populations needs to be elucidated.

Scope of the Book and Its Organization

This book covers four cross-cutting conceptual themes. First, we identify the *scope of the problem* in chapters 2, 3, and 4 to try to arrive at an answer to the question, "What proportion of motor vehicle accident survivors develop PTSD?" In this section, as in all sections, we present two answers to the questions: (a) the best answer we can find in the worldwide English language literature and (b) the answer we find from our own research data. We then try to reconcile these two responses if they are markedly different. In this first section, we also present a description of the population we studied and our methodology (chapter 4).

The second broad theme is a description of the *short-term psychosocial consequences* of having been in a serious MVA, covered in chapters 5, 6, and 11 (devoted to acute stress disorder) of Section 2. Again, we summarize our results and those from the literature.

The third theme is the *short-term history of MVA-related PTSD* (chapter 7) and factors that can influence this, such as physical injury (chapter 9), litigation (chapter 10), and delayed-onset PTSD (chapter 8).

In the third section of the book we turn from assessment to treatment. Thus, our fourth conceptual theme, *psychological treatment of the MVA survivor with PTSD*. Again, we try to review the English language literature (chapter 14) and then present our own treatment procedures and their results. The conceptual underpinning of our approach to treatment is presented in chapter 13. Chapters 15 and 16 present treatment procedures in great detail as well as uncontrolled data on the effectiveness of these treatments.

Clinical Hints

For the most part, this book is an accurate description of what we did, what we found, and how it fits into what is known from other sources. Thus, we have tried to make empirically based conclusions. However, scattered throughout the book are clearly labeled *clinical hints*. These are impressions that cannot be backed up firmly with data or suggestions of what to do when available data give no guidance. We hope they are useful.

As is obvious from the citations and references herein, we have published much of our data from the Albany MVA Project in piecemeal fashion over the past 3 to 4 years. In this volume we attempt to pull all of that data together in an integrated fashion. At the same time, we have tried to summarize, fairly, the English language literature on this topic and to integrate our data and the literature.

For Whom Was This Book Written?

We foresee three broad audiences for this book. First, we expect that those *psychologists, psychiatrists* and other *mental health professionals* who assess and treat the survivors of serious MVAs will find much value in this book. We have tried to describe our procedures fully so that others can incorporate them. Moreover, we describe our population carefully so that the clinician can determine whether his or her patient is similar. We provide MVA survivor norms on the psychological tests we used in chapter 5 and an empirically validated, step-by-step treatment regimen in chapter 16.

Second, we believe this book may be of value to *attorneys* who handle MVA survivor cases. Again, we describe what we would expect to find acutely and over at least a 1-year follow-up for MVA survivors in terms of psychosocial status. We also address the effects of litigation on the clinical course (chapter 10).

Third, we believe the *physicians* who treat MVA survivors—the orthopedists, the physiatrists, and the primary care physicians — can find value in this book, as they are likely to encounter at least 1 of the 3 million Americans per year who is involved in a serious MVA. We also believe the psyche and the soma interact in the long-term healing process (see chapter 9) and that physicians can optimize their care of the MVA survivor by being aware of the psychological issues likely to be present among MVA survivors.

Finally, we hope that this book sparks interest among researchers, both those who are established and their students. We provide some answers but realize we raise many questions. The survivors of serious MVAs are a large population that should be studied more.

2

The Magnitude of the Problem

Epidemiology of MVAs

MVAs are widespread in the United States as well as in all of the rest of the industrialized world. In fact, they are so ubiquitous that one could guess that the majority of American men will experience at least a minor MVA by age 30 and that many of their female counterparts will join them in this experience. Precise data are not available on the total number of MVAs occurring in the United States each year, although it is estimated that annually over 1% of the American population experience an MVA.

If we move from the minor MVA in which there is only some property damage (those we colloquially call "fender benders") to those more serious MVAs in which one or more individuals are injured enough to seek medical attention, then reasonable estimates are available from the U.S. Department of Transportation (DOT). Furthermore, the DOT has precise data on the number of MVAs resulting in fatalities and the number of individuals killed. Table 2-1 presents a summary of the data from the DOT on the estimated number of personal injury MVAs, number of persons injured, number of fatal MVAs, and number of fatalities from 1990 to 1995.

We have focused our own research on individuals who were injured in MVAs (driver, passenger, or pedestrian in which the vehicle was an automobile, truck, bus, or motorcycle) and who

Table 2-1

U.S. Department of Transportation Nationwide Summaries of Personal Injury Accidents and Fatal Accidents for 1990–1995

Year	Estimated no. of personal injury MVAs	Estimated no. of persons injured	No. of fatal MVAs	No. of fatalities
1990	2,122,000	3,231,000	39,836	44,599
1991	2,008,000	3,097,000	36,937	41,508
1992	1,991,000	3,070,000	34,942	39,250
1993	2,005,000	3,125,000	35,780	40,150
1994	2,092,000	3,215,000	36,223	40,676
1995	2,166,000	3,386,000	37,221	41,798

Note: Data From *Traffic Safety Facts 1994: A Compilation of Motor Vehicle Crash Data From the Fatal Accident Reporting System and General Estimates Systems.* National Highway Traffic Safety Administration, U.S. Department of Transportation, August 1995. (Supplemented with 1995 data.)

sought medical attention for those injuries within 48 hr of the accident. Thus, we considered a *serious motor vehicle accident* one in which one or more of the individuals involved was injured sufficiently to seek medical care. In this way we have excluded individuals involved in "minor" MVA from participation in our research (although we know of instances in which even this kind of accident has had noticeable psychological effects).

As we have sought to present our own research on MVA victims, a frequently raised issue has been the "seriousness of the accident." To the best of our knowledge there are no validated scales of accident severity. One could try to rank severity in terms of property damage: The greater the property damage, in all likelihood, the higher the speed of impact. However, degree of property damage is confounded by the value of the vehicle and by the number of vehicles involved and thus does not seem very useful. One could try to rate severity in terms of the total number of vehicles involved, total number of individuals involved, or total number of individuals injured. The last two of these are probably related.

If by *seriousness* one means the extent of physical injuries to the victim (which can be scaled) or the extent of psychological distress suffered by the victim, one could use these constructs. However, it becomes tautological to attempt to determine whether serious MVAs lead to PTSD because that would mean that MVAs, which lead to great psychological distress, cause PTSD.

One could also restrict *serious* to MVAs in which there is a fatality. This seems too restrictive because the number of MVAs involving fatalities are thankfully rare in comparison with personal injury MVAs, about 1 to 55 (see Table 2-1).

Our solution was to label an accident as *serious* if one of the individuals involved sought medical attention and to restrict our study sample to individuals who themselves sought medical attention.

It came to our attention that Bryant and Harvey (1995), working in Australia, have published a 5-point scale of MVA severity: 1 = *no injury*, 2 = *mild injury not requiring hospitalization*, 3 = *injury requiring hospitalization for less than 2 weeks*, 4 = *injury requiring hospitalization for more than 2 weeks*, and 5 = *the MVA involved a fatality.* This scale is thus tied in part to physical injury severity and to recuperation rate. There are better ways to scale injury severity (e.g., using the Abbreviated Injury Scale [AIS], described at length in chapter 3), which do not confound it with recuperation. Moreover, hospital admission and length of stay may be determined by third-party payer parameters rather than by injury parameters. No data are yet available on this scale regarding reliability (which should be very high) or validity.

Epidemiology of PTSD

One of the major potential consequences of serious MVAs is, of course, PTSD. Although psychological morbidity resulting from traumatic events has long been recognized, it was only with the publication of the *DSM–III* (APA, 1980) that major professional attention began to focus on this condition. (We might also note that "serious MVAs" were one of the stressors of "traumatic events outside the range of normal human experience," listed in the *DSM–III*).

Estimates of the incidence and prevalence of PTSD in the general U.S. population have varied widely. The largest American epidemiologic study devoted to mental disorders (Regier et al., 1984), the Environmental Catchment Area (ECA) study, assessed approximately 21,000 individuals across five geographic sites (New Haven, CT; Baltimore, MD; Durham, NC; St. Louis, MO; and Los Angeles, CA). Trained lay interviewers used the Diagnostic Interview Schedule (DIS) to conduct individual face-to-face interviews (Robins, Helzer, Croughan, & Ratliff, 1981; Robins, Helzer, Croughan, Williams, & Spitzer, 1981). The original DIS did not include questions specifically designed to detect PTSD. However, Helzer, Robins, and McEvoy (1987) added several questions to the DIS related to the respondent's having experienced an event that frightened him or her and that led to one or more PTSD symptoms (as defined in the *DSM–III*).The rapidity with which the symptoms began after the event, their duration, and their frequency were assessed in the 2,493 face-to-face interviews.

Helzer et al. (1987) found a prevalence of PTSD of 5 per 1,000 men and 13 per 1,000 women, for a population lifetime prevalence of about 1%. Only 5 of the 1,000 cases of PTSD were due to serious accidents, indicating that lifetime PTSD from MVAs is very infrequent.

This very low lifetime prevalence of PTSD from all causes has been criticized because of the assessment methodology; research has shown that the original DIS was relatively insensitive to PTSD in a Vietnam veteran population (Kulka et al., 1990).

Norris (1992) conducted a telephone survey of 1,000 adults in four southern cities, with a response rate was 71%. Half of the sample was male, half female; moreover, half was White and half Black. Research participants also were evenly balanced among young (18–39), middle-aged (40–59), and older (60+). Norris assessed lifetime occurrence of nine traumatic events. This was followed by a series of questions (the Traumatic Stress Schedule) to determine whether the individuals met the *DSM–III–R* (3rd ed., rev., APA, 1987) criteria for PTSD following the trauma. She found a lifetime prevalence of 7.4 per 100 for PTSD from all causes. Most relevant to us, 23.4% had experienced an MVA during their lifetime, 2.6% in the past year. Overall, 69% of participants had experienced some qualifying traumatic event in their lifetime and 21% in the past year.

Of those who experienced a serious MVA, 11.5% met the criteria for PTSD; for those who had been in an MVA within the past year, the value was 9.5%, meeting criteria for PTSD. Norris commented specifically on the relative high rate of PTSD possible from MVAs, which she calculated to be 2.7 per 100 lifetime.

Breslau, Davis, Andreski, and Peterson (1991) assessed by telephone interview 1,007 young adults (ages 21 to 30) who were enrolled in a health maintenance organization (HMO) in Detroit. The assessors were trained lay interviewers in the use of the DIS. Attention was paid to the possible occurrence of eight specific stressors, including "serious MVAs"; diagnoses were based on *DSM–III–R* (APA, 1987) criteria. Breslau et al. found that 39.1% of respondents had suffered at least one traumatic event (and 3.6% three or more traumatic events). They found that 9.2% of the total population had developed PTSD (23.6% of those suffering any traumatic event). In addition, 9.4% were involved in serious

MVAs, with 11.6% of those developing PTSD in approximately equal proportions for men and women. This led to a lifetime prevalence (for this young population) of 1.09 per 100 for PTSD, secondary to serious MVA with injury.

The National Co-Morbidity Survey

A major new American psychiatric epidemiology study, the National Co-Morbidity Survey (NCS), has recently been described (Kessler et al., 1994). Lifetime and 12-month prevalence estimates of 14 *DSM–III–R* (APA, 1987) psychiatric disorders were obtained by trained lay interviewers using the Composite International Diagnostic Interview with a sample of 8,098 individuals (ages 15 to 54). The survey was conducted from 1990 to 1992 by trained interviewers who were closely supervised; the sample demographics were designed to mirror the U.S. population.

Especially relevant to this book's topic was detailed assessment of lifetime prevalence of specific traumatic events suffered by the sample (and an open-ended "other traumatic event question") and subsequent assessment for possible PTSD using *DSM–III–R* criteria (Kessler et al., 1995). Respondents were asked to select their most upsetting traumatic event and assessed for the development of PTSD secondary to this event. Finally, they were asked the length of time (weeks, months, years) the symptoms of PTSD persisted for this event. Thus, the duration data are retrospective. Assessment for a large number of possible co-morbid conditions was also carried out. As is readily acknowledged in Kessler et al.'s (1995) report, the possibility of developing PTSD from other experienced traumatic events, other than the one identified as most traumatic, was not assessed.

Relevant to our concerns are the number of individuals who acknowledged being involved in a life-threatening accident (it is not clear whether all accidents were MVAs). Twenty-five percent of the men ($n = 703$) and 13.8% of women ($n = 422$) admitted to having been in life-threatening accidents. (The gender difference in prevalence is significant.) For men in life-threatening accidents, 44.6% selected it as the most traumatic event; for women the value was comparable, 44.5%. Finally, 6.3% of men who had life-threatening accidents developed PTSD ($n = 314$), as did 6.8% of their female counterparts ($n = 188$). These rates did not differ statistically. In fact, this value is probably an underestimate because the possibility of developing PTSD from a serious MVA was not assessed if the participant identified some other trauma as more serious. Moreover, despite careful attention to assessment of the experience of various trauma, in many instances the trauma occurred many years earlier so that the assessment for subsequent PTSD was retrospective by many years. Nevertheless, these data seem to indicate that, at a minimum, 1.6% of men and 1.2% of women will meet the criteria for PTSD secondary to a serious MVA over their lifetime.

The overall survey found that women who were exposed to any extreme trauma were more than twice as likely as men to develop PTSD (20.4% for women compared with 8.2% for men, $p = .001$). Of all of the male cases of PTSD ($n = 139$) identified in the NCS, 12.1% were due to accidents; for the 320 women with PTSD, 5.1% were due to accidents. Interestingly, of the male participants with a lifetime history of PTSD, 88.3% met the criteria for at least one other disorder; for women, the co-morbidity rate was 79%.

Finally, in the retrospective examination of remission of PTSD from all causes, there was a significant advantage for having received mental health treatment (but not necessarily for PTSD) up to about 6 years post-trauma. Beyond that point, about 40% of the sample continued to have PTSD as long as 10 years post-trauma. At 1 year about 30% had remitted, whereas at 2 years it was close to 40%. Remission rates specific to accident victims with PTSD were not available.

We believe the lifetime prevalence values, multiplied by the population of the United States from the last three studies (1% to 3%) gives some indication of the size of the potential problem, 2.5 to 7 million cases in the United States alone. Thus, we have a sizeable mental health problem in this country that has been all but ignored by American researchers and perhaps by the mental health treatment community. We hope this book will begin to reverse that neglect.

3

What Percentage of MVA Survivors Develop PTSD?

We address the question posed by this chapter by examining how such an answer has evolved in the literature. As diagnostic criteria and assessment tools have become more sophisticated, the resulting picture of MVA-related PTSD has begun to shift, too. This chapter begins by examining the pre-*DSM–III* (APA, 1980) literature, the post-*DSM–III*, and the epidemiological surveys and by providing a brief overview of our Albany MVA data. We also attempt to reconcile differences among the other studies and between the other studies and our own results to accurately represent the true picture of PTSD among survivors of serious MVAs.

The Pre-*DSM–III* Literature

Since the term *post-traumatic stress disorder* (PTSD) was introduced to the American mental health community in 1980 with the publication of the *DSM–III* (APA, 1980), it has made a useful demarcation in the literature. Prior to 1980, much of the psychological and psychiatric literature did not have great precision in its diagnostic labels. Nevertheless, there was a descriptive literature on MVA survivors. Table 3-1 provides a summary of this literature.

In Table 3-1 one finds little solid information based on current diagnostic standards. Modlin's (1967) report is probably the most

Table 3-1

Rates of PTSD in MVA Samples Evaluated Prior to DSM–III

Authors/country	Description of sample	MVA	M/F	Age	How assessed	Results
Thompson, 1965 United States	500 cases of "post-accident neurosis" evaluated for litigation	N/R	N/R	N/R	Clinical interview (DSM–I)	406 cases of anxiety state 25 cases of phobic neurosis 156 cases of superimposed depressive neurosis (52% improved with no Tx)
Modlin, 1967 United States	40 cases of "post-accident syndrome" out of 150 referred for evaluation for litigation	N/R	27/13	17–62	Clinical interview	Good, stable premorbid functioning; Sx: Anxiety, tension, irritability, impaired concentration repetitive nightmares, anhedonia, withdrawal, startle hypervigilant. (Probably PTSD 27%)
Allodi, 1974 Canada	50 cases referred for evaluation for accident litigation	30%	N/R	N/R	Clinical interview	98% had accident neurosis

| Parker, 1977
Australia | 750 cases referred
for evaluation of
accident litigation
296 with neurosis | N/R
(about half) | 170/126
57.4% | N/R | Clinical
interview | 12% had "traumatic"
neurosis for MVA
survivors
35% anxiety
35% phobia
34% irritability
18% anhedonia
15% insomnia |
| Mendolson, 1982
Australia | 101 accident victims
referred for evaluation
or treatment | 42/101
42% | N/R | N/R | Clinical
interview | 25/42 MVA victims
returned to work prior
to settlement |

Note: N/R = not reported; M/F = male/female. Tx = treatment; Sx = symptom.

useful, for of the 40 cases (of 150) he highlighted all appear to meet current criteria for PTSD. Otherwise, we are left with the author's diagnostic impression in the absence of symptomatic criteria. We find estimates of "accident neurosis" or "traumatic neurosis" ranging from 98% (Allodi, 1974) to 12% (Parker, 1977) of accident survivors who were evaluated because of litigation. (However, about a third of Parker's MVA survivors had symptoms consistent with PTSD.) One other point stands out in terms of possible pre-accident psychopathology. Although Modlin identified a group with good, stable premorbid functioning that developed PTSD, Parker (1977) reported that 20% of his sample had pre-accident neurotic symptoms, whereas Allodi (1974) found evidence of pre-accident "neurotic proneness" in 24% of his sample. Incidentally, almost all of the accident survivors reported in Table 3-1 were involved in compensation litigation. We return to this topic in chapter 10.

The Post-*DSM–III* Literature

Tables 3-2 and 3-3 list the studies that provide potential answers to the titular question. In Table 3-2 all of the samples consisted of either treatment-seeking individuals or individuals who were referred to mental health professionals for medicolegal evaluation.

An examination of Table 3-2 reveals that samples referred for mental health evaluation or treatment tended to yield a fairly high percentage of cases with PTSD, from a low of 14.5% (Golberg & Gara, 1990) to 100% in two treatment samples (Burstein, 1986, 1989; Kuch, Swinson, & Kirby, 1985). The average across nine samples was 59.9%. Almost all of the diagnoses were ascertained by clinical interview; almost all used objective criteria from *DSM–III* ($n = 5$) or *DSM–III–R* ($n = 2$). One ambiguous result is that of Brom, Kleber, and Hofman (1993) who assessed a Dutch sample solely by a Dutch version of the Impact of Event Scale (IES). We have taken their 22% who had severe symptoms (total scores greater than 30) to indicate PTSD. Unfortunately, the IES does not assess the hyperarousal symptoms so a precise estimate is hard to determine.

Table 3-3 provides a description of all of the other non-treatment-seeking samples, although it presents a somewhat different picture of prevalence of PTSD following an MVA. Values ranged from 0.9% (Malt, 1988) to 100% (Kuch et al., 1994). This latter study might belong in Table 3-2 because all participants were suffering from chronic pain. Across the eight studies, the average value was 29.5%. If we eliminate the very low value from Malt's study and the very high value from Kuch et al. (1994) from the remaining five studies we find an average of 26.4%.

All of the studies but two (Bryant & Harvey, 1995, 1996) used *DSM–III* or *DSM–III–R* criteria, and many used structured clinical interviews of demonstrated reliability and validity. Bryant and Harvey (1996) identified 31% of their hospitalized MVA survivor sample as scoring in the high IES (>30) range. In their earlier study Bryant and Harvey (1995), surveying formerly hospitalized MVA survivors 1 year after the MVA, found 41% were still "cases" (noticeably distressed and disturbed) on the basis of a General Health Questionnaire (GHQ) score of <3. Using their IES score of >30, 46.4% still had notable post-traumatic symptoms. (We address the possible diagnosis of PTSD using the IES in chapter 5.)

An interesting feature of the studies summarized in Table 3-3 is that 8 of 9 participants were hospitalized patients. Patients who were hospitalized, even for a brief (1 to 2 days) period, tended to be more seriously injured. It is not clear whether the 62 whiplash injury cases included in Mayou et al.'s (1993) 188 cases had been admitted to a hospital.

An examination of the low rate outliers (studies by Malt, 1988, in Norway and by Mayou et al., 1993, in the United Kingdom) reveals that part of the explanation for the low rate of case finding could lie in the diagnostic instruments used. Malt and colleagues (Malt, 1988; Malt et al., 1989; Malt et al., 1993) used clinical interviews or questionnaires. Mayou et al. used the Present State Examination (PSE; Wing, Cooper, & Sartorious, 1974) a well-known structured psychiatric interview. It could be that the PSE is not especially sensitive to PTSD. Samples clustering around the average mostly used structured psychiatric interviews. They came from the United Kingdom, Australia (*n* = 2), and the United States.

Table 3-2

Rates of PTSD Found in Treatment/Evaluation Seeking MVA Survivors

Authors/ country	Sample description	% MVA	M/F	M	Age range	Time since MVA	How assessed	Diagnostic criterion	PTSD
Kuch et al., 1985 Canada	30 MVA victims referred for evaluation (18) or treatment (12)	100	8/22	N/R	N/R	N/R	Clinical interview and questionnaire	DSM–III	100%
Tarsh & Royston, 1985 United Kingdom	35 cases of "accident neurosis" assessed for insurance claims; gross somatization	25	18/17	42	28–58	5 yr.	Clinical interview	N/R	N/R
Burstein, 1986 United States	19 MVA victims referred for treatment	100	4/15	37.5	N/R	29 wks	Clinical interview	DSM–III	100%
Platt & Husband, 1986 United States	31 MVA victims, referred for evaluation re: legal suits	100	9/22	37	18–63	7.4 mo.	Clinical interview	DSM–III	77.4% 24/31
Hoffman, 1986 Canada	98 accident victims referred for evaluation by lawyers	Some	N/R	N/R	N/R	N/R	Clinical interview	DSM–III	10.2% 10/98

26

Study	Sample	% MVA	Gender	Mean age	Age range	Time since accident	Assessment	Criteria	PTSD rate
Jones & Riley, 1987 Australia	327 accident victims referred for evaluation by lawyers (180 MVA)	55.7	58.6% male	N/R	N/R	N/R	Semi-structured clinical interview	DSM–III	12 clear cases of PTSD from MVA 6.7%
Burstein, 1989 United States	70 MVA victims referred for treatment	100	N/R	N/R	N/R	N/R	Clinical interview	DSM–III	100%
Goldberg & Gara, 1990 United States	55 MVA victims referred for evaluation/31 had lawsuits pending	100	14/41	37	N/R	15 mo. (2–60 mo.)	Clinical interview	N/R	14.5%
Horne, 1993 Australia	7 MVA victims seeking treatment	100	2/5	31.3	26–37	23 mo. (7–45 mo.)	Clinical interview	DSM–III–R	43%
Datal & Harrison, 1993 United Kingdom	56 MVA victims referred for evaluation by lawyers	100	N/R	N/R	N/R	2.7 yr. (1.3–7.0)	Interview	DSM–III–R	32.1%
Brom et al., 1993 The Netherlands	151 victims of "serious MVA" out of 738 solicited by letter to participate in treatment research	100	89/62	37.5	N/R	N/R probably weeks	Dutch IES	N/R	22% had severe Sx

Note: N/R = not reported. IES = Impact of Event Scale. Sx = symptom.

Table 3-3

Rates of PTSD Found in Unselected Samples of MVA Victims

Author/ country	Sample description	MVA	M/F	Mean and Age range	Time since MVA	How assessed	Dx Criterion	PTSD
Malt, 1988 Norway	113 hospitalized accident victims	46%	75.7% male	36.2 15–69	Within days of injury	Clinical interview/IES, STAI GHQ-20	DSM–III/ ICD–9	1% (3 cases with PTS-Sx)
Malt, et al., 1989 Norway	551 adults with accidental injuries who were hospitalized (out of 683, 83.5%)	43.6% 240	N/R	N/R 15–69	3 yr.	Questionnaire	? 26.7%[a] had some DSM–II	Dx
Feinstein & Dolan, 1991 United Kingdom	48 hospitalized PTS with leg fractures. Reassessed at 6 wks. and 6 months	56.3	34/14	30.5 16–60	~ 1 wk.	Clinical interview Questionnaire for PTSD Sx at FU	DSM–III–R	25% at 6 wks 14.6% at 6 mo.
Green et al., 1993 Australia	24 of 69 hospitalized MVA victims. Reassessed at 1 mo. and 18 mo.	100%	19/5	N/R	~ 1 wk.	DIS, GHQ	DSM–III–R	at 1 mo. 2/24 PTSD 7 sub-PTSD at 18 mo. 6 PTSD 1 sub-PTSD

Study	Sample	%	Sex	Age	Time	Measure	Dx criteria	Results
Mayou et al., 1993 United Kingdom	188 of 200 consecutive MVA victims admitted to hospital (includes 63 whiplash only) Reassessed at 3 mo. and 12 mo.	100%	68% male	30.1 18–70	9 days	PSE	DSM–III–R	14/174 8% at 3 mo. 19/171 11.1% within 1 yr.
Malt et al., 1993 Norway	192 MVA victims who were hospitalized	100%	N/R	N/R 15–69	3 yr.	Clinical interview GHQ-20	N/R	Less than 5%
Epstein, 1993 United States	15 PTS hospitalized in trauma center. Reassessed every 10 wks. for 9 months	N/R (most)	10/5	34.4 20–82	Few days	Structured interview	DSM–III–R	40% (6 total cases within FU)
Kuch et al., 1994 Canada	55 MVA victims with minimal injury and chronic pain	100%	19/36	38.0 N/R	2 yr. or longer	SCID for PTSD and phobia	DSM–III–R	100%
Bryant & Harvey, 1995c Australia	56 hospitalized MVA victims (of 131)	100%	45/11	34.4 15–79	1 yr.	IES and GHQ	None GHQ > 3 high IES score	41% GHQ > 3 46.4% IES > 30
Bryant & Harvey, 1996 Australia	114 successive (post-traumatic amnesia of <1 day) hospitalized MVA victims	100%	82/32	29.3 16–60	1–15 days	Questionnaires IES, STAI, & interview	None (high IES scores)	31% had high IES (> 30)

Note: N/R = not reported. Dx = diagnosis; Sx = symptom; STAI = State–Trait Anxiety Inventory; GHQ = General Health Questionnaire; PSE = Present State Examination. FU = follow-up; DIS = Diagnostic Interview Schedule; ICD = International Classification of Diseases. SCID = Structured Clinical Interview for *DSM–III–R*.
[a] data not certain.

Epidemiologic Surveys

In chapter 2, we presented a detailed review of four American epidemiologic surveys that focused on PTSD. Their results are summarized in Table 3-4. Again, we find a range of values, with Breslau et al.'s (1991) survey of young urban adults yielding the lowest lifetime prevalence of involvement in serious MVAs. This is understandable given the attenuated age range.

The two more representative epidemiologic studies reveal that being involved in a serious MVA over one's lifetime is a fairly common occurrence for Americans, 19.4% according to Kessler et al. (1995) and 23.4% according to Norris (1992). We also found that a fairly sizable proportion of individuals who were in MVAs and found them traumatic developed PTSD: 6.5% of MVA victims in Kessler et al.'s study compared with 11.5% in Norris's study. The lower value from Kessler et al. (1995) could be resultant of a failure to assess for PTSD when the respondent nominated another event as more traumatic than the MVA. There is no way to know from these epidemiologic studies the extent to which the MVA survivors who were studied had been injured and whether they had been hospitalized. The average value from the two studies—about 9% of MVA survivors developing PTSD—is certainly within the range of values reported in Table 3-3.

The Albany MVA Project

We present our data on the Albany MVA Project in detail in chapter 4. However, for the purposes of this discussion we must jump ahead somewhat. Among the 158 MVA survivors we assessed, 62 (39.2%) met the criteria for PTSD 1 to 4 months post-MVA on the basis of the CAPS interview, and another 45 (28.5%) met the criteria for subsyndromal PTSD. Moreover, 8 of those with inital subsyndromal PTSD developed full PTSD during the follow-up, giving us a total of 70 (44.3%) cases of PTSD in the sample. (Delayed-onset PTSD is discussed in chapter 8.) Ours was not a

Table 3-4

Summary of Motor Vehicle Accident Related PTSD From American Epidemiologic Surveys

| Authors | Sample | | Diagnostic instrument | Rate of MVAs | Rate of PTSD from MVAs | Overall rate of PTSD |
	Size	How selected				
Helzer et al., 1987	2,493	ECA sample in St. Louis; face-to-face interview	DIS + extra Quest. *DSM–III*		0.5/1000 overall	5/1000 male 13/1000 female
Breslau et al., 1991	1,007	HMO member in Detroit; telephone interview	DIS *DSM–III–R*	9.4/100	11.6/100 1.09/100 overall	9.2/100
Norris, 1992	1,000	Adults in 4 southern cities 50% male 50% Black; telephone interview	Traumatic Stress Schedule *DSM–III–R*	23.4/100	11.5/100 3% overall	
Kessler et al., 1995	5,877	National probability sample; telephone interview	Composite International Diagnostic Interview *DSM–III–R*	25/100 male 13.3/100 female	6.3/100 male 8.8/100 female 1.6% male 1.2% female overall	5.0/100 male 10.4/100 female

treatment-seeking sample or a sample referred for specific medicolegal evaluation. About half of the participants were referred from various practitioners, whereas the other half were self-referred based on advertisements, media coverage, and so forth.

The values given above were based on *DSM–III–R* (APA, 1987) criteria using a "rule of 3" on CAPS items to decide whether or not a symptom was present to a sufficient degree to be counted. These are the criteria that we used and discuss throughout this book. The results of using modified diagnostic criteria (*DSM–IV*) or modified scoring rules for the CAPS are presented in Table 3-5 ("rule of 4" rather than "rule of 3"; see chapter 4 for details).

One can see from Table 3-5 that the fraction of the sample changes as PTSD changes somewhat with differing diagnostic criteria. *DSM-IV* added the requirement (A-2) that the subjective reaction to the traumatic event be one of "intense fear, helplessness or horror." This change leads to a 10% decrease in the number of individuals who meet the full diagnostic criteria. Likewise, changing the scoring rule on the CAPS leads to a 15% decrease.

If we compare our Albany results (39.2%) for rate of developing PTSD initially from an MVA, we are on the high side for non-treatment-seeking samples (average 29.5%; see Table 3-3). Moreover, whereas all of our sample had sought medical attention as a result of the MVA, only 24 (15.2%) were actually admitted to a hospital; another 94 (59.5%) were seen in the emergency room and released. It could be that our relatively high level of case finding is due to the diagnostic instrument we used, the CAPS. Perhaps it is more sensitive to cases of PTSD.

Most of the non-treatment-seeking samples were seen initially within a few days of the MVA, and many were followed up on one or more occasions. The follow-up is, of course, necessary to establish the diagnosis of PTSD because the diagnosis requires that symptoms be experienced for at least 1 month. In our Albany study we delayed the initial assessment at least 1 month post-MVA to be certain the individual could meet the temporal requirement.

To return to our opening question, it appears that 10% to 45% of survivors of serious MVAs (defined as one in which someone

Table 3-5

Rates of PTSD Among Albany MVA Project Participants as a Function of Diagnostic Criteria

| | | | Diagnosis | | | | |
| Diagnostic criteria | PTSD | | Subsyndromal PTSD | | Non-PTSD | |
	Frequency	%	Frequency	%	Frequency	%
DSM–III–R CAPS rule of 3	62	39.2	45	28.5	51	32.3
DSM–III–R CAPS rule of 4	53	33.5	34	21.5	71	45.0
DSM–IV CAPS rule of 3 (ignore criterion A-2)	61	38.6	44	27.8	53	33.5
DSM–IV CAPS rule of 3 (with criterion A-2)	55	34.8	50	31.6	53	33.5

is injured sufficiently to require medical attention) may develop PTSD either acutely or within a year of the MVA. This wide range of percentages highlights the large degree of mental and emotional suffering resulting from MVAs in this country.

Section Two

Psychological Effects of MVAs

4

The Albany MVA Project

A s mentioned in chapter 1, we studied a cohort of survivors of serious MVAs for about 5 years. Under the aegis of a grant from the National Institute of Mental Health (NIMH), from September 1991 through May 1996, we recruited and assessed 158 survivors of recent MVAs and followed them for 1 year or longer. We also assessed 93 individuals who matched our MVA sample demographically but who had not been involved in an MVA, even a minor fender bender, within the previous year. In this section we present basic descriptive information on our MVA victim sample and the controls, and we describe the assessment procedures in detail. Thus, any reader who seeks to apply our assessment procedures and our norms can find the detailed description of what was done.

Entry Criteria

To be included in the study the individual had to have been in an MVA 1 to 4 months prior to the assessment, had to have sought medical attention within 48 hours of the MVA, and had to be at least 17 years of age. We chose the interval of 1 to 4 months post-MVA for two reasons: First, an individual must be symptomatic for at least 1 month to meet the *DSM–III–R* criteria for PTSD (APA, 1987). Thus, our research participants could be legitimately diagnosed, whereas other prospective studies of traumatized populations (e.g., Rothbaum, Foa, Riggs, Murdock, & Walsh, 1992) cannot legimately make a diagnosis of PTSD for assault survivors 1 to 2 weeks post-assault because insufficient time has elapsed since the trauma. Likewise, studies that accrue samples of MVA survivors in emergency rooms (e.g., Mayou, Bryant, & Duthie, 1993), or while they are acutely hospitalized (e.g., Bryant & Harvey, 1996; Epstein, 1993), cannot make the diagnosis of PTSD at those points.

Although ideally we would have assessed everyone at the 1-month anniversary, this was not possible in a community volunteer sample. We set an arbitrary window of 1 to 4 months to see participants close in time to the MVA.

Second, we were very interested in learning how the participants evaluated themselves prior to the accident. Many studies of individuals with PTSD have made attempts to assess, retrospectively, the participant's pretrauma status. We feared that living with PTSD for many months or even years could affect the participant's pre-MVA recollections. We compromised by allowing a maximum of 4 months to elapse between the MVA and initial assessment. In assessing pre-MVA psychopathology, we have the advantage that our instrument, the Structured Clinical Interview for *DSM–III–R* (SCID; Spitzer, Williams, Gibbon, & First, 1990), was designed to assess lifetime psychopathology and is judged to do so adequately.

The MVA Survivor and Control Samples

The demographic characteristics of our sample are reported in Table 4-1. We divided the MVA sample into three subgroups which seem helpful as will become apparent in coming chapters: those with full PTSD, those with what we termed subsyndromal PTSD—positive for Criterion B (*reexperiencing symptoms*) and either Criterion C (*avoidance* and *psychic numbing*) or Criterion D (*hyperarousal*), but not both—and non-PTSD (positive for only one criterion or none of the criteria).

The data in Table 4-1 shows that the non-MVA controls matched the overall MVA sample well on basic demographic variables of age, gender, and ethnicity. The controls were

Table 4-1

Demographic Characteristics of Subsamples of Motor Vehicle Accident Survivors and Controls

Characteristic	MVA victims			All MVA victims	Non-MVA controls
	PTSD	Subsyndromal PTSD	Non-PTSD		
Gender (M/F)	13/49	14/31	23/28	50/108	28/65
% male in subsample	21.0	31.1	45.1	31.6	30.1
Age M(SD)	34.8 (11.2)	35.4 (11.7)	36.2 (14.7)	35.4 (12.5)	37.7 (14.0)
Range	18–73	17–65	17–71	17–73	20–78
Ethnic Status					
Caucasian/minority	50/12	42/3	48/3	140/18	84/9
% minority in subsample	19.4	6.7	5.9	11.4	9.7
Education Level					
High school or less	14	13	14	41	11
Some college through BA	29	19	27	75	41
Graduate training	19	13	10	42	41
CAPS score M(SD)	59.4 (21.4)	29.9 (11.2)	9.6 (7.8)	—	—

somewhat better educated. The percentage of the sample that was minority (African American, Asian, and Hispanic) matches the 1990 U.S. Census value (about 10% of adults) for minorities in the four counties surrounding Albany.

Two other points show up in these basic demographics: There were significantly more women in the MVA–PTSD subgroup (79%) than in the other two subgroups combined (61.5%), χ^2 (1, $N = 158$) = 5.38, $p = .020$. Minorities were disproportionately represented in the MVA–PTSD subgroup (19.4%) compared with the other two subgroups combined (6.3%), $\chi^2(1, N = 158)$, = 6.41, $p = .011$.

The gender finding is consistent with data from the NCS (Kessler et al., 1995), which also found women disproportionately represented among trauma survivors who developed PTSD over their lifetime: 5.0% of men versus 10.4% of women.

Two other basic characteristics of our sample should be noted: Among all participants, 149 (94.3%) were either drivers or passengers in the automobile or truck involved in the accident, 6 were pedestrians, 2 had been riding bicycles and were struck by motorized vehicles, and 1 was on a motorcycle. Among the 149, 120 were drivers, whereas only 29 were passengers. One hundred eighteen (74.7%) of our sample were initially treated in an emergency room, whereas the others saw a variety of health care providers after their MVA. Of the 118, 24 (15.2% of the total MVA sample) were admitted to the hospital.

Over half of the sample was referred by local health care practitioners and the rest were self-referred on the basis of advertising or local media coverage. Referral sources were asked to bring the project to the attention of all MVA survivors (readily identified in New York because of no-fault insurance as the third-party payer) not just those in obvious distress. We do not know what proportion of those informed of and referred to the project followed up on the referral.

All participants (MVA survivors and controls) were paid for their participation: $50 for the first interview and first follow-up and $75 for the second (12-month) follow-up. We do not know what bias the payment may have introduced. We do believe the honorarium was an important incentive for a portion of the population, especially those with low family income. In fact, we might not have been able to attract the latter without the incentive. (It works out to about $6 to $7 per hour, including travel time.)

The Assessment Procedures

The bulk of our assessments were structured interview schedules administered by trained and experienced doctoral-level interviewers. All four assessors were doctoral-level psychologists, each of whom had over 5 years of experience assessing Vietnam veterans for possible PTSD. We describe the assessments in the order in which participants experienced them.

The MVA Interview

We developed a structured interview to assess details of the MVA, immediate physical and medical consequences and treatments, subjective reactions to the accident, and effects of the MVA on subsequent travel behavior. A copy of the MVA Interview is contained in Appendix A.

The interview begins by having the participant tell his or her account of the accident, including details of the circumstances leading up to the accident. We paid special attention to individuals' thoughts and sensory experiences to have the raw material for the idiosyncratic audiotapes used in the psychophysiological assessment (described in chapter 12). For our sample, 35 (22.2%) were single vehicle accidents, 98 (62%) involved two vehicles, and 25 (15.8%) three or more vehicles.

Clinical Hint

We believed it was very important for the participant to tell his or her story first and in great detail (after all, the incident is what brought them to the study).

We made no attempt to check on the veracity of the participant's report but found no obvious reasons to doubt them. We also had promised the participants confidentiality and that we would send a copy of our full report to any professionals of their choosing, free of charge, with their written permission. Participants typically had the opportunity to review the full written report before it was committed to our files.

In assessing the impact of the MVA on travel behavior, we paid special attention to two points: (a) whether travel behavior (post-MVA) was foregone or endured with great distress and (b) whether the avoidance was due to physical limitations (e.g., unable to drive because of a broken leg or no vehicle yet available to replace the damaged one) or to psychological limitations. These results are reported in chapter 5.

The Role of Alcohol and Drugs

Our sample was probably atypical of all injured MVA survivors in that only 8 (5.1%) admitted to being under the influence of alcohol or drugs at the time of the accident. In 16 instances, our participants were fairly certain that the other driver had been using alcohol or drugs, on the basis of police reports or observations at the time of the accident.

Clinician-Administered PTSD Scale (CAPS)

We next administered the CAPS, a structured interview for assessing the symptoms of PTSD, developed by personnel at the National Center for PTSD (Boston Branch; Blake et al., 1990a).[1]

Psychometric evaluations showed test–retest reliabilities among the three independent clinician assessors of .90 to .98; the internal consistency alpha was .94. Validation of the CAPS versus the Mississippi Scale for PTSD was .91, and the SCID PTSD module was .89 (Weathers, Blake, et al., 1992; Weathers & Litz, 1994). One of the psychologists who participated in the development of the CAPS trained the other three assessors in its use.

For each of the 17 symptoms of PTSD the CAPS assesses both a frequency of occurrence (or percentage of time or of relevant

---

[1]Information on the availability of the CAPS and of the newer version, adapted to *DSM–IV,* can be obtained from Frank Weathers, National Center for PTSD, Behavioral Science Division (Boston), 150 South Huntington Avenue, Boston, MA 02130.

activities for which the symptom is present) over the past month and the severity of symptoms at their worst over the previous month. Both frequency and severity are rated on a 0 to 4 scale; an individual symptom can have a score of 0 to 8 and a total CAPS score (sum of all 17 symptom scores) of 0 to 136 (our MVA-PTSD subgroup had a mean CAPS score of 59.4; see Table 4-1). In addition to ratings of symptoms and a diagnosis, the CAPS also obtains ratings of overall impairment in vocational and social spheres and overall severity.

We adopted the scoring rule that the total CAPS score for a symptom had to equal 3 (either a 2 on frequency and 1 on severity or a 1 on frequency and 2 on severity) or greater for the symptom to count toward the presence of PTSD. Thus, items that had a score of 1-1 (2) were not counted as clinically meaningful. An internal analysis of data from 100 cases showed slight differences in verifiers (role impairment) if one used a rule of 3 rather than rule of 2. Moving to a rule of 4 (scores of 1-3, 2-2, or 3-1 on an individual symptom) for a symptom to count for the diagnosis identifies a significantly more impaired and distressed group (Blanchard, Hickling, Taylor, Forneris, et al., 1996).

To give one a clearer sense of what our MVA subgroups were like in terms of PTSD symptoms, in Table 4-2 shows the percentages of each MVA subgroup that was positive for each of the 17 symptoms.

We compared the three subsamples by nonorthogonal chi-squares: One compared those with full PTSD to the syndromal PTSDs; the other compared the syndromal PTSDs to the non-PTSDs. The probabilities for these comparisons are in Table 4-2.

Table 4-2 presents five specific findings: First, the major difference between the survivors with full PTSD and those with the syndromal form of PTSD lies in the Criterion C symptoms of avoidance and psychic numbing. The two groups of survivors were markedly different on all seven symptoms. Second, these two survivor groups were not different on five of six hyperarousal symptoms; only on impairment of concentration did they differ significantly. Third, the full PTSDs and syndromal PTSDs differed on three of the four reexperiencing symptoms (at <.05) with flashbacks being the common symptom.

Table 4-2

Percentages of Motor Vehicle Accident Survivors Who Were Positive for Each of the 17 Symptoms of PTSD at Initial Assessment

Symptom	MVA subgroups			Comparisons			
		Subsyndromal		PTSD vs. Sub-PTSD		Sub-PTSD vs. Non-PTSD	
	PTSD $(n=62)$	PTSD $(n=45)$	Non-PTSD $(n=51)$	χ^2	p	χ^2	p
Reexperiencing symptoms							
1. Intrusive recollection	67.7	35.6	07.8	10.88	.00100	11.13	.00090
2. Distress at reminders	96.8	84.4	13.7	5.15	.02330	48.01	.00000
3. Flashbacks	43.5	42.2	03.9	0.02	.89120	20.52	.00001
4. Recurrent distressing dreams	51.6	31.1	05.9	4.47	.03450	10.44	.00120
Avoidance & numbing symptoms							
5. Avoid thoughts/ feelings	83.9	26.7	09.8	35.50	.00000	04.66	.0308

	Col1	Col2	Col3	Col4	Col5	Col6	Col7
6. Behavioral avoidance	75.8	35.6	09.8	17.45	.00003	09.28	.00230
7. Event amnesia	38.7	04.4	11.8	16.64	.00005	01.68	.19530
8. Loss of interest/ anhedonia	74.2	11.1	09.8	41.60	.00000	00.04	.83430
9. Estrangement	72.6	0.0	7.8	56.37	.00000	03.68	.05500
10. Emotional numbing	62.9	6.7	5.9	34.58	.00000	00.03	.87410
11. Foreshortened future	37.1	2.2	0.0	18.23	.00002	01.15	.28450
Hyperarousal							
12. Sleep disturbance	69.4	60.0	23.5	01.01	.31520	13.18	.00030
13. Irritability/anger	79.0	62.2	17.6	03.65	.05600	20.05	.00001
14. Difficulty concentrating	74.2	31.1	13.7	19.65	.00001	04.23	.03980
15. Hypervigilance	53.2	68.9	15.7	2.66	.10280	28.05	.00000
16. Exaggerated startle	66.1	60.0	13.7	0.42	.51550	22.38	.00000
17. Physical reaction to reminders	75.8	62.2	13.7	2.30	.12980	24.27	.00000

Turning to the comparisons of individuals with subsyndromal PTSD and those classified as non-PTSD, we find significant differences on all four reexperiencing symptoms and on all of the hyperarousal symptoms. Finally, those with subsyndromal PTSD had more avoidance, both of thoughts and feelings and of situations, than those with non-PTSD. In essence, individuals with subsyndromal PTSD tended to have reexperiencing symptoms and hyperarousal symptoms. They had markedly less avoidance than those with full PTSD and very few psychic numbing symptoms.

Table 4-2 shows that less than half of the sample with PTSD acknowledged having 3 of the 17 possible symptoms of PTSD. These three included flashbacks (43.5%), event amnesia (38.7%), and sense of foreshortened future (37.1%).

Table 4-3 presents the distribution of total CAPS scores for all three MVA survivor subgroups. This information can serve as norms on total CAPS scores for others working with MVA survivors.

Table 4-3 also reveals that a few of our survivors who met the full criteria for PTSD were not very symptomatic. Also, there is a substantial overlap of total CAPS scores between the upper third of those with syndromal PTSD and those who met the full criteria. As is detailed in chapter 8, some of these individuals with syndromal PTSD were found to develop delayed-onset PTSD during the follow-up.

CAPS Reliability Check

We sought to establish interrater reliability on the CAPS by tape-recording all interviews. A set of 15 audiotapes (5 from each of the 3 primary interviewers) was randomly selected and re-scored by an advanced graduate student in clinical psychology who was blind to diagnosis. Kappa for agreement on diagnosis was .810, $p < .0005$. Pearson correlation coefficients for scores on individual symptoms range from .82 to .99, with a mean (using Fisher's r-to-z transformation) of .975, $p < .001$. Thus, this crucial variable was satisfactorily reliable, for both symptom scores and diagnosis.

Table 4-3

Total CAPS Scores of MVA Survivor Subgroups

	Cumulative percentage of Subgroups		
Score	PTSD ($n = 62$)	Subsyndromal PTSD ($n = 45$)	Non-PTSD ($n = 51$)
0–5	—	—	41.2
6–10	—	2.2	51.0
11–15	—	8.9	76.5
16–20	—	24.4	90.2
21–25	1.6	40.0	98.0
26–30	6.5	53.3	100.0
31–35	12.9	66.7	—
36–40	21.0	82.2	—
41–45	30.6	91.1	—
46–50	38.7	97.8	—
51–55	46.8	97.8	—
56–60	56.5	100.0	—
61–65	64.5	—	—
66–70	69.4	—	—
71–75	80.6	—	—
76–80	83.9	—	—
81–85	85.5	—	—
86–90	87.1	—	—
91–95	91.9	—	—
96–100	95.2	—	—
100–105	98.4	—	—
105+	100.0	—	—
M	59.4	29.9	9.6
SD	21.4	11.2	7.8

CAPS-IV

The National Center for PTSD has standardized and published a new version of the CAPS for *DSM–IV* (APA, 1994). A recent small study conducted in our center using the CAPS-IV yielded a kappa of .808, $p < .005$, for diagnostic agreement among trained doctoral students administering the CAPS after treatment.

Previous Trauma and Prior PTSD

We next assessed for prior trauma and prior PTSD. Participants were asked about any previous MVAs. For any MVA in which either the participant or someone else sought medical attention, we assessed for possible PTSD from that accident.

We then inquired about other previous trauma, using the questions developed by Breslau et al. (1991), with particular attention to other accidents or injuries, destruction of property due to fire or natural causes, assaults, or other injuries to the participant or a close family member. When there was a noticeable trauma, we assessed for possible PTSD.

Table 4-4 summarizes the results of this assessment for the three MVA subgroups and the controls. (Interestingly, two of the controls had been involved in previous MVAs in which there was a fatality.)

From the table one can see that a large proportion of our population (at least half of each subgroup), MVA survivors and controls, had been involved in prior serious MVAs. Also, a large proportion had experienced at least one prior traumatic event, including prior serious MVAs, by our criteria. However, as a group the MVA survivors were significantly more likely to have experienced a prior serious MVA or any prior trauma than the non-MVA controls. Prior PTSD was disproportionately present in the history of the MVA survivors who had the more severe reactions (PTSD or syndromal PTSD) to the current MVA. These results, which show that prior PTSD sensitizes an individual to develop PTSD with a new trauma (the current MVA), are consistent with the work of Breslau et al. (1991), who initially reported this finding.

Psychosocial History

This portion of the assessment was not conducted with a structured interview. Instead, we gathered a brief psychosocial history with emphasis on developmental milestones such as school

Table 4-4

Previous Trauma (Including Previous Serious MVAs) and Previous PTSD for all Motor Vehicle Accident Survivor Groups and Controls

Measure	MVA subgroups			Non-MVA controls	Comparisons			
		Subsyndromal			MVA vs. Controls		PTSD vs. Sub & Non	
	PTSD	PTSD	Non-PTSD		χ^2	p	χ^2	p
Prior serious MVA	38 (61.3)	34 (75.6)	36 (70.6)	48 (51.6)	06.98	.00830	2.35	.125
Prior PTSD from MVA	6 (9.7)	7 (15.6)	0 (0)	6 (6.5)	00.26	.60700	0.28	.594
Other prior trauma	46 (74.2)	31 (68.9)	30 (58.8)	33 (35.5)	24.67	.00000	1.96	.162
Any prior trauma								
Including MVA	55 (88.7)	41 (91.1)	45 (88.2)	64 (68.8)	16.31	.0001	0.03	.862
Any prior PTSD	11 (17.7)	13 (28.9)	2 (3.9)	7 (7.5)	05.59	.018	2.32	.127

Note: Values in parentheses are the percentages of the subsample represented by the tabulated frequencies.

attendence, moves, divorces, death of parents, marriage, child-births, and work history. We also explored relationships with extended family.

As part of this effort we also assessed for previous medical problems and individuals' ratings of their physical health before and after the MVA and previous psychological or psychiatric treatment for themselves and family members.

LIFE-Base

The LIFE-Base is a semistructured interview developed by Keller et al. (1987) to assess current psychosocial status in their longitudinal follow-up studies. It was modified for our purposes to assess status for the month before the accident and for current (post-MVA) status. Performance at work, school (for part-time or full-time students), and home (of household activities) was assessed on a 5-point scale (1 = *high level of performance with no impairment,* 2 = *satisfactory level of performance with no impairment,* 3 = *mild impairment,* 4 = *moderate impairment* [person misses a lot of work or has considerable difficulty carrying out duties], and 5 = *very poor performance with severe impairment*). Quality of social relations before and after the accident with all relevant first-degree relatives (parents, siblings, children, and spouse or partner) was assessed. Again, ratings were made on a 5-point scale (1 = *very good, close emotional relationship;* 5 = *very poor relationship; feels no emotional closeness, avoids family member or almost always hostile contact*). We averaged the ratings across all first-degree relatives to derive a measure of perceived social support.

We also assessed quality of relationships with friends and of recreational activities again on similar 5-point scales. Finally, a Global Assessment Scale (GAS; Endicott, Spitzer, Fleiss, & Cohen, 1977) rating (0 to 100 in 10-point increments) was made.

The assessors were trained by personnel at Brown University under Keller's supervision to use the LIFE-Base and the LIFE.[2] The latter was adapted to use for follow-up of the MVA survivors and to assess PTSD symptoms on a weekly basis as well as psychosocial status variables on a monthly basis.

---

[2]We acknowledge the assistance of Martin Keller and Tracie Shea in providing our training and assistance in adapting the LIFE to our use.

Structured Clinical Interview for *DSM–III–R* (SCID)

We used the SCID-NP (nonpatient edition, version 1.0; Spitzer, Williams, Gibbon, & First, 1990) to assess current and lifetime *DSM–III–R* (APA, 1987) disorders. Two of the assessors were trained in its use by personnel from New York State Psychiatric Institute. They trained the other two, who had also reviewed the training videotapes ("SCID-101").

SCID-II

Finally, we assessed for possible personality disorders (Axis II disorders) using the SCID-II (version 1.0; Spitzer, Williams, Gibbon, & First, 1990). A screening questionnaire was mailed to the participants before the initial appointment. From it (a series of 113 yes–no questions, grouped by *DSM–III–R* personality disorder) we determined whether the participant had answered affirmatively to enough items so that he or she might be positive for the disorder. Thus, we formally assessed only for personality disorders that were likely to be present. Symptoms were scored *absent, subthreshold,* or *present* on the basis of the interview.

We also adopted a convention of labeling a participant as subthreshold for a personality disorder if he or she was (a) positive for one less than the required minimum number of symptoms to make the diagnosis or (b) positive for the minimum number of symptoms needed for the diagnosis if both fully present and subthreshold ratings were counted.

This concluded the interview. It took from 2 hours to 5 hours to complete. The participant was given an appointment for the psychophysiological assessment and a feedback appointment with the assessor. (The psychophysiological assessment procedures and results are discussed in chapter 12.)

We created a long narrative of all of the interview material and made diagnoses. We gave any participant with a positive Axis I diagnosis, including PTSD, a referral for treatment.

The participant returned in about 1 week and was asked to read the narrative. Corrections were made in the final version at that point. In this way, participants had full knowledge of the report if it was sent to any third party.

Psychological Tests. A second part of our overall assessment battery consisted of several standardized psychological tests, including the following:

* Beck Depression Inventory (Beck, Ward, Mendelson, Mock, & Erbaugh, 1961): a 21-item self-report measure with well-established reliability and validity (Beck, Steer, & Garbin, 1988).
* State–Trait Anxiety Inventory (Spielberger, Gorsuch, & Lushene, 1970): a 40-item self-report measure that yields values measuring both one's current state anxiety level and one's overriding trait anxiety level.
* Impact of Event Scale (Horowitz, Wilmer, & Alvarez, 1979): a 15-item scale widely used in PTSD research, which yields a score on *intrusion* or reexperiencing symptoms and a score on *avoidance* symptoms. The two are summed for a total score.
* Keane's PTSD Scale (P–K Scale; Keane, Malloy, & Fairbank, 1984): a 49-item scale for which the items have been shown empirically to differentiate Vietnam veterans with PTSD from similar Vietnam veterans who do not have PTSD.
* Reaction Index (Frederick, 1985): a 20-item scale used to detect possible cases of PTSD.

To make our results maximally useful to others, we present norms for each of our MVA subgroups and for the controls on each test, as well as the means and standard deviations, in chapter 5.

Assessment of Non-MVA Controls. The non-MVA controls underwent many of the same structured interviews. For this group we began with the psychosocial history, followed by the assessment of prior traumatic events and possible PTSD, then the SCID, SCID-II, and finally the LIFE-Base. They also participated in the psychophysiological assessment and heard a randomly selected audiotape developed for an MVA victim.

Follow-Up Assessments

The primary purpose of this research project was to examine the short-term natural history of PTSD and other disorders caused by an injury-producing MVA. Thus, the project was designed to re-assess all MVA survivors, both those who initially met the criteria for PTSD and the others, at 6-month intervals over 1 year. The 6-month intervals were chosen for several reasons: (a) to minimize the burden on the participants (and thus reduce the costs of the research, as each re-assessment costs over $200 out of pocket) and (b) to take advantage of a follow-up methodology used successfully in the mood disorders, the LIFE Longitudinal Interval Follow-Up Evaluation (Keller et al., 1987). Keller's research had shown that with his structured form of interviewing, 6-month intervals were a viable strategy. Thus, although shorter intervals, such as used by Epstein (1993) in his small sample, might yield more sensitive data, 6 months was demonstrably viable for this kind of work.

Participants were given an appointment for a re-assessment 6 months from the date of the initial assessment. About 1 week before the appointment, a set of questionnaires (repeats of the ones described earlier) was mailed to the participant along with a reminder of the appointment. This was followed with a phone call.

We had taken the precaution of obtaining the name, address, and phone number of someone the MVA victim said would know their whereabouts. These were used to track individuals. Despite our best efforts (including completing some follow-up interviews by telephone for individuals who had moved), we lost 13 individuals at the 6-month follow-up and an additional 13 individuals at the 12-month follow-up. At the 12-month follow-up, 1 participant had died; 13 refused to participate; and 12 had moved, left no forwarding address, and were unreachable through family contacts. (Part of this stemmed from the failure of one assessor to continue in the research and to actively pursue his participants.) The demographic characteristics of the samples assessed at each of the follow-up points are described in Table 4-5.

Although there were no significant differences in most of the demographic variables between dropouts and completers at 6 months or 12 months, there was a trend, particularly at 12 months, for disproportionate loss among individuals initially diagnosed with full PTSD ($p = .09$). There was significantly

Table 4-5

Demographic and Diagnostic Information on Completers and Dropouts at Each Assessment

		Sample			
Variable	Initial	6-mo. completers	6-mo. dropout	12-mo. completers	12-mo. dropout
Initial diagnosis					
PTSD	62 (39.2%)[a]	55 (37.9%)	7 (11.3%)[b]	48 (36.4%)[a]	14 (22.6%)[b]
Subsyndromal	45 (28.5%)	43 (29.7%)	2 (4.4%)	42 (31.8%)	3 (6.6%)
Non-PTSD	51 (32.3%)	47 (32.4%)	4 (7.8%)	42 (31.8%)	9 (17.6%)
Total	158	145	13 (8.2%)	132	26 (16.4%)
Gender (M/F)	50/108	48/97	2/1	44/88	6/20
% female	68.4%	66.9%	84.6%	66.7%	76.9%
Age *M(SD)*	35.4 (12.5)	36.0 (12.7%)	29.3 (7.7%)	36.2 (12.6)	31.7 (11.8)

Ethnicity					
Caucasian/minority	140/18	131/14	9/4	123/9	17/9
% minority	11.4%	9.7%	30.8%	6.8%	34.6%
Education					
Some college/HS or less	117/41	38/106	10/3	100/32	17/9
% college	74.1%	73.8%	76.9%	75.8%	65.4%
Marital status					
Married/not married	65/93	62/83	3/10	57/75	8/18
% married	41.1%	42.8%	23.1%	43.2%	30.8%

[a]Percentages of the total sample at that assessment. For follow-ups, the frequencies are of those available based on initial diagnosis. [b]Percentages for dropouts are for initial diagnostic subsample who dropped out.

greater loss of minority MVA survivors, $\chi^2(1, N = 158) = 16.63$, $p = .0005$. Thus, dropouts were more likely to be single, female, younger, and a member of a minority group and to have initially been diagnosed with PTSD.

LIFE Interviews

As noted earlier, all four assessors were trained to interview using the LIFE by personnel at Brown University under the guidance of Keller.

The essence of the LIFE is to use personal event anchors to assist participants in recalling when symptomatic changes occurred. Thus, major holidays (e.g., Thanksgiving, Christmas, Fourth of July), birthdays (the participants' as well as those of close family members), anniversaries, and so forth are used as anchors.

Individuals are assessed for their current status on the variable of interest (say, the intrusive recollection symptom of PTSD). If it is different from the status at the previous assessment, the participant is then helped to identify when (on a week by week basis) the change occurred. He or she is also asked to cite any other worsening, or lessening, of the symptom. If the symptom has not changed, the individual is also asked whether the symptom has been better or worse over the interval and to pinpoint the times of any changes.

We used the LIFE Interview directly for tracking Axis I comorbidity, treatments received (psychological, drug, or both), and psychosocial variables. The latter were assessed on a monthly basis.

We adopted the LIFE interviewing format to examine each of the 17 symptoms of PTSD as well as the physical injuries and travel behaviors. Weekly grid sheets were created for each variable of interest. On these weekly grids we also noted when any legal events related to the MVA occurred (visits to lawyers, depositions, etc.) and when any new MVAs or other stressful events (so defined by the participant) occurred involving the participant or close family members. The locally designed follow-up interview and the grid sheets used for the tracking of PTSD symptoms and other variables are contained in Appendix B.

We also assessed the patient for PTSD in a formal manner using the CAPS-2 (Blake et al., 1990b), a version of the CAPS designed for follow-up studies and detecting change. We used CAPS-based diagnoses for all of the follow-up analyses (see chapter 7), not "follow-up grid-based" diagnoses.

Through tracking all 17 symptoms of PTSD, it was possible to determine with some precision when a participant who had initially met criteria for PTSD no longer met the full criteria (and also when someone deteriorated from syndromal PTSD to meeting the full PTSD criteria; see chapter 8 for a discussion of delayed-onset PTSD). Although Keller's procedures were designed to track full diagnostic disorders, the procedures lend themselves well to this symptom-by-symptom approach.

- Psychological tests: The participants completed the BDI, STAI, and IES at each follow-up.
- Follow-up psychophysiological assessment: The psychophysiological assessment was repeated at the 12-month follow-up only.
- Follow-up at 18-months: We made an attempt to follow-up all of those participants with an initial diagnosis of PTSD for one additional 6-month interval, thus generating an 18-month follow-up for these participants. We had the inevitable additional loss of research participants but gathered data on 35 with initial PTSD, using the same procedures.

Longer Term Questionnaire Follow-Up

The development of a standardized and validated questionnaire for assessing PTSD, the PTSD *Checklist* (PCL; Weathers, Litz, Herman, Huska, & Keane, 1993; Weathers, Litz, Huska, & Keane, 1994) of the National Center for PTSD (Boston Branch) led to a decision to try to gather one last round of follow-up data.

Re-standardization of the PCL on a new cohort of MVA survivors (and sexual assault survivors; total $n = 30$) who were assessed with the CAPS revealed high intercorrelations of total PCL score with total CAPS score ($r = .929$, $p < .0001$). We found that a cut-off score of 44 had the greatest predicitive power, rather than the 50 recommended by Weathers et al. (1993) on the basis of their standardization with Vietnam veterans.

We mailed a small packet of questionnaires including the PCL, BDI, STAI, IES, and questions about additional treatment and new MVAs to all original participants. They were offered $5 to complete the questionnaires and return them to us. These data thus represent a follow-up of 16 to 24 months. We collected 100 of 157 questionnaires, for a 64% return rate, from two mailings if the first packet was not returned by the post office as undeliverable.

Clinical Hint

It is obvious that our overall assessment procedures were very long and detailed, testing the stamina and endurance of both assessor and MVA survivor. Because this was a research project we tried to err on the side of thoroughness, sacrificing some degree of patient convenience. As the following chapters show, we believe there is potential value in each set of information gathered. However, for the practicing clinician, we could see omitting the psychological tests and possibly the psychophysiological assessment, as well as the SCID-II. We believe the remaining information is needed to adequately characterize and understand the MVA survivor.

5

What Are the Psychosocial Effects of MVAs on Accident Survivors?

In chapter 3 we described the primary effect a traumatic event may have on an individual, namely, the development of PTSD or a subsyndromal form of it. We also found that the rate with which MVA survivors develop PTSD is highly variable. In the present chapter we examine other psychosocial consequences that may befall an MVA survivor, including the development of disorders in addition to PTSD, or *co-morbid* psychiatric disorders, effects on driving and travel, and other psychosocial effects such as impaired performance of major role functions.

We begin the chapter with a discussion of the largest and most soundly conducted study of co-morbidity associated with PTSD from various causes, the National Co-Morbidity Study (NCS; Kessler et al., 1995). Next, we focus more closely on the MVA literature and the co-morbidity found as a consequence of MVAs. Then, following the pattern of chapter 3, we describe our own relevant data.

The National Co-Morbidity Study

The NCS (Kessler et al., 1995) provides a good overview of the psychiatric co-morbidity experienced among those with PTSD from a wide array of traumatic events, including MVAs. The interviews for the NCS were conducted in such a way that it is possible to obtain good estimates of whether PTSD or the various co-morbid disorders assessed was primary—that is, if the MVA survivor had lifetime PTSD and major depression—and whether the major depression preceded or followed the onset of the PTSD.

In the NCS study, both men and women with PTSD were more likely to have mood disorders (major depressive episode, dysthymia, or mania) than those participants who did not have PTSD. In fact, about 48% of those with PTSD of either gender had co-morbid major depression and 22% had co-morbid dysthymia. It was estimated, statistically, that from 53% to 78% of the mood disorders were secondary to the PTSD.

For anxiety disorders, the rate of co-morbidity for those with PTSD ranged from 7% (for men with panic disorders) to 31.4% (for women with simple phobia). Kessler et al. (1995) estimated that from 30% to 56% of the anxiety disorders were secondary to the PTSD. Finally, for substance use disorders, the rate of co-morbidity ranged from 27% (women with drug abuse or dependence) to 52% (men with alcohol abuse or dependence). The substance use disorders were estimated to be secondary to the PTSD, from 52% to 84% of the instances, on a par with the mood disorders. Separate data on MVA survivors were not available in the NCS report.

Co-Morbidity Among MVA Survivors

Co-morbid psychiatric conditions were not routinely reported in the studies of MVA survivors described in chapter 3 (Tables 3-2 and 3-3). A summary of the available information is provided in Table 5-1 for studies of MVA survivors who were seeking evaluation or treatment and in Table 5-2 for the other basic descriptive studies of MVA survivors. The basic descriptions of the samples and rate of PTSD are repeated in Tables 5-1 and 5-2.

Among the treatment- and evaluation-seeking samples presented in Table 5-1, mood disorders were the most reported major co-morbid condition, with 3% to 51% of the sample having notable depressive disorders. Like the NCS sample, the MVA survivors described in Table 5-1 also reported having notable anxiety disorders. Unlike the NCS sample, however, there was a large degree of co-morbid somatoform disorders (9% to 29%) and many patients with pain problems (not necessarily somatoform pain disorders).

Among the unselected samples represented in Table 5-2, mood disorders were much less prevalent, ranging from 4% to 7%. There was much more emphasis in these studies on identifying the fraction of the sample that represented a "psychiatric case" by one measure or the other. These were individuals with sufficient symptoms, subjective distress and role impairment, to be detected but not necessarily specified. On this dimension the rate of "caseness" ranged from 13.3% (Mayou et al., 1993) to 62.5% (Feinstein & Dolan, 1991), with an average across the studies of 33.4%.

Co-Morbidity in the Albany MVA Study

As mentioned earlier, in the Albany MVA Study, we devoted a fair degree of effort to examining our study samples (MVA survivors and controls) for both co-morbid psychiatric conditions and the general psychosocial impact of the MVA on the individual. This work was previously summarized by Blanchard, Hickling, Taylor, and Loos (1995).

Co-Morbid Mood Disorders

Our findings on co-morbid mood disorders for our MVA sample and the controls, on the basis of SCID interviews, are tabulated in Table 5-3. In all cases we have compared the frequencies with two orthogonal contrasts using chi-square: a comparison of all MVA survivors with controls and then a comparison of those MVA survivors with PTSD with those with subsyndromal PTSD or non-PTSD. Statistics are listed only for significant comparisons.

In Table 5-3 three findings stand out. First, the MVA survivors showed more current major depression than the controls. This finding was primarily due to the high percentage of major depression among MVA survivors with PTSD (53.2%), which was significantly greater ($p < .0001$) than that found in the other two groups (4.1%). Second, this high percentage of current major depression among MVA–PTSDs was due to two factors: (a) More

Table 5-1

Co-Morbidity Found in Treatment/Evaluation Seeking MVA Survivors

Author/country	Description of sample	PTSD	Co-morbidity	Driving phobia
Kuch et al., 1985 Canada	30 MVA victims referred for evaluation (18) or treatment (12)	100%	Depressed mood Muscle pain	77%
Tarsh & Royston, 1985 United Kingdom	35 Cases of "accident neurosis" assessed for insurance claims; gross somatization	N/R	Severe depression–1 (3%) Paranoid psychosis–1 (3%) Hypochondriasis–10 (29%) Widespread mild depression	N/R
Platt & Husband, 1986 United States	31 MVA victims for evaluation r.e. legal suits	77.4%	7 women (of 22) met criteria for major depression (32%)	N/R
Jones & Riley, 1987 Australia	327 accident victims referred for evaluation by lawyers	N/R	13.5% mood disorders 6% anxiety disorders 9% somatoform disorders 67% depressive symptoms 73% sleep disturbance 72% HA 75% irritability	N/R

Table 5-1 (Continued)

Co-Morbidity Found in Treatment/Evaluation Seeking MVA Survivors

Author/country	Description of sample	PTSD	Co-morbidity	Driving phobia
Goldberg & Gara, 1990 United States	55 MVA victims referred for evaluation; 31 had lawsuits pending	14.5%	Depression 28/55 (51%) Limb pain 11/55 (20%) Post-concussive syndrome 12/55 (22%)	N/R
Horne, 1993 Australia	7 MVA victims seeking treatment	43%	3 with phobic anxiety	N/R
Datal & Harrison, 1993 United Kingdom	56 MVA victims referred for evaluation by lawyers	32.1% 26.8%	7.1% mood disorder 17.9% anxiety disorder somatoform pain disorder 5.4% adjustment disorder	10.7 (6/56) with phobic travel anxiety
Hickling & Blanchard, 1992 United States	20 MVA victims referred for treatment of HA or other pain	50% (15% sub-PTSD)	45% major depression 20% dysthymia 20% panic disorder 10% alcoholism 25% OBS	60%

Note: N/R = not reported.

Table 5-2

Co-Morbidity Found in Unselected Samples of MVA Victims

Author/country	Description of sample	PTSD	Co-morbidity	Driving phobia
Malt, 1988 Norway	113 hospitalized accident victims	1%	1% major depression 3% atypical anxiety 3% dysthymia 5% adjustment disorder (depressed) 9% atypical OBS	N/R
Malt et al., 1989 Norway	551 adults with accidental injuries who were hospitalized (out of 683, 83.5%)	N/R	33.7% psychiatric case 26.7% some DSM–III Dx	N/R
Feinstein & Dolan, 1991 United Kingdom	48 hospitalized Pts with leg fractures. Reassessed at 6 wks and 6 months	25% at 6 wk. 14.6 % at 6 mo.	62.5% were "cases" CIS > 14 25% cases at 6 wks. 10/48 (21%) cases at 6 mo. 12.5% had depressive Sx at 6 wks.	N/R
Green et al., 1993 Australia	24 of 69 hospitalized MVA victims. Reassessed at 1 mo. and 18 mo.	8% at 1 mo. 25% at 18 mo.	33% had clinically significant Sx	N/R

Table 5-2 (*Continued*)
Co-Morbidity Found in Unselected Samples of MVA Victims

Author/country	Description of sample	PTSD	Co-morbidity	Driving phobia
Mayou et al., 1993 United Kingdom	188 of 200 consecutive MVA victims admitted to hospital (includes 63 whiplash only). Reassessed at 3 mo. and 12 mo.	8% at 3 mo. 11.1% at 12 mo.	6.9% mood or anxiety disorders 25/188 (13.3%) psychiatric cases	18.4% travel anxiety at 1 year
Mayou et al., 1991 United Kingdom	418 MVA victims admitted to hospital (of 864) assessed 4–6 yr. post-MVA by questionnaire	N/R	N/R	2% stopped driving 8% much avoidance
Malt et al., 1993 Norway	192 MVA victims who were hospitalized	< 5%	68/183 (37%) were psychiatric cases by GHQ 48/183 (26%) had "nervousness"	N/R
Kuch et al., 1994 Canada	55 MVA victims with minimal injury and chronic pain	100%	Assessed only for accident phobia	38.2% accident phobia
Bryant & Harvey, 1995 Australia	56 hospitalized MVA victims (of 131; 1 year after MVA)	41% had high GHQ > 3	31% substance abuse	N/R
Bryant & Harvey, 1996 Australia	114 consecutive hospitalized MVA victims	31% had high IES > 30	37% high State Anxiety (50+) 25% high Trait Anxiety (50+)	N/R

Table 5-3

Co-Morbid Mood Disorders Among MVA Survivors and Controls

Disorders	MVA victims						Non MVA controls		Comparisons			
	PTSD		Subsyndromal PTSD		Non-PTSD				MVA vs. Control		PTSD vs. Subsyndromal and Non-PTSD	
	Freq.	%	Freq.	%	Freq.	%	Freq.	%	χ^2	p	χ^2	p
Current major depression	33	53.2	3	6.7	1	2.0	4	4.3	15.65	<.0001	50.60	<.0001
Onset before MVA	6	9.7	2	4.4	0		—		—	—	4.52	.034
Onset after MVA	27	43.5	1	2.2	1	2.0	—		—	—	47.8	<.0001
Current dysthymia	3	4.8	3	6.7	3	5.9	2	2.2		ns		ns
Current bipolar disorder	0		1	2.2	0		1	1.1		ns		ns
Any current mood disorder	35	56.5	7	15.6	4	7.8	6	6.5	18.30	<.0001	34.80	<.0001
Lifetime major depression	31	50.0	16	35.6	6	11.8	25	26.9		ns	12.40	.0004
Lifetime dysthymia	3	4.8	3	6.7	3	5.9	2	2.2		ns		ns
Lifetime bipolar disorder	4	6.5	2	4.4	0		3	3.2		ns		ns
Any pre-MVA mood disorder	32	51.6	20	44.4	7	13.7	29	31.2		ns		ns

Note. Freq. = frequency. Adapted from "Psychiatric Morbidity Associated With Motor Vehicle Accidents," by E. B. Blanchard, E. J. Hickling, A. E. Taylor, and W. R. Loos, 1995, *Journal of Nervous and Mental Disease, 183,* 495–504. Copyright 1995 by Williams & Wilkins. Adapted with permission.

MVA survivors who developed PTSD were clinically depressed at the time of the MVA (9.7%) than among the other two MVA survivor groups (2.1%); and (b) of greater importance, 43.5% of MVA survivors with PTSD developed a major depression after the MVA. We feel fairly confident in these figures because great care was taken with individuals who were currently depressed to determine when the depressive episode started. Third, the MVA survivors who developed PTSD had a greater history of major depression than found in the other two survivor groups, 50% versus 23% ($p = .0004$).

Thus, our first finding is not surprising, the MVA–PTSD group was clearly more vulnerable to developing a major depression with the traumatic event, given their history. It appears that prior major depression is a clear risk factor for developing PTSD from an injury-producing MVA. We address this issue in detail in chapter 6. The finding that pre-trauma major depression is a risk factor for PTSD has been previously noted in Breslau et al.'s (1991) report on a young urban sample assessed retrospectively.

The high level of co-morbid major depression with PTSD has also been noted in two epidemiologic studies of PTSD: Breslau et al. (1991) reported that 36.6% of her sample with PTSD also met the criteria for major depression. Kessler et al. (1995) in the NCS found that 47.9% of men and 48.5% of women with PTSD also had co-morbid major depression. These values are similar to ours and to reports in Table 5-1 (e.g., Goldberg & Gara, 1990, 51%; Hickling & Blanchard, 1992, 45%) but not to those in Table 5-2. We should note that Kessler et al. (1995) calculated that the PTSD was primary to the current co-morbid mood disorders in 53% to 78% of instances, echoing our finding.

Co-Morbid Anxiety Disorders

Similar information on co-morbid anxiety disorders is presented in Table 5-4, again for the three MVA survivor groups and the controls.

Two findings stand out in Table 5-4: First, there were no differences between the MVA survivors as a group and the controls on anxiety disorders. There were, however, a number of low-level significant differences between the MVA survivors with PTSD and the other two MVA survivor groups. Those with PTSD

Table 5-4

Co-Morbid Anxiety Disorders Among MVA Survivors and Controls

| Disorders | MVA victims | | | | | | Non-MVA controls | Comparisons | | | |
| | PTSD | | Subsyndromal PTSD | | Non-PTSD | | | MVA vs. Control | | PTSD vs. Subsyndromal and Non-PTSD | |
	Freq.	%	Freq.	%	Freq.	%	Freq.	%	χ^2	p	χ^2	p
Current panic disorder	4	6.5	1	2.2	0	0	0	0		ns	3.60	.058
Onset after MVA	3	4.8		0	0	0	0	0		ns	4.76	.024
Lifetime panic disorder	7	11.3	3	6.7	0	0	6	6.5		ns	4.24	.040
Current agorphobia with panic		0		0		0		0	—	—	—	—
Current social phobia	5	8.1	3	6.7	1	2.0	3	3.2		ns		ns
Current simple phobia	13	21.0	6	13.3	1	2.0	6	6.5		ns	6.37	.012
Current OCD	2	3.2		0		0	1	1.1		ns		ns
Current GAD	2	3.2	1	2.2	2	3.9	5	5.4		ns		ns
Any current anxiety disorder	17	27.4	10	22.2	4	7.8	13	14.0		ns	3.93	.047
Any lifetime anxiety disorder	18	29.0	11	24.4	3	5.9	15	16.1		ns	4.87	.027

showed a higher rate of current panic disorder (6.5% vs. 1%) with most of that panic having started after the MVA (three out of four cases). There was also more current simple phobia (21.0% vs. 7.3%). These combine to lead to more current and more lifetime anxiety disorders among those with PTSD than among the other MVA survivors.

Breslau et al. (1991) found more panic disorder, obsessive compulsive disorder (OCD), and generalized anxiety disorder (GAD) among their young urban adults with PTSD than among the comparison group. Likewise, Kessler et al. (1995) in the NCS found higher levels of co-morbid anxiety disorders (panic disorder, GAD, simple phobia, social phobia, and agoraphobia) among those with PTSD versus those without it. Their levels of co-morbid anxiety disorders were generally 1.5 (panic disorder) to 5 (GAD) times greater than we found.

Co-Morbid Alcohol and Drug Abuse and Dependence

In Table 5-5 are the data on alcohol and drug abuse and dependence co-morbidity. The only significant finding was a higher lifetime level of drug dependence among our MVA survivors (13.9%) than among our controls (2.2%, $p = .0022$). There were no differences among the MVA survivor subgroups. There was also remarkably little current alcohol or drug abuse and dependence (3.2%). This may well represent an unavoidable recruiting bias: Individuals who were heavily involved in misusing substances at the time of their MVA may be unlikely to volunteer for research. In fact, only 8 (5.1%) individuals admitted to having alcohol or other drugs in their system at the time of the MVA, and only 2 were cited by the police for driving under the influence.

Breslau et al. (1991) found more substance abuse and dependence among her research participants with PTSD (43.0%) than those without it (24.7%). Kessler et al. (1995) made similar observations in the NCS. Other Axis I co-morbidity data are presented in Table 5-6.

Co-Morbid Personality Disorders

The results of the SCID-II interviews on co-morbid personality disorders, or Axis II disorders, are reported in Table 5-7. In

Table 5-5

Co-Morbid Substance Abuse/Dependence Among MVA Survivors and Controls

Disorders	MVA victims			Non-MVA controls	Comparisons			
					MVA vs. Control		PTSD vs.	Subsyndromal and Non-PTSD
	PTSD	Subsyndromal PTSD	Non-PTSD					
	Freq. %	Freq. %	Freq. %	Freq. %	χ^2	p	χ^2	p
Current alcohol abuse or dependence	1 1.6	1 2.2	2 3.9	0		ns		ns
Current drug abuse or dependence	0	1 2.2	0	0		ns		ns
Lifetime alcohol abuse	1 1.6	0	0	2 2.2		ns		ns
Lifetime alcohol dependence	9 14.5	8 17.8	1 2.0	6 6.5		ns		ns
Lifetime drug abuse	2 3.2	0	1 2.0	0		ns		ns
Lifetime drug dependence	9 14.5	4 8.9	9 17.6	2 2.2	9.38	.0022		ns

Note: Freq. = frequency. Adapted from "Psychiatric Morbidity Associated With Motor Vehicle Accidents," by E. B. Blanchard, E. J. Hickling, A. E. Taylor, and W. R. Loos, 1995, *Journal of Nervous and Mental Disease, 183,* 495–504. Copyright 1995 by Williams & Wilkins. Adapted with permission.

Table 5-6

Other Co-Morbidity Comparisons Among MVA Survivors and Controls

Disorders	MVA victims			Non-MVA controls	Comparisons			
	PTSD	Subsyndromal PTSD	Non-PTSD		MVA vs. Control		PTSD vs. Subsyndromal and Non-PTSD	
					χ^2	p	χ^2	p
Lifetime somatoform disorder	0	0	0	0	—	—	—	—
Current/lifetime eating disorder	5 (8.1)	2 (4.4)	2 (3.9)	2 (2.2)	—	ns	—	ns
Current/lifetime psychotic disorder	0	0	0	0	—	—	—	—

Note: Values in parentheses are the percentage of the subsample the tabulated frequency represent.

71

Table 5-7, one finds relatively low levels of Axis II disorders among the various subgroups and no significant differences on any of the comparisons. Overall, 13.3% of the MVA survivors met the criteria for one or more personality disorder. Among those who were diagnosed with PTSD, obsessive–compulsive personality disorder was the most common (9.7%).

A noteworthy absence in our Axis II findings is any noticeable frequency of antisocial personality disorder (1.9% of all MVA survivors). This may again represent a recruiting bias: Antisocials may not readily volunteer for a research project. Breslau et al. (1991) did find that a high percentage of their young adults with PTSD had a family history of antisocial behavior (41.3%). Kessler et al. (1995) in the NCS found that 43.3% of their male research participants with PTSD and 15.4% of their female participants with PTSD met the *DSM–III–R* criteria for conduct disorder, and its presence was a clear significant risk factor for PTSD among both sexes.

Psychometric Measures of Psychological Distress

As Tables 5-1 and 5-2 show, there is a sizable literature on psychiatric co-morbidity among MVA survivors who develop PTSD. The material in this section departs from that literature, and its notion of categorical diagnoses, to examine psychological distress from the dimensional perspective of the psychological test. Only one such measure has found widespread use in the MVA–PTSD literature, Horowitz et al.'s (1979) Impact of Event Scale (IES). Table 5-8 contains summarized data from other studies of MVA survivors on the IES.

Despite fairly widespread use (seven studies) of the IES, it is a bit difficult to determine what score one might expect of an MVA survivor with PTSD. Of the three studies that speak to this (Burstein, 1986; Epstein, 1993; Green et al., 1993) the total IES scores of MVA–PTSDs ranged from 34 to 49, with a mean of 41.1. The highest score resulted from a psychological treatment-seeking sample (Burstein, 1986), which might be expected to be highly distressed.

Table 5-7

Co-Morbid Personality Disorders Among MVA Survivors and Controls

Disorders	MVA victims			Non-MVA controls	Comparisons			
	PTSD	Subsyndromal PTSD	Non-PTSD		MVA vs. Control		PTSD vs. Subsyndromal and Non-PTSD	
	Freq. %	Freq. %	Freq. %	Freq. %	χ^2	p	χ^2	p
Borderline personality disorder	2 3.2	1 2.2	0 0	1 1.1		ns		ns
Antisocial personality disorder	2 3.2	0 0	0 0			ns		ns
OC personality disorder	6 9.7	3 6.7	2 3.9	5 5.4		ns		ns
Paranoid personality disorder	2 3.2	2 4.4	0 0	1 1.1		ns		ns
Avoidant personality disorder	3 4.8	3 6.7	2 3.9	1 1.1		ns		ns
Dependent personality disorder	2 3.2	0 0	2 2.2			ns		ns
Any Axis II personality disorder	11 17.7	5 11.1	5 9.8	8 8.6		ns		ns

Note: Freq. = frequency. Adapted from "Psychiatric Morbidity Associated With Motor Vehicle Accidents," by E. B. Blanchard, E. J. Hickling, A. E. Taylor, and W. R. Loos, 1995, Journal of Nervous and Mental Disease, 183, 495–504. Copyright 1995 by Williams & Wilkins. Adapted with permission.

Table 5-8

Summary of Findings With Impact of Event Scale Among Motor Vehicle Accident Survivors

Study and country	Population	% MVA	% PTSD	Impact of Event Scale		
				PTSD M (SD)	vs. Other M (SD)	Total victim sample M (SD)
Burstein, 1986 United States	19 MVA survivors with PTSD referred for treatment vs. 11 with sudden loss and PTSD	100.0	100	MVA-PTSD 49.3 vs.	Loss PTSD 48.0	— —
Malt, 1988 Norway	113 hospitalized accident victims 46 from MVA	40.7	1		21% 9+ on intrustion 44% 9+ on avoidance	Intrusion: 5.5 (6.0) Avoidance: 9.3 (8.5)
Feinstein & Dolan, 1991 United Kingdom	48 MVA survivors with leg fractures	100.0	25 at 6 weeks	Initial IES predicts PTSD at 6 weeks		Intrusion: 24.4 Avoidance: 14.9
Green et al., 1993 Australia	24 hospitalized MVA survivors	100.0	8 at 1-mo. 29 sub-PTSD	PTSD 34.4 (15.7) vs. 18.3 (9.5) vs. 16.1 (9.0) vs.	Non-PTSD 7.0 (5.8)[a] total 6.3 (5.8)[a] intrusion 2.5 (3.3)[a] avoidance	— —

74

Table 5-8 (*Continued*)

Summary of Findings With Impact of Event Scale Among Motor Vehicle Accident Survivors

Study and country	Population	% MVA	% PTSD	Impact of Event Scale		
				PTSD _M (SD)_	vs. Other _M (SD)_	Total victim sample _M (SD)_
Brom et al., 1993 The Netherlands	151 (of 738) survivors of serious MVAs	100.0	N/R			Dutch version of IES Intrusion: 10.7 Avoidance: 7.8 Total 19.5
Epstein, 1993 United States	15 accident survivors hospitalized on trauma unit	100.0[b]	40	PTSD 21.5 (10.5) vs. 18.7 (7.1) vs.	Non-PTSD 10.2 (6.9)[a] intrusion 7.5 (3.6)[a] avoidance	
Bryant & Harvey, 1996 Australia	114 hospitalized MVA survivors	100.0	N/R			31% had high (total IES scores): 30+ 25% had high (intrusion): 20+ 18% had high (avoidance): 20+

Note: N/R = not reported. [a]Significant difference. [b]Data not certain.

The Albany MVA Project

To make our psychometric data maximally useful, we present the distribution of scores on each of the psychological tests administered to our MVA survivors, by diagnostic subgroup, and on controls (when appropriate). The values for the IES are presented in Table 5-9.

In Table 5-9, we find a mean IES score for our PTSD subgroup of 35.4, which is within the range reported in Table 5-8 for com-

Table 5-9

Impact of Event Scale Scores of Albany MVA Survivor Victim Subgroups

| | | Cumulative percentage of subgroup | |
Score	PTSD (*n* = 61)	Subsyndromal PTSD (*n* = 44)	Non-PTSD (*n* = 50)
0–5	4.9	20.0	64.0
6–10	11.5	37.8	78.0
11–15	14.8	55.6	82.0
16–20	23.0	60.0	86.0
21–25	27.9	75.6	90.0
26–30	41.0	80.0	90.0
31–35	52.5	88.9	92.0
36–40	63.9	91.1	98.0
41–45	70.5	97.8	100.0
46–50	78.7	100.0	—
51–55	82.0	—	—
56–60	91.8	—	—
61–65	96.7	—	—
66–70	98.4	—	—
71+	100.0	—	—
M	35.4	17.8	8.2
SD	17.7	13.0	11.4

parable populations. We found 59% of our PTSD group to have total IES scores of greater than 30, the level used by Bryant and Harvey (1996) to indicate PTSD.

Use of IES to Diagnose PTSD

Some authors have used IES scores above a certain level to infer whether an individual meets criteria for PTSD (e.g., Brom et al., 1993; Bryant & Harvey, 1996). We examined our data to see how well certain scores on the IES discriminated among MVA survivors with diagnoses based on the CAPS interview of PTSD, subsyndromal PTSD, and non-PTSD. The results are presented in Table 5-10.

Table 5-10 shows that 58% of our PTSDs were correctly identified with an IES total score of greater than 30. Unfortunately, 28% of those with IES scores of 31 or higher did not meet the full criteria for PTSD, including 10% who were non-PTSD. Similarly, at the other end of the scale, we found 23% of our PTSDs had IES scores of 20 or less. Although those with PTSD amount to only 12% of all participants with IES scores of 20 or lower, the false-negative rate seems high.

Table 5-10

Comparison of IES Scores to CAPS Diagnoses Among MVA Survivors

	Diagnosis based on CAPS		
IES score	PTSD	Sub	Non
20 or lower	14 (23%)	27 (60%)	43 (86%)
21–30	11 (18%)	9 (20%)	2 (4%)
31 or higher	36 (58%)	9 (20%)	5 (10%)

Note: Percentages refer to column values. Sub = subsyndromal; Non = 5 non-PTSD.

Clinical Hint

We believe the IES is a useful psychometric measure but do not believe it can be used as a substitute for a structured clinical interview in making a definitive diagnosis.

In Tables 5-11 through 5-15 we present the data on our other test measures. These data are presented in the form of norms for each test so that the clinician could compare his or her individual case with norms from a set of MVA survivors.

Table 5-11

Beck Depression Inventory Scores of Albany MVA Survivor Subgroups and Controls

		Cumulative percentage of subgroup		
Score	PTSD ($n = 61$)	Subsyndromal PTSD ($n = 44$)	Non-PTSD ($n = 50$)	Non-MVA controls ($n = 95$)
0–3	3.3	25.0	50.0	50.5
4–6	18.0	56.8	74.0	77.9
7–9	23.0	68.2	82.0	87.4
10–12	36.1	75.0	86.0	93.7
13–15	54.1	86.4	94.0	100.0
16–18	75.4	97.7	96.0	—
19–21	85.2	97.7	100.0	—
22–24	91.8	97.7	—	—
27–30	91.8	97.7	—	—
31–33	95.1	100.0	—	—
34–36	95.1	—	—	—
37–39	98.4	—	—	—
40+	100.0	—	—	—
M	15.5	7.6	5.0	4.4
SD	9.0	6.4	5.6	4.2

Table 5-12

STAI-State Anxiety Scores on Albany MVA Survivor Subgroups and Controls

		Cumulative percentage of subgroup		
Score	PTSD (*n* = 61)	Subsyndromal PTSD (*n* = 44)	Non-PTSD (*n* = 50)	Non-MVA controls (*n* = 95)
20–30	1.6	0	8.0	10.5
31–35	1.6	6.8	38.0	26.3
36–40	9.8	25.0	58.0	40.0
41–45	14.8	40.9	74.0	55.8
46–50	21.3	50.0	82.0	69.5
51–55	34.4	63.6	86.0	75.8
56–60	47.5	72.7	88.0	83.2
61–65	57.4	79.5	90.0	91.6
66–70	65.6	86.4	90.0	96.8
71–75	77.0	90.9	94.0	97.9
76–80	80.3	95.5	96.0	97.4
81–85	85.2	97.7	98.0	100.0
86–90	90.2	100.0	100.0	—
99–95	91.8	—	—	—
96–100	96.7	—	—	—
101+	100.0	—	—	—
M	64.4	52.5	42.7	45.8
SD	17.9	14.4	14.5	13.1

In Table 5-16 are the comparisons of the group means for each of the psychometric measures. In each instance the one-way ANOVA across the groups was significant at $p < .01$ or better. Follow-up comparisons by Duncan's multiple-range test revealed that in each instance MVA survivors with PTSD had higher scores (more distress) than MVAs with subsyndromal PTSD, who were higher than those with non-PTSD. The latter did not differ from the nonaccident controls in any case. In one instance (Keane's PTSD Scale) the subsyndromals did not differ from the controls.

Table 5-13

STAI Trait Anxiety Scores on Albany MVA Survivor Subgroups and Controls

		Cumulative percentage of subgroup		
Score	PTSD (*n* = 61)	Subsyndromal PTSD (*n* = 44)	Non-PTSD (*n* = 50)	Non-MVA controls (*n* = 95)
20–30	1.6	2.3	8.0	7.4
31–35	4.9	9.1	38.0	24.2
36–40	6.6	20.5	50.0	37.9
41–45	16.4	29.5	60.0	48.4
46–50	21.3	52.3	76.0	64.2
51–55	37.7	63.6	88.0	78.9
56–60	47.5	72.7	88.0	88.4
61–65	55.7	81.8	92.0	92.6
66–70	80.3	88.6	96.0	92.6
71–75	93.4	90.9	100.0	96.8
76–80	96.7	95.5	—	97.9
81–85	98.4	95.5	—	100.0
86–90	98.4	97.7	—	—
91–95	98.4	97.7	—	—
96–100	98.4	100.0	—	—
100+	100.0	—	—	—
M	60.2	53.2	43.3	46.6
SD	13.6	14.7	12.3	12.8

The score for MVAs with PTSD on the Keane PTSD scale was certainly at variance with the standardization data for this scale compared with the scores of the Vietnam veterans. For that sample, a score above 35 correctly identified 85% with PTSD. The difference might be explained by the duration of the diagnoses: Our sample was approximately 2 months post-trauma (and predominantly female), whereas Keane et al.'s (1984) sample was exclusively male and on average 15 years post-trauma.

Table 5-14

Reaction Index Scores on Albany MVA Suvivor Subgroups

| Score | Cumulative percentage of subgroup | | |
	PTSD ($n = 61$)	Subsyndromal PTSD ($n = 44$)	Non-PTSD ($n = 50$)
1–5	1.8	7.1	29.2
6–10	1.8	16.7	47.9
11–15	3.6	31.0	77.1
16–20	10.7	52.4	85.4
21–25	16.1	59.5	93.8
26–30	39.3	73.8	97.9
31–35	48.2	85.7	100.0
36–40	58.9	97.6	—
41–45	60.7	100.0	—
46–50	69.6	—	—
51–55	87.5	—	—
56–60	94.6	—	—
61–65	96.4	—	—
66–70	100.0	—	—
M	38.5	21.5	11.2
SD	14.9	10.8	7.8

Other Psychosocial Effects of MVAs and the Concept of *Caseness*

One of the important aspects of all diagnoses in the newer *DSMs* has been that, in addition to meeting symptomatic and temporal criteria, an individual must also experience subjective distress or major role performance impairment (e.g., impaired functioning at work or school, impaired relationships with family and friends, and impaired use of leisure time or recreational activities) to warrant a diagnosis. These two latter factors, subjective distress and role impairment, define the concept of *caseness*; that

Table 5-15

Keane's MMPI PTSD Scale Scores of Albany MVA Survivor Subgroups

	Cumulative percentage of subgroup		
Score	PTSD ($n = 62$)	Subsyndromal PTSD ($n = 45$)	Non-PTSD ($n = 50$)
0–5	17.7	46.7	66.0
6–10	40.3	64.4	88.0
11–15	58.1	77.8	92.0
16–20	72.6	91.1	94.0
21–25	88.7	95.6	98.0
26–30	91.9	97.8	100.0
31–35	96.8	97.8	—
36–40	98.4	100.0	—
41–49	100.0	—	—
M	14.7	9.0	5.2
SD	10.4	8.3	6.0

Note: MMPI = Minnesota Multiphasic Personality Inventory.

is, the symptoms interfere in the latter two spheres of an individual's life enough to warrant being called a case.

There has been some study of caseness in MVA survivors; most of it has been obtained using questionnaires or interview schedules such as Mayou et al.'s (1993) study in which they used the Present State Examination (Wing et al., 1974) to determine caseness or Malt et al.'s (1993) use of the GHQ-20 (Goldberg, 1972) to determine caseness (also used by Green et al., 1993, and by Bryant & Harvey, 1995, in their Australian studies).

For example, Mayou et al. (1993) identified 25 cases (out of 188 MVA survivors seen in the emergency room) for a caseness rate of 13.9% initially. Green et al. (1993) found 9 cases out of 24 assessed (37.5%), whereas Malt et al. (1993) found 37.2% of his sample had

Table 5-16

Psychological Test Measures of Subjective Distress for All Motor Vehicle Accident Survivor Subgroups and Controls

Measure	MVA subgroups						Non-MVA controls	
	PTSD		Subsyndromal PTSD		Non-PTSD			
	M	SD	M	SD	M	SD	M	SD
Beck Depression Inventory	15.5_a	9.0	7.6_b	6.4	5.0_c	5.6	4.4_c	4.2
Trait anxiety	60.2_a	13.6	53.2_b	14.7	43.3_c	12.3	46.7_c	12.8
State anxiety	64.4_a	17.9	52.5_b	14.4	42.7_c	14.5	46.0_c	13.1
Impact of Event total score	35.4_a	17.7	17.8_b	13.0	8.2_c	11.4	—	
Avoidance	18.3_a	9.0	9.2_b	7.0	4.1_c	5.9	—	
Intrusion	17.1_a	9.0	8.6_b	6.5	4.1_c	6.0	—	
Keane's MMPI PTSD Scale	15.0_a	10.3	9.0_b	8.3	5.2_c	6.0	$6.4_{b,c}$	6.1
Reaction Index	38.5_a	14.9	21.5_b	10.8	11.2_c	7.8	—	

Note: Values sharing the same subscript are not significantly different at the .05 level by Duncan's multiple-range test. Adapted from "Psychiatric Morbidity Associated With Motor Vehicle Accidents," by E. B. Blanchard, E. J. Hickling, A. E. Taylor, and W. R. Loos, 1995, *Journal of Nervous and Mental Disease, 183,* 495–504. Copyright 1995 by Williams & Wilkins. Adapted with permission.

GHQ scores indicating caseness. Bryant and Harvey (1995) found that 41% of their sample met criteria for caseness 1 year after the MVA.

In the Albany MVA Project we approached the concept of caseness and psychosocial impact using the LIFE-Base interview (Keller et al., 1987) at the initial assessment (see chapter 4 for description of items). We derived ratings on four psychosocial variables: (a) performance in major role function (either work, school if full-time or part-time student, or homemaking if the individual did not work out of the home and was not a student), (b) average relationship with all first-degree relatives plus spouse or partner if living in a long-term relationship, (c) relationships with friends, and (d) participation in recreational activity. The values for these ratings for each of the MVA survivor subgroups and the controls are reported in Table 5-17.

In Table 5-17, we find the PTSD group reported being more impaired than the other two MVA subgroups and the controls on all four measures. For major role performance the difference between the PTSDs and subsyndromal PTSDs was a full-scale unit: the difference between a satisfactory level of performance with no impairment (value of 2.0) and mild impairment (value 3.0; worked less than expected, had mild difficulties carrying out duties, or both). Likewise, it was almost a full scale unit on participation in recreational activities—the difference between *good* (2.0; participates in several activities) versus *fair*—(3.0; occasional participation in recreational activities with limited enjoyment).

The other two MVA survivor groups did not differ. They functioned at a significantly poorer level than the controls on major role performance and participation in recreation.

The only other study to examine similar factors was the prospective follow-up by Mayou et al. (1993) in the United Kingdom. When Mayou et al. examined all of their research participants who met the criteria for PTSD during the year-long follow-up ($n = 19$) and compared them with the other MVA survivors ($n = 150$), they found significantly ($p < .01$ or better) greater levels of impairment among the PTSDs for effects on leisure (74%) and effects on work (67%; percentages are for those with PTSD who acknowledged moderate to great impairment effects).

Table 5-17

LIFE-Base Ratings of Role Performance for All Motor Vehicle Accident Survivor Subgroups and Controls

| Measure | MVA subgroups | | | | | | Non-MVA controls | |
| | PTSD | | Subsyndromal PTSD | | Non-PTSD | | | |
	M	SD	M	SD	M	SD	M	SD
Work, school, homemaking performance	3.1$_a$	1.4	2.1$_b$	1.2	1.9$_b$	1.2	1.4$_c$	0.7
Relations with family (Average across all first-degree relatives and mate)	2.3$_a$	1.0	2.1$_b$	0.8	1.9$_{b,c}$	0.7	1.8$_c$	0.6
Relations with friends	2.4$_a$	1.2	1.8$_b$	1.0	1.9$_b$	1.1	1.6$_b$	0.8
Recreational activity	3.3$_a$	1.4	2.4$_b$	1.1	2.2$_b$	1.4	1.8$_c$	1.1
Global Assessment Scale Rating	53.6$_a$	14.7	65.3$_b$	15.7	76.7$_c$	16.1	81.2$_c$	14.0

Note: All measures except GAS rating are on 1 (*very good*) to 5 (*very poor*) scales. Values which share the same subscript are not significantly different at the .05 level by Duncan's multiple-range test. Adapted from "Psychiatric Morbidity Associated With Motor Vehicle Accidents," by E. B. Blanchard, E. J. Hickling, A. E. Taylor, and W. R. Loos, 1995, *Journal of Nervous and Mental Disease, 183,* 495–504. Copyright 1995 by Williams & Wilkins. Adapted with permission.

Taking the results of the two studies together, it is clear that meeting the criteria for PTSD subsequent to an MVA usually implies major impact on the individual's life. (See the Case of Mary J. for an example of this impact.)

Effects of MVAs on Travel Behavior

A consequence one might logically expect of serious MVAs is altered travel behavior, especially varying degrees of phobic avoidance. Given the dependence of many Americans on the private automobile, it is possible that this problem assumes greater importance in the United States than in other Western nations. Earlier we presented the rates of driving phobia and related travel behavior alterations found in the various MVA survivor studies (see Tables 5-1 and 5-2). Two of the studies on treatment-seeking MVA survivors (Hickling & Blanchard, 1992; Kuch et al., 1985) report very high levels of driving phobia (77% and 60%, respectively). It could well be that the interference of avoidence of travel in everyday life and the distress experienced by those who do not avoid were some of the primary reasons for seeking treatment.

In the most detailed examination of this topic, Mayou and Bryant (1994) presented data from their 1-year prospective follow-up of MVA survivors (see also Mayou et al., 1993). At the 1-year follow-up, 65% of individuals who had been drivers in their accidents and 44% of persons who had been passengers reported lingering effects on their driving behavior. Moreover, 18.7% of the 1-year sample showed either phobic avoidance of certain travel behavior (avoiding certain routes or travel conditions, for example, driving at night or on high-speed highways) or extreme distress if those conditions had to be endured. Finally, 42% of motorcyclists (who composed 37.4% of the total follow-up sample) had stopped riding motorcycles. Two individuals who were "learner car drivers" had not returned to driving because of fear. Interestingly, individuals who had been passengers in the accidents experienced greater levels of effects on travel (84% had noticeable difficulty as a passenger at the 1-year follow-up). Mayou and Bryant (1994) found that experiencing phobic travel anxiety was associated with having other diagnosable disorders over the course of the year, with being female, and with having "initial 'horrific' memories" of the MVA.

In another experiment, Kuch et al. (1994) studied 55 MVA survivors who had minimal injury and chronic pain. They found that 21 participants (38.2%) met *DSM–III–R* criteria for simple phobia. They provided a definition of *accident phobia:* (a) intensification of symptoms associated with exposure to driving; (b) fear-related substantial reduction of miles normally traveled; (c) when driving, restrictions to certain roads or weather conditions; and (d) excessive cautioning of the driver when the patient was a passenger and possibly restriction of seats taken in the vehicle. Of their 21 accident phobics 8 also met the criteria for PTSD.

The Albany MVA Study

The effects of the MVA on the travel behavior of our sample of MVA survivors are presented in Table 15-18 as a function of subgroup. We defined *driving phobia* as either complete elimination of all driving or severe restriction of all driving (e.g., only drove from home to work and home to grocery store, both of which were close by). We also described a category we termed *driving reluctance,* which included avoidance of the MVA site, avoidance of MVA-related weather conditions (e.g., snow and heavy rain), avoidance of certain road and traffic conditions (e.g., high-speed highways or similar roads at heavy traffic times), and avoidance of all travel (driving or passenger role) for pleasure. As an example, one young man avoided the intersection at which his accident happened. This necessitated his driving an extra 8 miles to enter the major north–south throughway every day he went to work. Thus, our definition of *driving phobia* is more restrictive than Kuch et al.'s (1994) *accident phobia.* Our *driving reluctance* would more closely approximate Kuch et al.'s (1994) *accident phobia.*

As seen in Table 5-18, *driving phobia,* as we termed it, was found only among MVA survivors with PTSD (15.3% of PTSDs). We also found some driving reluctance among the subsyndromal PTSD and even the non-PTSD groups, but it was significantly higher among the subgroup with full PTSD. One can also see that

Table 5-18

Effects of Accident on Driving Behavior of Motor Vehicle Accident Groups

| | MVA Subgroups | | | | | | Comparisons | |
| | PTSD | | Subsyndromal PTSD | | Non-PTSD | | PTSD vs. Sub and Non | |
Measure	Freq.	%	Freq.	%	Freq.	%	χ^2	p
Does not drive (no license, injuries)	3	4.8	1	2.2	6	11.8		ns
Driving phobia	9	15.)	0	0	0	0	14.46	.00014
Driving reluctant								
Avoids MVA site	20	33.9	9	20.4	4	8.9	8.11	.00440
Avoids highways, etc.	14	23.7	6	13.6	2	4.4	6.47	.01100
Avoids driving/riding for pleasure	26	44.1	6	13.6	1	2.3	17.02	.00004
Any noticeable driving reluctance	55	93.2	35	79.5	8	17.8	12.23	.00047

Note: Values in parentheses are the percentage of the subsample of possible drivers (eliminating those in first row) that the tabulated frequencies represent. Adapted from "Psychiatric Morbidity Associated With Motor Vehicle Accidents," by E. B. Blanchard, E. J. Hickling, A. E. Taylor, and W. R. Loos, 1995, *Journal of Nervous and Mental Disease, 183,* 495–504. Copyright 1995 by Williams & Wilkins. Adapted with permission.

almost all (93.2%) of the subsample with MVA-related PTSD acknowledged noticeable effects of the MVA on their travel behavior. We also found some of this in the other two subgroups of MVA survivors (79.5% in sub-PTSD; 17.8% in non-PTSD).

Our results are similar to Kuch et al.'s (1994) results if one defines *accident phobia* as they did. However, we found that 93% (55/59) of the accident phobics (driving reluctant) met the criteria for PTSD as compared with Kuch et al.'s 38.2%. We also found 4 individuals (6.5% of total PTSDs) who met the criteria for PTSD but not for accident phobia.

Without question, one of the serious, interfering effects of MVAs is the change in travel behavior. Particularly for individuals with limited access to public transportation or who live in widely spread out communities, daily travel by a motor vehicle is almost a necessity. For example, one woman gave up driving entirely after her MVA. Later, during the follow-up, she had returned to driving of necessity because her husband became ill and could not drive. Most of our participants engaged in some type of "exposure therapy," forcing themselves to travel while enduring the distress or finding alternative routes.

As this chapter documents, survivors of serious MVAs experience noticeable psychosocial effects of the accident in addition to developing PTSD. The two that are most prevalent are also primary reasons why MVA survivors seek mental health services: the subjective distress that accompanies the co-morbid mood disorders and the role interference and subjective distress one finds among the driving reluctant and driving phobic.

6

Who Develops PTSD From MVAs?

The question that introduces this chapter becomes important if there are limited treatment resources available for MVA survivors. We know from chapter 3 that from 5% to 45% (a sizable proportion) of MVA survivors who seek medical attention will develop PTSD in the year following the accident and that another 15% to 30% will develop a subsyndromal form of PTSD (Green et al., 1993; Hickling & Blanchard, 1992) and consequently experience notable subjective distress and role impairment.

Given this potential degree of morbidity and limited treatment resources, one must consider a triage effort of referring those most likely to develop diagnosable conditions to treatment promptly while withholding such a referral from those expected to do well. Under these circumstances, it becomes important to know who, among MVA survivors, is at relatively greater risk, and who is at lesser risk, to develop PTSD. (The prediction of who remits relatively quickly, with or without treatment, and who continues to suffer more chronically from PTSD or subsyndromal PTSD is a related issue we consider in chapter 7.)

As before, we present possible answers to our question that have been provided by other studies of MVA survivors and answers from studies of victims of other kinds of trauma. Finally, we summarize our own data on this important topic.

Review of Motor Vehicle Accident Literature

Our compilation of studies on MVA survivors that have addressed the prediction of who develops PTSD from a group of accident survivors is summarized in Table 6-1. We have also included material that speaks explicitly to variables that did not predict PTSD.

An examination of the material in Table 6-1 reveals only limited help. One major point emerges from these data: High scores on the factors measured by the IES, intrusion and avoidance, in the time shortly after the accident tended to be the most consistent predictors of later PTSD. Thus, Feinstein and Dolan (1991) and Green et al. (1993) found that high IES scores at less than 1 week and at 1 month post-MVA, respectively, predicted later PTSD. Epstein (1993) also found higher scores on IES intrusion and avoidance in six cases wherein individuals developed PTSD over his follow-up. Consistent with this, Mayou et al. (1993) found that "horrific and intrusive memories" at the initial assessment (usually in the emergency room) predicted PTSD. Finally, Kuch et al. (1994) found that accident phobia predicted PTSD; the essence of the accident phobia was *avoidance*.

Although this information is very clinically useful, it is a bit tautological: higher scores on two of the four symptom clusters which define PTSD (intrusive recollection and avoidance) predict the later presence of PTSD. A similar finding is that of Green et al. (1993), that early presence of a subclinical form of PTSD (similar to our subsyndromal PTSD) predicts full PTSD later.

In addition to the finding that some early level of characteristic symptoms predicts later PTSD, two other factors emerge from Table 6-1: "Perceived threat of life" in the MVA (Green et al., 1993) was a predictor. Scotti et al. (1992) made a similar observation. Interestingly, it is now part of the required criteria in the *DSM–IV* (APA, 1994) definition (Criterion A-2). Death of someone in the accident also seemed to lead to difficulty but was not a significant predictor in Bryant and Harvey's (1996) study.

On one point there was noticeable disagreement, the role played by the extent of physical injury. Malt et al. (1993) found that severity of injury predicts the degree of "nervousness." Malt et al. (1989) identified death of one of the participants in the accident as a predictor of later difficulty. Foeckler, Garrard, Williams, Thomas, and Jones (1978) interviewed 29 drivers who were involved in fatal accidents. Although no formal diagnostic evaluations were conducted, they noted that 16 of 29 (55%) individuals had a "crisis" (probably noticeable psychological distress) after the fatal MVA. Ten (34%) seemed to have some clear reexperiencing symptoms, whereas 10 (the degree of overlap between these two subsets was not clear) had long-term (at least 1 year) depression. This is graphically depicted in numerous anecdotes in Gilliam and Chesser's (1991) *Fatal Moments: The Tragedy of the Accidental Killer.*

Prediction of Who Develops PTSD From Studies of Other Trauma

Within the vast literature on PTSD, there are other studies involving other traumatic events that provide some guidance on this topic. For example, Breslau et al. (1991) identified six independent predictors of the development of PTSD in a traumatized population: female sex, neuroticism, early separation from parent, preexisting anxiety or depression, a family history of anxiety, and a family history of antisocial behavior. Kessler et al. (1995) in the NCS found that being female, currently married for men, and previously married for women were predictors. Likewise, co-morbid anxiety disorder, mood disorders, and substance use disorders were predictors. Kilpatrick, Saunders, Amick-McMullan, Best, Veronen, and Resnick (1989) found that whether a woman was injured or not during a criminal assault predicted the development of consequent PTSD.

The Albany MVA Study

Our philosophy in addressing this question of prediction of who develops PTSD, and who does not, was to cast a very broad net with regards to potential predictors. Thus, we included the following as potential predictors: (a) pre-MVA variables derived from the psychosocial history, psychiatric history, and LIFE-Base

Table 6-1

Predictors of Development of PTSD Among MVA Survivors

Study (country)	Population	PTSD	Which variables predict PTSD	Which variables do not predict
Malt et al., 1989 Norway	551 adults (240 MVA) hospitalized for accidental injuries.	N/R	Death in the accident predicts worse family relations.	N/R
Feinstein & Dolan, 1991 United Kingdom	48 hospitalized patients with leg fractures (27 MVA)	25% "caseness"	Initial (< 1-week) IES score predicts 6-month PTSD severity and extent of injury.	Demographics, initial injury severity, subjective rating of severity and extent of injury.
Mayou et al., 1993 United Kingdom	188 consecutive MVA survivors (of 200) admitted to hospital or whiplash (n = 63)	8% at 3 months	Initial (< 1 week) "horrific and intrusive memories"	No memory of MVA (23.4%), neuroticism, previous psychological problems, baseline depression
Green et al., 1993 Australia	24 hospitalized MVA survivors	8 % at 1 month 30% at 18 months	Subclinical PTSD at 1-month predicts PTSD at 18 mos; high IES score at 1-month; perceived threat to life.	Extent of injury, extent of physical impairment
Malt et al., 1993 N.	192 MVA survivors	Less than 5%	"Nervousness" predicted by older age and severity	N/R

94

Table 6-1 *(Continued)*

Predictors of Development of PTSD Among MVA Survivors

Study (country)	Population	PTSD	Which variables predict PTSD	Which variables do not predict
Kuch et al., 1994 Canada	55 MVA survivors with minimal injury and chronic pain	14.5%	Presence of accident phobia predicts PTSD	N/R
Epstein, 1993 United States	15 MVA survivors hospitalized on trauma unit	40%	High avoidance and intrusion scores on the IES	N/R
Scotti et al., 1992 United States	80 college undergrads (61 had been in MVA)	N/R	High level of PTSD symptoms predicted by anxiety severity (car totaled and degree of injury) and perceived threat of harm	N/R
Bryant & Harvey, 1996 Australia	114 successive MVA victims hospitalized	31% had high IES (> 30) scores	Trait anxiety (.41), fear of new MVA (.40), head injury (−.27) predict IES intrusion	Death of loved one in MVA, extent of injury

Note: N/R = not reported.

and (b) variables related to the MVA and its immediate consequences, such as degree of physical injury. In all, we derived
36 variables.

Because our study involved assessing individuals 1 to 4
months post-MVA, by which time they could meet the criteria for
PTSD, we did not believe we could use concurrently administered psychological tests (like the IES) or specific PTSD symptoms because these variables were a part of the criterion we
sought to predict.

We then calculated the simple univariate correlation of each
predictor with our criterion variables, either the dichotomous
variable of whether the participant met the criteria for PTSD
or the continuous variable of total CAPS score, representing
the total amount of psychological distress due to post-trauma
stress (PTS) symptom effects. The simple univariate correlations
are summarized in Table 6-2. (This work was previously presented in Blanchard, Hickling, Taylor, Forneris, Loos, & Jaccard,
1996.)

In Table 6-2, one notes a number of significant, but low-level,
correlations with one of the two criterion variables, either total
CAPS score as a measure of PTS symptoms or the dichotomous
variable of diagnosis of full PTSD. Variables emerged from simple demographics: gender (which appeared in Breslau et al.,
1991, and Kessler et al., 1995) and ethnic status (which was
apparent in chapter 3), but not from pre-MVA functioning. Prior
(pre-MVA) psychiatric disorders (mood, anxiety, and PTSD) also
emerged as significant predictors, echoing the findings of Breslau
et al. (1991) and Kessler et al. (1995).

Finally, a number of variables emerged from those we labeled
as *accident-related*, including three of the strongest individual
predictors: MVA survivor's fear of death, consistent with the
studies of Mayou et al. (1993) and Scotti et al. (1992); degree of
physical injury, consistent with Malt et al. (1989) and Scotti et al.
(1992) and contradicting Mayou et al. (1993) and Feinstein and
Dolan (1991); and litigation initiated. In fact, this latter variable
(litigation initiated) had the highest single correlation coefficient
($r = .371$) with total CAPS score, accounting for 13.6% of the variance. (As noted earlier, there were no variables related to the
intrusion or avoidance symptoms of PTSD because we believed

they would be highly redundant with the criterion at the time they were measured.)

As a next step, we eliminated all potential predictors that did not individually account for at least 2% of the variance in one of the two criteria, that is, a simple correlation of .141 or greater. This left us with a potential predictor pool of 19 variables. Finally, in the multiple regression we required that a variable account for at least 2% of new variance in the squared multiple correlation and that the change in the squared multiple correlation represented by the variable be significant at $p < .05$. There was considerable overlap among the pre-MVA psychiatric status variables; this was permitted because it was not clear which ones might be important. For example, prior major depression and prior PTSD, both potential predictors according to the literature, are subsumed under prior mood disorder and prior anxiety disorder, respectively, and also both are jointly subsumed under any prior Axis I disorder.

There were two different prediction problems: (a) to predict the dichotomous criterion of whether the participant met the full *DSM–III–R* (APA, 1987) diagnostic criteria for PTSD and (b) to predict the degree of PTS symptoms as indicated by the CAPS scores at the time of the initial assessment. For the first problem the appropriate statistic was logistic regression because the criterion was dichotomous. For the second problem the appropriate analysis was multiple regression.

Prediction of PTS Symptoms (Total CAPS Score)

We used stepwise multiple regression to predict our measure of PTS symptoms across the entire sample. The final equation, containing eight variables, yielded a multiple correlation of .617, $F(8, 149) = 11.48$, $p < .0001$, accounting for 38.1% of the variance in total CAPS score at the initial assessment. It is summarized in Table 6-3.

If we rely on the size of the standardized regression weights and zero order correlations as a rough indicator of the relative importance of predictor variables, we find the litigation variable (whether the MVA survivor had contacted a lawyer—and thus

Table 6-2

Description of Potential Predictors and Their Simple Correlations With Criterion Variables

		Simple correlation with	
			Dx. of PTSD
Variable and how measured	Total CAPS score	1 = PTSD	0 = Non-PTSD
Demographics			
Age	−.102		−.038
Gender: 1 = female, 0 = male	.187*		.185*
Marital status: 1 = married, 0 = unmarried (single, divorced, separated)	−.056		−.040
Education level: high-school diploma or less = 1 Some college or bachelor's degree = 2 Bachelor's degree and more = 3	.016		.082
Ethnic status: 1 = Caucasian, 0 = Minority (African American, Hispanic, Asian)	−.266*		−.201*
Pre-MVA Functioning			
Pre-MVA GAS rating: 0–100	−.048		−.094
Pre-MVA Work status: −1 = full-time employment student or volunteer 2 = full-time with layoffs of more than 3 months			

Table 6-2 (*Continued*)
Description of Potential Predictors and Their Simple Correlations With Criterion Variables

Variable and how measured	Total CAPS score	Dx. of PTSD 1 = PTSD	Dx. of PTSD 0 = Non-PTSD
		Simple correlation with	
3 = part-time employment or volunteer (30 hrs/wk or less) full-time homemaker			
4 = unemployed but expected to work by self or others			
5 = unemployed, not expected to work (e.g., disabled)	.100		.013
Pre-MVA health status: 0–100 (100 = super healthy)	–.153		–.148
Pre-MVA family relations: Average rating of relationship with all first degree relatives including spouse or partner (1 = very good, 5 = very poor)	.026		–.018
Family size/number of relatives rated in item above	–.015		.040
Pre-MVA relations with friends: 1 = very good 5 = very poor)	.005		.045

(Table 6-2 continues)

99

Table 6-2 *(Continued)*

Description of Potential Predictors and Their Simple Correlations With Criterion Variables

		Simple correlation with		
		Total CAPS score	Dx. of PTSD	
Variable and how measured			1 = PTSD	0 = Non-PTSD
Pre-MVA psychiatric status				
Prior major depression	1 = yes, 0 = no	.237**		.254**
Depressed at time of MVA	1 = yes, 0 = no	.161*		.169*
Prior mood disorder	1 = yes, 0 = no	.270**		.237**
Prior anxiety disorder	1 = yes, 0 = no	.242**		.176*
Prior substance abuse/dependence	1 = yes, 0 = no	.127		.045
Any prior Axis I disorder	1 = yes, 0 = no	.258**		.231**
Any prior Axis II disorder	1 = yes, 0 = no	.144		.105
Prior serious MVA	1 = yes, 0 = no	−.130		−.122
Any prior trauma	1 = yes, 0 = no	.139		.111
Prior PTSD	1 = yes, 0 = no	.211**		.121
Prior psychological/psychiatric treatment	1 = yes, 0 = no	.056		.002
Accident-related variables				
Number of vehicles involved: 1-up		.152		.112
Were others hurt or killed?	1 = yes, 0 = no	.254**		.220**
Driver or passenger/pedestrian	1 = yes, 0 = no	−.061		−.044
Were traffic citations issued?	1 = yes, 0 = no	.050		.003

100

Table 6-2 *(Continued)*

Description of Potential Predictors and Their Simple Correlations With Criterion Variables

		Simple correlation with	
			Dx. of PTSD
Variable and how measured		Total CAPS score	1 = PTSD 0 = Non-PTSD
Was subject cited?	1 = yes, 0 = no	.042	.049
Degree of responsibility for MVA			
Subject	0–100	–.011	.088
Other drivers	0–100	.172*	.049
Road conditions	0–100	–.217**	–.151
Was subject unconscious?	1 = yes, 0 = no	.216**	.170*
Has subject begun litigation (contacted lawyer)?	1 = yes, 0 = no	.370**	.224**
Subject rating of fear of death			
0 = none, 100 = certain I would die		.275**	.310**
Subject rating of degree of control during MVA			
0 = none, 100 = complete control		–.037	.042
Degree of physical injury (AIS scores) 0–up		.250**	.245**
Did subject experience whiplash injury?	1 = yes, 0 = no	.201*	.132

Note: $^*p < .05$. $^{**}p < .01$.   From "Who Develops PTSD From Motor Vehicle Accidents?" by E. B. Blanchard, E. J. Hickling, A. E. Taylor, W. R. Loos, and C. A. Forneris, 1996, *Behaviour Research and Therapy, 34,* 1–10. Copyright 1996 by Elsevier Science. Adapted with permission.

Table 6-3

Summary of Final Multiple Regression to Predict PTS Symptoms in MVA Survivors

Variable	B	β	t	p	R	R^2	Change in R^2	Sig. of F for change
Litigation	13.872	.256	3.83	.0002	.369	0.136	—	—
Prior mood disorder	9.480	.158	2.41	.0172	.459	0.210	0.074	0.0002
Fear of dying (in MVA)	0.091	.146	2.19	.0300	.502	0.252	0.042	0.0041
Ethnicity	-15.675	-.193	2.97	.0035	.534	0.285	0.033	0.0083
Road conditions								
Responsible for MVA	-0.114	-.149	2.28	.0242	.558	0.311	0.026	0.0173
Extent of injury (AIS Score)	1.005	.216	3.16	.0019	.578	0.335	0.024	0.0225
Prior PTSD	10.822	.170	2.58	.0107	.600	0.360	0.025	0.0158
Whiplash injury	8.828	-.164	2.49	.0138	.617	0.381	0.021	0.0269
Constant	25.724							

Note: From "Who Develops PTSD From Motor Vehicle Accidents?" by E. B. Blanchard, E. J. Hickling, A. E. Taylor, W. R. Loos, and C. A. Forneris, 1996, *Behaviour Research and Therapy, 34,* 1–10. Copyright 1996 by Elsevier Science. Adapted with permission.

was contemplating litigation—by the time of the initial assessment, about 2 months post-MVA on average) was the strongest predictor.

This predictor was a bit problematic and points to the difficulty inherent in trying to draw causal conclusions from correlational research. The direction of causality was unclear. It could be that those seriously enough injured or distressed enough to meet the criteria for a diagnosis of PTSD (and thus to have relatively high CAPS scores) were more likely to seek the services of a lawyer and begin litigation. The correlation between degree of injury (AIS score) and CAPS score was. 185 ($p = .020$.) However, it is possible that those who decided to seek litigation were subsequently inclined to portray themselves as more symptomatic, hence having higher CAPS scores, even to an independent assessor, and thus more likely to meet the criteria for PTSD.

The existence of "no fault" insurance in the state in which this study was conducted (New York) means that most of the medical care needed for recovery would be paid automatically, removing that incentive from MVA survivors to seek legal services. However, no fault does not compensate for pain and suffering and does not, in some cases, cover full rehabilitative (e.g., physical therapy) services. We return to the topic of effects of litigation in chapter 10. We save further discussion of predictors until after the logistic regression analysis to predict the diagnosis of PTSD so as to combine discussion of predictors that appear in both analyses.

Logistic Regression to Predict PTSD Diagnosis

As described earlier, we used stepwise logistic regression to predict the categorical or dichotomous variable of who is likely versus unlikely to develop PTSD among our MVA survivors. We could have followed the example of Kilpatrick et al. (1989) in their work with criminal assault survivors and used multiple regression with the dichotomous criterion. However, we believe logistic regression, which was developed for use with a dichotomous criterion, is more appropriate and yields an equation that optimizes correct classification of individuals as PTSD or non-PTSD. We should note that with a sample containing 39.2% PTSDs, one could be correct 60.8% of the time by considering everyone non-PTSD. Table 6-4 summarizes the results of the logistic analysis.

The variables are listed in the order they entered the equation so as to jointly maximize the correct classification of those with PTSD and overall correct classification.

With this prediction equation, the four variables that entered (extent of injury, litigation, fear of death, and prior major depressive episode) correctly classified 69.6% of participants overall, including 56.5% of the PTSDs and 78.1% of the non-PTSDs, Model $\chi^2(4, N = 158) = 36.4, p < .0001$.

Three of the four variables would be expected on the basis of prior PTSD (and non-MVA) research: extent of injury, fear of death during the MVA, and history of prior major depressive episode. That the litigation variable, our best single predictor, entered was no surprise statistically.

Logistic regression yields coefficients for an equation to predict the natural logarithm of an odds ratio, that is, the probability of an individual's being classified as PTSD or non-PTSD divided by the probability of being non-PTSD. Again, when we used base rates, the odds ratio of PTSD to non-PTSD was 0.392 to 0.608, or 0.645 to 1; or conversely the odds of being non-PTSD were 1.55 to 1.

As an example, consider the situation in which both of the dichotomous predictors, prior major depression and initiation of litigation are positive (value of 1), and the fear of dying and extent of injury variables are at the mean for the population plus one standard deviation (67.4 and 10.05, respectively). This yields the following equation:

ln (odds ratio) = −0.768 + 0.014 (67.4) + 0.634 (1.0) + 0.794 (1.0) + 0.104 (10.05)

or

ln (odds ratio) = −0.6488;
odds ratio = 1.913 to 1.

This means that likelihood of such an MVA victim's meeting the criteria for PTSD is 1.91 to 1.

Table 6-4

Summary of Final Logistic Regression to Predict PTSD Disorder in MVA Survivors

Variable	B	Wald	Sig.	R	PTSD	Non-PTSD
Fear of dying (in MVA)	0.014	8.67	.0032	.1775	40.3	84.4
Prior major depression	0.634	10.30	.0013	.1981	45.2	85.4
Litigation	0.794	4.53	.0333	.1094	50.0	83.3
Extent of injury	0.104	5.34	.0209	.1256	56.5	78.1
Constant	−2.768					

Note: Sig. = significance. From "Who Develops PTSD From Motor Vehicle Accidents?" by E. B. Blanchard, E. J. Hickling, A. E. Taylor, W. R. Loos, and C. A. Forneris, 1996, *Behaviour Research and Therapy, 34,* 1–10. Copyright 1996 by Elsevier Science. Adapted with permission.

As a second example in the opposite direction, consider the case in which both dichotomous predictors are negative (value of zero) and the fear of dying and extent of injury variables are at one standard deviation below the population mean (-12.4 and 0.89, respectively). This yields the following equation:

ln (odds ratio) = 2.768 + 0.014 (-12.4) + 0.634 (0) +
0.794 (0) + 0.104 (-0.89) or
ln (odds ratio) = -3.03416
odds ratio = 0.0481.

This means that the likelihood of this second MVA victim's meeting the criteria for PTSD is 0.05 to 1.0, or about 1 chance in 20.

Four of the significant predictors to enter the equation to predict PTS symptoms also were predictors in the logistic regression analysis for the diagnosis of PTSD. We have already discussed the litigation variable. The three other significant predictors were not unexpected: The presence of a prior major depressive episode has been shown by others (Breslau et al., 1991; North et al., 1994) to predict the development of PTSD in newly traumatized individuals. For the regression analysis to predict PTS symptoms, the variable becomes prior mood disorder, a slightly broader category. The results in chapter 5 certainly point to strong association in our data between prior depression and development of PTSD after an MVA. Likewise, fear of dying in the MVA was found to be a predictor by Mayou et al. (1993) in their study of MVA survivors and was related to the idea put forth by March (1993). Although the prior evidence on the predictive value of extent of injury was mixed as noted earlier (Malt et al., 1993, reported finding an association, whereas Mayou et al., 1993, and Feinstein & Dolan, 1991, did not), finding that it entered was not unexpected. In an earlier study examining that variable and fear of dying only with our first 100 MVA survivors, we found both made independent contributions to prediction (Blanchard, Hickling, Mitnick, Taylor, Loos, & Buckley, 1995).

Prediction of PTS Symptoms. The results of predicting the extent of PTS symptoms were stronger than those for predicting diagnostic status but more complicated. Because we had a continuous dependent variable, total CAPS score, and thus could use multiple regression, we expected better results.

As noted earlier in chapter 5, presence of prior PTSD from other, earlier trauma is consistent with the pioneering work of Breslau et al. (1991). Thus, finding it in our analyses was not unexpected. It may be that both prior PTSD and prior major depressive episode leave "psychic scars" with an individual and that these psychic scars constitute vulnerabilities to new traumatic events. In both instances there is substantial distress and symptoms, more than the everyday stress of life.

The significant correlation with ethnicity is difficult to understand. It may be a function of a small minority population (11% of the sample) and some unknown selection bias. However, a recent report by Breslau, Davis, and Andreski (1995) found in a sample of over 1,000 young urban adults that Black participants were more likely to experience new trauma in a 3-year prospective follow-up. Replication of our results with larger samples of injured minority MVA survivors would be needed to have confidence in this finding.

The attribution of responsibility for the accident to road conditions yielded a low-level, negative correlation ($r = -.217, p < .01$) with PTS symptoms. This implies that the greater the attribution to road conditions the fewer PTS symptoms. This could mean that when road conditions (e.g., snowy or icy roads, poorly banked curves, or poorly marked roads) were substantial contributors to the MVA, the MVA victim realized that he or she was not personally very responsible and thus took on less blame and was consequently less symptomatic. Again, caution is warranted in assuming causality from correlations.

The whiplash variable did not appear in the cross-validation analyses (Blanchard, Hickling, Taylor, Loos, & Forneris, 1996), and thus one should be cautious in relying on it. It may enter separately as this kind of soft tissue injury receives a very low AIS score yet can be very debilitating.

Overall, we were pleased with the results. They represent, to the best of our knowledge, the first systematic attempt at prediction of PTSD and PTS symptoms shortly after an MVA trauma. The elegant work of Kilpatrick et al. (1989) with criminal assault survivors is comparable (and in many ways stronger because of the straightforward nature of their results); however, their time since trauma averaged 9.4 years in that study and they used multiple regression rather than logistic regression as the analytic tool. Mayou et al. (1993) studied a population similar to ours but did not examine the same range of predictors nor attempt the multivariate prediction.

There are two obvious limitations to these data and their generality. First, we had a self-selected sample of injured MVA survivors rather than a random sample. This could introduce unknown biases. Second, the recent trauma of the MVA may distort the individual's recall of their psychiatric and psychosocial history. To compensate we have used a psychiatric diagnostic instrument (SCID) that seems to yield reliable historical data in psychiatric patients and a psychosocial rating instrument (LIFE-Base) that also yields reliable data. Moreover, our research participants had been living with the sequelae of their trauma for only weeks to a few months, not years as in the study of many other traumatized populations.

Death of an MVA Participant. In our sample of 158 MVA survivors, only 2 survivors had been involved in fatal accidents. Both developed PTSD. Among our controls, 2 had been involved in fatal MVAs earlier in their lives; 1 of these 2 developed PTSD from that accident. We strongly believe participants in fatal accidents, even when they are not responsible (not the driver), are at great risk for developing PTSD. Bryant and Harvey's (1996) findings are at odds with this, but they were not concerned with predicting PTSD, only IES scores. (Larger samples are probably needed to address this issue in a definitive fashion.)

Clinical Hint

For the clinician called on to evaluate newly injured MVA survivors, say within a week of the MVA, we would recommend six (or perhaps eight) variables be assessed to determine the likelihood that the new MVA survivor may have short-term (the next few months) difficulties.

1. Is the patient having reexperiencing symptoms (intrusive recollections, nightmares, flashbacks, or distress when reminded of the accident)?

2. Does the patient seek to avoid thoughts or behavioral reminders of the accident?
3. How serious were the physical injuries? The more serious (higher AIS score), the higher the likelihood of difficulty.
4. How frightened or terrified by the prospect of dying in the MVA was the patient?
5. Has the patient suffered from a previous major depression?
6. Has the patient previously been traumatized and had diagnosable PTSD?
7. Is the patient female?
8. Was anyone killed in the accident?

Positive responses to each of these questions seem to increase the risk of later PTSD and thus might trigger early intervention.

What Is the Short-Term History of MVA-Related PTSD and What Predicts Remission?

To this point we have been concerned with the initial impact of an MVA on the survivor in terms of post-trauma–specific problems such as developing PTSD or subsyndromal PTSD and in terms of the development of co-morbid conditions and the overall psychosocial impact on the survivor. In this chapter we begin to examine the longer term consequences for those MVA survivors who were psychological causalities of the trauma. The primary question becomes what happens to those individuals who initially developed PTSD or even subsyndromal PTSD over time, or what is the natural history of PTSD? Corollary questions of interest are (a) what is the impact of psychological and pharmacological treatment on that natural history and (b) what variables or factors predict relatively early remission versus prolonged periods of being symptomatic?

Short-Term Natural History of PTSD

We depart from our usual format of examining the specific MVA survivor literature followed by a selected review of the literature on other kinds of trauma survivors by reversing the order and describing the other literature first. Three studies are especially pertinent. First, the National Vietnam Veterans Readjustment Study (NVVRS; Kulka et al., 1988), conducted with face-to-face interviews of 3,016 veterans approximately 15 to 20 years after

their exposure to combat in Southeast Asia, revealed that approximately 15% of those who served in Vietnam (exposed to combat)
were, in 1986 to 1988, suffering from PTSD. Furthermore,
approximately 30% of those surveyed (a carefully selected representative sample of all of the Americans who served in Southeast
Asia) had met the criteria for combat-related PTSD at some point
in their lives. Thus, over nearly 20 years approximately 50% had
remitted sufficiently such that they no longer met the full PTSD
criteria, at least as determined retrospectively.

Rothbaum, Foa, Riggs, Murdock, and Walsh (1992) conducted
a prospective study of female sexual assault victims with the initial assessment an average of 12 days ($SD = 9.4$) after the assault.
These victims were re-assessed every week for 12 weeks for the
symptoms of PTSD. Although these women could not technically
meet the criteria for PTSD at the initial assessment (because of
not having been symptomatic for 1 month [Criterion E]), if one
looks only at the symptom picture (done by Rothbaum et al.),
then 94% met the criteria initially. By 4 weeks this percentage was
reduced to 64%, by 3 months it was down to 47%, and by 6
months (see Rothbaum & Foa, 1993) it was down to 42%. In a
comparable report on assault victims (see Rothbaum & Foa, 1993)
the initial percentage with PTSD (again relaxing the Criterion E
requirement) was 65%; by 3 months this was down to 14.6%, and
by 6 months to 11.5%. Obviously, assault, especially sexual
assault, leads a very high percentage of the victims to develop
PTSD initially; however, the recovery or remission curve seems
to be fairly steep, with over 50% of those initially meeting the full
PTSD criteria remitted by 3 months.

McFarlane (1988) conducted a prospective follow-up of
Australian fire fighters exposed to large-scale and devastating
brush fires. He assessed them at three time points (4 months, 11
months, and 29 months post-trauma) with the IES and the GHQ,
which he alleged permit reasonable diagnostic approximations.
Of the 315 individuals assessed at all three time points, 95 (30.2%)
developed PTSD initially and another 62 (19.7%) developed it
later. Of those 95 with initial PTSD, 45 (47.4%) had remitted 7
months later and 18 (18.9%) others had remitted by 29 months,
with 32 (33.7%) showing persistent, chronic PTSD. Sixty-two
(19.7% of the total sample) developed delayed-onset PTSD. Of

those 62, 17 (27.4%) remitted 18 months later, whereas 45 persisted.

The MVA Literature

Table 7-1 summarizes the available data from the MVA literature on the short-term natural history and remission of PTSD. Examination of Table 7-1 reveals a mixed picture with regard to remission of PTSD. Three studies (Brom et al., 1993; Feinstein & Dolan, 1991; Mayou et al., 1993) found remission rates among those with PTSD of 41.7%, 38.5%, and 63.6%, respectively, over prospective follow-ups of 6, 12, and 6 months, respectively. The average remission rate was 47.9%, whereas the sample retention rate was 82%.

There is a clear exception to these findings: Green et al. (1993) followed hospitalized MVA victims for 18 months in Australia. They reported no remission; moreover, 5 of 7 (71%) of patients with subclinical PTSD at 1 month had deteriorated to full PTSD by 18 months. Mayou et al. (1993) also reported cases of delayed-onset PTSD. (We address this topic in chapter 8.)

For the most part it appears that a lower percentage of MVA survivors, compared with assault or rape victims, develop PTSD from their traumatic experiences. (see chapter 3). However, the remission curve for MVA-related PTSD appears less steep than that for assault victims: About 50% of persons with PTSD (whom we refer to also as *PTSDs*) remitted by 6 months to 1 year compared with assault-related PTSDs, who showed 50% remission at 3 months.

We use two terms in this chapter that warrant definition: *remission* and *recovery*. We mean by *remission* that the individual no longer meets the full diagnostic criteria for PTSD or subsyndromal PTSD. Given the categorical nature of that change, and of the diagnostic criteria for PTSD, one could have remission accompanied by a dramatic reduction in overall level of symptoms, or one could have remission resulting from a slight change in one symptom. This is awkward clinically because in the former instance almost everyone would agree that meaningful improvement has occurred, whereas in the latter one might not agree about improvement.

Table 7-1
Summary of MVA Studies on Remission of PTSD

Study and country	Population	PTSD	Follow-up interval	PTSDs remitted	Sample loss	Predictors of remission
Malt (1988) Norway	113 hospitalized accident victims (46% MVA)	1%	28 mo. (16–51 mo)	N/R	6/113 = 5%	N/R
Feinstein & Dolan (1991) United Kingdom	48 patients with leg fractures (56% MVA)	25% at 6-weeks	6 mo.	5/12 remitted (41.7%) IES total 24.4, 6 wk.–18.5, 6 mo.–15.9	7/48 = 14.6%	N/R
Mayou et al. (1993) United Kingdom	188 consecutive MVA victims either admitted to hospital or whiplash (n = 63)	8.0% at 3 mo.	12 mo.	5/13 remitted (38.5%)	14.5%	N/R

Table 7-1 *(Continued)*
Summary of MVA Studies on Remission of PTSD

Study and country	Population	PTSD	Follow-up interval	PTSDs remitted	Sample loss	Predictors of remission
Brom et al. (1993) The Netherlands	151 victims of serious MVA—83 in symptom monitoring	N/R (22% with severe symptoms)	6 mo.	Total IES: Initial, 17.4 6-mo., 7.4 8% had severe symptoms remission, 63.6%	24%	N/R
Green et al. (1993) Australia	24 of 69 hospitalized MVA victims	1 mo. 8.3% 18 mo. 25%	18 mo.	No remission 5/7 subclinical PTSD are worse at 18 mo.	25%	N/R

Note: N/R = not reported.

115

We use the term *recovery* to indicate that an individual falls in our non-PTSD category. Some symptoms may still be present but not enough to warrant a diagnosis.

The Albany MVA Study

As noted in chapter 4, we conducted two extensive follow-up assessments, at 6 months after the initial assessment and again at 12 months (there was a more limited assessment of initial PTSDs only at 18 months). As noted in chapter 4 (Table 4-5), we retained 91.8% of the sample at 6 months and 84.6% at 1 year. Thus, our retention rates are comparable, or better, than most of the studies in Table 7-1. We did have a noticeable loss among our MVA survivors initially diagnosed with PTSD: We lost 22% of the initial PTSDs by the 12-month follow-up. Because there are two somewhat different samples for each follow-up point, we present the data for the 6-month follow-up and for the 12-month follow-up separately. It then follows that we also present the information on the prediction of remission separately for the 6-month and 12-month follow-up samples.

Six-Month Follow-Up

Figure 7-1 shows the remission curve for those individuals initially diagnosed with PTSD. Using Guilford's chi-square for correlated proportions (Guilford, 1965, p. 242, formula 11.13), we tested each month's proportion against the initial diagnostic data. We found a significant ($p < .05$) drop by Month 2 (5 of 55 had remitted). By Month 3, 20% had remitted fully ($n = 5$) or in part ($n = 6$); by Month 6, 54.5% had remitted, 17 (30.9%) fully and 13 (23.9%) partially to subsyndromal PTSD.

Thus, our 6-month data show that a slightly greater percentage of our initial PTSDs had remitted than the average for other MVA follow-up studies (47.9%). It is also the case that our MVA survivors with PTSD did not remit as rapidly, as a group, as sexual or other assault victims.

The 6-month follow-up data for those initially diagnosed with subsyndromal PTSD are displayed in Figure 7-2. This group

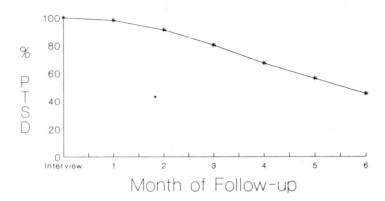

Figure 7-1.   Six-month follow-up: Remission curve for individuals
initially diagnosed with PTSD.

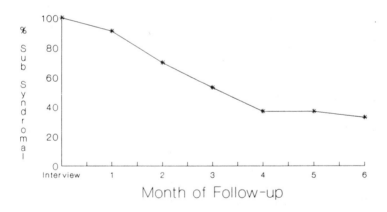

Figure 7-2.   Six-month follow-up data for individuals initially
diagnosed with subsyndromal PTSD.

showed more rapid remission of symptoms than those with full
PTSD. By the first month of the follow-up, the proportion who
remitted (9.3%) was significant at the $p < .05$ level. At 3 months
46.5% have remitted; by 6 months the proportion was 67.4% (but
2 participants had worsened and now met the criteria for
delayed-onset PTSD).

Prediction of Short-Term Remission

We cover four separate prediction problems in this section: For the initial PTSDs and initial subsyndromal PTSDs, we sought to predict the dichotomous variable of remitted or not (for the PTSDs we thus combined those who at 6 months were either non-PTSD or subsyndromal PTSD; for the initial subsyndromals, we combined the unremitted subsyndromals with the deteriorated—to full PTSD—patients). We also sought to predict 6-month continuing level of PTS symptoms (CAPS) score.

As in chapter 6, we used logistic regression to predict the dichotomous outcome variable and stepwise multiple regression to predict CAPS score, our measure of PTS symptoms. Also, as in chapter 6, we have "cast a wide net" for potential predictors relying on (a) demographic variables; (b) accident-related variables; (c) variables related to the physical effects of the MVA including the degree of recovery from physical injury, measured by the Physical Injury Quotient (see chapter 9) at each month; (d) subjective reactions to the MVA; (d) pre-MVA psychopathology; (e) psychopathology diagnosed at the initial assessment; (f) psychosocial factors; and (g) new MVA-related and other psychosocial stresses since the MVA. The simple correlations of each of the 45 predictors with the two criteria for each subgroup (PTSD and subsyndromal PTSD) are presented in Table 7-2.

As before, we eliminated any potential predictor that did not account for at least 4% of variance in the criterion ($r = .20$ or higher). This reduced the potential predictor pool to 35 variables. (This work is summarized by Blanchard, Hickling, Forneris, Taylor, Buckley, Loos, & Jaccard, 1997).

Logistic Regression to Predict Remission of Initial PTSDs. The results of this analysis are summarized in Table 7-3 and show that with four variables one can correctly characterize 83.6% of the initial PTSDs, including 80% of those who did not remit and 86.7% of those who remitted in part or altogether. This compares favorably with a base rate of 54.6% correctly classified if we had classified everyone as a remitter.

As shown in Table 7-3, the four variables are CAPS score at the initial assessment; the initial Abbreviated Injury Scale score, the degree of physical injury remission, physical injury quotient

(PIQ) at 4 months, and whether a close family member had suffered some traumatic experience over the 6-month follow-up. These data suggest that the physical status and psychological status interact (the topic of chapter 9) but have independent effects on remission. They also suggest that initial degree of injury, both physical and psychological, are powerful predictors of short-term status. One can apply the detailed description of how to use logistic regression beta weights, presented in chapter 6, to the data in Table 7-3.

Multiple Regression to Predict 6-Month CAPS Score. The next set of analyses were designed to predict the CAPS score at 6 months for those survivors initially diagnosed with PTSD. The results of the stepwise multiple regression are in Table 7-4.

The dominant variable was the initial CAPS score with a simple correlation of .603 ($p < .001$). Degree of physical injury recovery by Month 4 produced a final multiple correlation of .647, accounting for 42% of the variance.

As an exploratory step, we recalculated the regression with the initial CAPS score omitted. The results are reported in Table 7-5. Interestingly, with initial CAPS removed we found a larger final multiple correlation of .709, accounting for 50.3% of the variance. Noticeably different variables entered, including whether the survivor met criteria for major depression at the time of the initial assessment and whether he or she had experienced a pre-MVA major depression or alcohol abuse. Reaction to being in a vehicle (perceived vulnerability) at the time of the initial assessment and family relationship after the MVA also entered.

Logistic Regression to Predict Remission of Individuals With Initial Subsyndromal PTSD. The results of this prediction problem are summarized in Table 7-6. With three variables—two related to co-morbid disorders present at the initial assessment and the third, the PIQ, at 2 months—one can correctly classify 86.1% of the sample. This compares with a baseline level of correct classification of 67.4% if everyone is classified a remitter.

Multiple Regression to Predict CAPS Score of Individuals With Initial Subsyndromal PTSD. The final prediction effort for this section is shown in Table 7-7. With five variables we found a

Table 7-2

Values of Individual Predictors of Remission of MVA-Related PTSD and Subsyndromal PTSD at 6 Months

Predictor	PTSD		Subsyndromal	
	Diagnosis	CAPS 6 mo.	Diagnosis	CAPS 6 mo.
Demographics				
Age	.042	−.001	.095	.113
Sex	.040	.165	.271'	.097
1 = female				
0 = male				
Education level	−.190	−.220'	.109	.109
1 = High school				
2 = Bachelor's degree or less				
3 = Graduate degree				
Marital status	.040	−.039	.049	−.086
1 = Married				
0 = Unmarried				
Race	−.188	−.163	−.082	.030
1 = Caucasian				
0 = Other				
Accident-related variables				
No. Vehicles involved	.009	.071	.309*	.377*

Role in MVA				
1 = Driver	.078	−.012	.077	.291'
0 = Other				
Physical effects of MVA				
Abbreviated injury scale	.306*	.162	.116	.088
Whiplash injury				
1 = yes	.052	.127	.236	.319*
0 = no				
Loss of consciousness				
1 = yes	.389**	.163	−.097	−.131
0 = no				
Physical injury quotient				
Month 1	.144	.080	.355*	.449**
Month 2	.251'	.237'	.473***	.489***
Month 3	.234'	.291*	.455**	.425**
Month 4	.288*	.321*	.457**	.452**
Month 5	.250'	.288*	.439**	.484***
Month 6	.300*	.301*	.414**	.474***
Subjective reactions to MVA				
Degree of responsibility (%)	−.322*	.413**	−.170	.078
Fear of death at time of MVA (%)	.061	.053	−.157	−.252'
Degree of control Sub. had (%)	−.057	−.151	.082	.011
Subjective reactions to MVA (at time of assessment)				
Current vulnerability in vehicle (%)	.322*	.342*	.041	−.020
Present total functioning as percentage of pre-MVA functioning (sub. est.)	−.178	−.198	−.406**	−.522**
Post MVA GAS/pre-MVA GAS	−.269*	−.306*	−.101	.018

(Table 7-2 continues)

Table 7-2 *(Continued)*

Values of Individual Predictors of Remission of MVA-Related PTSD and Subsyndromal PTSD at 6 Months

Predictor	PTSD		Subsyndromal	
	Diagnosis	CAPS 6 mo.	Diagnosis	CAPS 6 mo.
Psychopathology (pre-MVA)				
Pre-MVA depression				
1 = yes	−.184	−.225'	−.057	.112
0 = no				
Pre-MVA PTSD				
1 = yes	−.078	−.070	−.066	−.125
0 = no				
Any Pre-MVA Axis I Disorder				
1 = yes	−.101	−.070	−.047	.030
0 = no				
Any Pre-MVA Axis II Disorder				
1 = yes	.188	.171	−.097	.269'
0 = no				
Pre-MVA Mental Health Tx.				
1 = yes	.069	.050	.248	.300*
0 = no				
Psychopathology (at time of assesment)				
Initial CAPS	.415**	.603***	.319*	.515***

Current major depression				
1 = yes	.256'	.433**	.318*	.146
0 = no				
Major depression at time of MVA				
1 = yes	−.035	.038	.222	.230
0 = no				
Current alcohol abuse/dependence				
1 = yes	.149	.244'	−.107	−.143
0 = no				
Current substance abuse/dependence				
1 = yes	—	—	−.107	−.143
0 = no				
Current anxiety disorder (except PTSD)				
1 = yes	−.022	.008	−.332*	−.192
0 = no				
Psychosocial effects of MVA				
Post-MVA role duunctioning work/school/home (1–5)	.240'	.382**	.250	.191
Pre-MVA family relations (1–5)	.171	.148	.092	.334*
Post-MVA family relations (1–5)	.252'	.396*	.068	.293'
Pre-MVA friend relations (1–5)	.033	−.016	.109	.145
Post-MVA friend relations (1–5)	.227'	.207	.068	.108
Post-MVA Factors				
Received psychological and/or drug Tx. post-MVA				
1 = yes	.000	.066	.433**	.455**
0 = no				

(Table 7-2 continues)

123

Table 7-2 (Continued)

Values of Individual Predictors of Remission of MVA-Related PTSD and Subsyndromal PTSD at 6 Months

Predictor	PTSD		Subsyndromal	
	Diagnosis	CAPS 6 mo.	Diagnosis	CAPS 6 mo.
Settled legal suit				
1 = yes	-.124	-.138	.222	.027
0 = no				
Settled traffic charges or insurance issues				
1 = yes	.219	.070	.145	-.096
0 = no				
New MVA (subject)				
1 = yes	-.035	.040	.212	-.111
0 = no				
New MVA family member				
1 = yes	-.009	-.083	.007	-.225
0 = no				
New other trauma (subject)				
1 = yes	.232'	.102	.087	.044
0 = no				
New other trauma (family member)				
1 = yes	.305*	.121	-.100	-.055
0 = no				

Note: For diagnosis 1 = PTSD, 0 = Sub/non-PTSD. 'p ≤ .10, *p ≤ .05, **p ≤ .01, ***p ≤ .001.

Note: For diagnosis 1 = PTSD, 0 = Sub/non-PTSD. $'p < .10, p < .05, **p < .01, ***p < .001.$

Table 7-3

Summary of Logistic Regression to Predict Remission of PTSD Among MVA Survivors Over Initial 6-Month Follow-Up

Variable	B	Wald	Sig.	R	Cumulative % correct classification		
					PTSD	Sub-PTSD or non-PTSD	Total
	—	—	—	—	0	100.0	54.6
Initial CAPS score	0.0520	6.976	.0083	.2562	60.0	80.0	70.9
New trauma to family	2.4868	6.708	.0096	.2492	64.0	83.3	74.6
Abbreviated Injury Scale score	0.1252	2.5772	.1084	.0873	72.0	86.7	80.0
Physical injury quotient (Month 4)	2.7914	4.1073	.0427	.1667	80.0	86.7	83.6
Constant	−6.2987	12.2139	.0005	—			
Total correct classification = 83.6%							

Table 7-4

Multiple Regression Analysis to Predict 6-Month Follow-Up CAPS Score Among MVA Survivors With Initial PTSD Diagnosis

Variable	B	β	t	p	R	R^2	Change in R^2	Sig. of F for change
Initial CAPS	0.7642	.5681	5.32	< .0001	.603	.346	—	—
Physical injury quotient (Month 4)	24.5288	.2377	2.23	.0305	.647	.419	.055	.0305
Constant	−22.0673							

Note: From "Prediction of Remission of Acute Post-Traumatic Stress Disorder in Motor Vehicle Accident Victims," by E. B. Blanchard, E. J. Hickling, C. A. Forneris, A. E. Taylor, T. C. Buckley, W. R. Loos, and J. Jaccard, 1997, *Journal of Traumatic Stress, 10,* Table 4. Copyright 1997 by Plenum. Adapted with permission.

Table 7-5

Multiple Regression Analysis to Predict Six-Month Follow-Up CAPS Score Among MVA Survivors With Initial PTSD Diagnosis (Omitting Initial CAPS Score)

Variable	B	β	t	p	R	R^2	Change in R^2	Sig. of F for change
Major depression at initial assessment	10.7757	.3546	3.24	.0022	.433	.188	—	—
Perceived vulnerability in vehicle at initial assessment	0.3494	.2859	2.80	.0073	.538	.290	.102	.0085
Pre-MVA major depression	−10.4822	−.3511	−3.40	.0014	.623	.388	.098	.0061
Post-MVA family relations	9.3342	.3038	2.82	.0069	.678	.459	.071	.0132
Alcohol abuse	47.6363	.2152	2.07	.0434	.709	.503	.044	.0434
Constant	−12.1297							

Note: From "Prediction of Remission of Acute Post-Traumatic Stress Disorder in Motor Vehicle Accident Victims," by E. B. Blanchard, E. J. Hickling, C. A. Forneris, A. E. Taylor, T. C. Buckley, W. R. Loos, and J. Jaccard, 1997, *Journal of Traumatic Stress, 10*, Table 4. Copyright 1997 by Plenum. Adapted with permission.

Table 7-6

Logistic Regression to Predict Remission of Subsyndromal PTSD Among MVA Survivors Over Initial 6-Month Follow-Up

| | | | | | Cumulative % correct classification | | |
					Sub-PTSD or PTSD	Non-PTSD	Total
Variable	B	Wald	Sig.	R	0	100.0	67.4
Physical Injury Quotient (Month 2)	4.579	8.1828	.0042	.3375	64.3	89.7	81.4
Major depression at initial assessment	6.193	.0161	.8990	.0000	71.4	89.7	83.7
Anxiety disorder at initial assessment	−9.821	.0355	.8506	.0000	71.4	93.1	86.1
Constant	−9.409	.0372	.8470				
Total correct classification = 86.1%							

Table 7-7

Multiple Regression Analyses to Predict 6-Month Follow-Up CAPS Score Among MVA Survivors With Initial Subsyndromal PTSD Diagnoses

Variable	With functioning measure				Without functioning measure			
	B	β	t	p	B	β	t	p
Participant's assessment of functioning at time of initial assessment	−0.0320	−1.0434	−0.29	.7706				
Pre-MVA family relations	5.6556	.3071	2.91	.0060	5.6399	.3063	2.94	.0055
Participant received mental health Tx. after MVA	12.8075	.3438	2.98	.0051	13.2811	.3566	3.37	.0017
No. of vehicles in MVA	9.3836	.3821	3.29	.0022	9.7514	.3970	3.84	.0004
Initial CAPS score	0.4513	.3434	2.67	.0113	0.4783	.3639	3.41	.0016
Constant	−30.3311				34.2559			

Note: From "Prediction of Remission of Acute Post-Traumatic Stress Disorder in Motor Vehicle Accident Victims," by E. B. Blanchard, E. J. Hickling, C. A. Forneris, A. E. Taylor, T. C. Buckley, W. R. Loos, and J. Jaccard, 1997, *Journal of Traumatic Stress, 10*, Table 6. Copyright 1997 by Plenum. Adapted with permission.

129

final multiple correlation of .776, accounting for 60.1% of the variance in CAPS score. Again, initial CAPS score was entered as was the survivor's subjective assessment of how well he or she was functioning at the time of initial assessment. Pre-MVA family relationships, the number of vehicles in the MVA, and whether the survivor received mental health treatment after the MVA were also entered.

Interestingly, the latter variable had a negative beta weight. This means receiving treatment was associated with a higher follow-up CAPS score. A further examination showed that survivors with subsyndromal PTSD who received mental health services tended to be more symptomatic (higher CAPS scores at initial assessment). Thus, those who were worse initially continued to be worse 6 months later.

Mental Health Treatment and Initial Remission. An interesting aspect of the short-term follow-up data is that receiving mental health treatment was essentially irrelevant, on a group basis, for the MVA survivors initially diagnosed with PTSD. The phi coefficient for receiving mental health treatment of any sort after the MVA and remission of PTSD was 0 (see Table 7-3). Data on this point are displayed in more detail in Table 7-8. There was the same rate of remission among survivors with initial PTSD for those who received any treatment versus those who did not (54.5%).

These results are consistent with the data on early intervention with troubled MVA survivors reported by Brom et al. (1993): They found no difference in reduction of IES scores for individuals who received brief treatment versus those who received no treatment. Brom et al.'s data are at odds with the data from the NCS reported by Kessler et al. (1995), who found an advantage in remission rates for those with PTSD who received mental health treatment at some time (but the treatment was not necessarily for the PTSD) versus those who never received treatment: at 6 months 20% remission for treated versus 15% for never treated; at 12 months 35% remission for treated versus 26% for never treated. The data on treatment and remission are retrospective, unfortunately; moreover, the treatment was not necessarily treatment for PTSD.

Table 7-8

Results of Uncontrolled Evaluation of Mental Health Treatments of MVA Survivors Initially Diagnosed With PTSD

Variable	Treatment status (frequencies)			
	Treated		Not treated	
Initial diagnostic status				
PTSD	22		33	
6-mo. FU diagnostic status				
PTSD	10		15	
Sub-PTSD	4		4	
Non-PTSD	8		14	
Initial CAPS score M (SD)	63.0	(22.6)	57.5	(22.0)
6-mo. FU CAPS score M (SD)	39.3	(29.8)	35.3	(30.3)

Note: FU = Follow-up. From "Prediction of Remission of Acute Post-Traumatic Stress Disorder in Motor Vehicle Accident Victims," by E. B. Blanchard, E. J. Hickling, C. A. Forneris, A. E. Taylor, T. C. Buckley, W. R. Loos, and J. Jaccard, 1997, *Journal of Traumatic Stress, 10,* Table 7. Copyright 1997 by Plenum. Adapted with permission.

One-Year Follow-Up

The last major topic in this chapter is the results from the one-year follow-up. We collected data on 83.5% of our initial sample of 158 MVA survivors (see chap. 3, Table 3-5). Unfortunately, there was some differential attrition. We lost a significantly larger proportion of our minority participants than we did those of Caucasian background. There was also a trend ($p = .09$) for differential loss among those initially diagnosed with PTSD. We lost 22% of those participants. Of those for whom we were unable to obtain 12-month data, 12 had moved and left no forwarding address and were unreachable through family contacts, 13 refused or had dropped out, and 1 had died. Details of this part of the project can be found in Blanchard, Hickling, Barton, Taylor, Loos and Jones-Alexander (1996).

Month-by-Month Remission Results

The month-by-month diagnostic status data for the 48 MVA survivors who were initially diagnosed with PTSD are reported in Figure 7-3. The figure shows that by 6 months the degree of remission had essentially plateaued, with the fraction of the sample still meeting the criteria for full PTSD ranging from 41.7% (Months 10, 11, and 12) to 50% (Month 7). The diagnostic breakdown based on the 12-month CAPS interview was 16 (33.3%) with full PTSD, 7 (14.6%) with subsyndromal PTSD, and 25 (52.1%) without PTSD.

Effect of Initial Diagnostic Criteria on 12-Month Remission Rate. In chapter 4 we outlined how the rate of initial diagnosis of PTSD from an MVA could vary by as much as 15% depending on whether one used *DSM–III–R* (APA, 1987) or *DSM–IV* (APA, 1994) criteria and whether one used in scoring CAPS symptoms a "rule of 3" or a "rule of 4." If one used *DSM–IV* criteria instead of the *DSM–III–R* we used throughout, the rate of remission at 12 months would be 67.3% rather than 66.7%. If one used the "rule of 4" to make the initial diagnosis, then the remission rate would

12 Month Follow-up of Initial PTSD Subjects

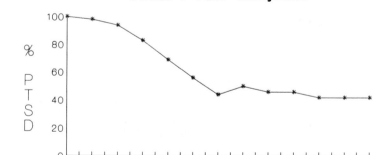

Figure 7-3. Month-by-month remission data for survivors initially diagnosed with PTSD.

be 64.3% rather than 66.7%. Thus, one obtains essentially the same rate of remission regardless of the initial diagnostic criteria applied.

Similar month-by-month results for those 42 survivors initially diagnosed with subsyndromal PTSD are plotted in Figure 7-4. We changed the format of the graph to show the percentage of the subsample that had deteriorated enough to meet the full PTSD criteria. (We discuss these individuals with delayed-onset PTSD in detail in chapter 8).

Examination of Figure 7-4 reveals again an essential plateau of the remission curve with the fraction of individuals who had not remitted (or who worsened) ranging from 33.3% (Month 6) to 23.8% (Month 10). The diagnostic breakdown from the 12-month CAPS interview was 3 (7.1%) with full PTSD, 9 (21.4%) still with subsyndromal PTSD, and 30 (71.4%) without PTSD.

18-Month Follow-Up on Initial PTSDs. As noted earlier, we followed up on 35 of those with initial PTSD (73% of those available at 12 months, but only 56.5% of the initial sample) with interviews at 18 months. The results for this longer follow-up are shown in Figure 7-5.

Figure 7-5 presents again our plateau effect: From the 12-month point to the 18-month CAPS, the proportion of the

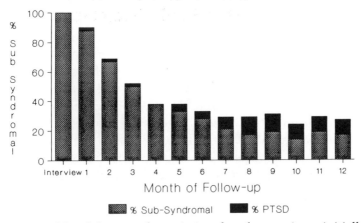

12 Month Follow-up of Initial Sub-syndromal Subjects

Figure 7-4.   Month-by-month remission data for survivors initially diagnosed with subsyndromal PTSD.

12-18 Month Follow-up of
Initial PTSD Subjects

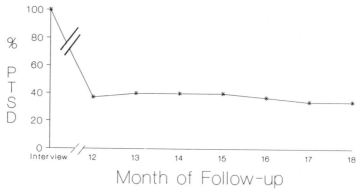

Figure 7-5.   Long-term follow-up data for initial PTSDs.

sample that remained with full PTSD ranged from 34.3% (Months 17 and 18) to 40% (Months 14 and 15).

Altogether it is apparent that a majority of MVA survivors who initially develop PTSD remit over the first 6 to 8 months (our assessment took place at approximately 2 months post-MVA) following the trauma. Thereafter there continues to be a gradual remission rate, with a 12-month remission rate of about 60%. Kessler et al. (1995) noted continued gradual improvement as far as 6 years post-trauma in their retrospective study of a large sample of mixed-trauma victims with PTSD.

The relatively high rate of remission over the first 6 months, combined with the data in Table 7-8 showing no appreciable beneficial effect of early treatment, have led us to focus our treatment efforts on individuals who remain distressed 6 months or after an MVA.

We interpret, with considerable caution, the finding that, on a group basis, receiving mental health treatment over the first 6 months after an MVA is not beneficial or is irrelevant in comparison with no treatment. The high remission rate would necessitate an extremely large treatment effect to show a statistically significant effect. There may have been a treatment effect in the first 6 months that we could not discern in our data.

Because the rate of spontaneous remission appears to slow after the first 6 months (as discussed the next section), it may be easier to show a treatment effect in periods after the first 6 months.

Prediction of Remission by 12 Months

We repeated our analysis of variables that might predict remission by 12 months. We restrict this discussion to the prediction of remission of initial PTSDs only, again focusing on logistic regression to predict the dichotomous outcome of meeting criteria for PTSD or not and on multiple regression to predict the continuous variable of 12-month CAPS score.

We cast an even wider net for potential predictors, examining the simple correlation of 101 potential predictors. To control for random relations, we restricted the final potential predictor battery to variables that accounted for 4% or more of the variance in one of the two criteria ($r = .20$). In addition, for the multiple regression analysis, we specified that each new variable entered must account for at least 3% of new variance.

The final predictor battery is presented in Table 7-9. As is obvious, a wide array of variables had significant bivariate relations with one of the two criteria; in fact, 45 variables met the initial screening criteria. There was clear redundancy among the variables; this was planned in an effort to find the best overall prediction equations.

Logistic Regression to Predict 12-Month Diagnostic States

The results of the logistic regression are reported in Table 7-10. From Table 7-10 one can see that base rates would correctly classify 66.7% of the sample if everyone had remitted. Using three variables, the overall accuracy improves to 79.2%, and the correct classification of those who still meet criteria for full PTSD improves from 0% with base rates to 62.5% correctly classified. Interestingly, all three variables came from the initial assessment: the foreshortened future symptom from Criterion C for PTSD, the irritability symptom from Criterion D for PTSD, and the degree of vulnerability the individual felt when in an automobile (as driver or passenger) at the time of the initial assessment. The

Table 7-9

Predictor Battery to Predict 12-Month Follow-Up Status of MVA Survivors Initially Diagnosed as PTSD

Predictor	Initial PTSDs	
	Diagnosis at 1 year	12-month CAPS score
Physical effects of MVA		
Abbreviated Injury Scale		.22
Loss of consciousness	.25	
Physical Injury Quotient		
Month 10	.24	.20
Month 12	−.23	.25
Month 11	.21	
Subjective reactions to MVA		
Degree of responsibility	−.28	−.38
Fear of death at time of MVA	.30	.21
Degree of control subject had		−.23
Estimate of how life-threatening MVA was	.36	
Subjective reactions to MVA (at time of assessment)		
Current vulnerability in vehicle	.27	.39
Present total functioning as % of Pre-MVA functioning		.26
Psychopathology (pre-MVA)		
Past alcohol abuse		.26

Past major depression	−.37	−.20
Any pre-MVA Axis II disorder	.34	.33
Psychopathology (at time of initial assess.)		
Initial CAPS	.31	.56
Major depression: current		.26
Alcohol abuse: current	.21	.56
Psychosocial effects of MVA		
Post-MVA family relations		.21
Post-MVA friend relations (Month 3)	−.23	
Pre-MVA friend relations	−.23	
Post-MVA Factors		
Received psychological treatment and/or drug Tx. over 1-year post-MVA		.23
New MVA (subject)	.24	
New trauma (family member)		−.23
Involved in litigation at 1-year	.30	.29
Initial CAPS Scores		
Symptom 1		.20
Symptom 2		.29
Symptom 3		.31
Symptom 4		.25
Symptom 5		.27
Symptom 6	.22	.39
Symptom 7		.24
Symptom 10	.26	.42

(Table 7-9 continues)

137

Table 7-9 (Continued)

Predictor Battery to Predict 12-Month Follow-Up Status of MVA Survivors Initially Diagnosed as PTSD

Predictor	Initial PTSDs	
	Diagnosis at 1 year	12-month CAPS score
Symptom 11	.40	.40
Symptom 12	.31	.40
Symptom 13	.41	.33
Symptom 14	.31	.42
Symptom 15		.22
Symptom 17		.20
Numbing cluster (DSM–III–R)	.24	.38
Avoidance cluster (DSM–III–R)	.23	.45
Avoidance/numbing (DSM–IV)	.30	.50
Reexperiencing (DSM–III–R)		.33
Reexperiencing (DSM–IV)		.36
Hyperarousal (DSM–III–R)	.38	.52
Hyperarousal (DSM–IV)	.39	.51

Note: For diagnosis at 1 year 0 = subsyndromal or non-PTSD and 1 = PTSD.

Table 7-10

Logistic Regression to Predict PTS Symptoms on 1-Year Clinical Status Among Initial PTSDs

Predictor	B	SE	Wald	df	Sig.	% correctly identified		
						PTSD	Less than PTSD	Overall
Base rate	—	—	—	—	—	0	100	66.7
Initial CAPS-13, Irritability	0.5251	0.1944	7.294	1	.0069	50.0	78.1	68.8
Initial CAPS								
Foreshortened future	0.4723	0.1889	6.254	1	.0124	56.3	90.6	79.2
Vulnerability in automobile at initial assessment	0.0379	0.0186	4.141	1	.0419	62.5	87.5	79.2
Constant	−6.6571	2.0234	10.824	1	.0010			

Note: Sig. = significance. From "One-Year Prospective Follow-Up of Motor Vehicle Accident Victims," by E. B. Blanchard, E. J. Hickling, K. A. Barton, A. E. Taylor, W. R. Loos, and J. Jones-Alexander, 1996, *Behaviour Research and Therapy, 34,* 775–786. Copyright 1996 by Elsevier Science. Adapted with permission.

physical injury variables that played a large role in the 6-month predictor analysis were absent in this analysis. Again, the reader is referred to chapter 6 for details on how to use the coefficients from the logistic regression.

Multiple Regression to Predict 12-Month CAPS Scores

The results of the multiple regression analysis to predict 12-month CAPS score are summarized in Table 7-11. Four variables emerged from this analysis as significant predictors. Two were related to initial CAPS score, which was a strong predictor of the 6-months CAPS score: the sum of the initial CAPS scores for the hyperarousal (Criterion D) symptoms and the sum of the initial CAPS scores for the avoidance symptoms of Criterion C. Two other variables from the overall assessment entered the final equation: the presence of any Axis II disorder and the presence of an alcohol abuse diagnosis at the initial assessment. This latter variable was also a predictor of 6-month CAPS score for initial PTSDs.

Thus, the initial level of PTSD symptom severity predicts both later symptom severity and overall remission. The alcohol abuse and Axis II diagnosis may serve as moderator variables: The presence of either of these indicates long-standing overall difficulty in functioning and thus is associated with continued symptoms.

Clinical Hint

It seems clear that initial severity of PTSD symptoms is a major predictor of short-term and longer term remission. More severely symptomatic individuals are more likely to continue to be symptomatic over time. Severity of physical injury and relative degree of healing play a role in short-term recovery but are not influential in the longer term. Finally, indications of chronic psychological problems prior to the MVA are associated with poorer recovery.

Another point that seems clear to us is that individuals who have not improved on their own by 6 to 8 months after an MVA are unlikely to remit spontaneously with further passage of time.

Table 7-11

Summary of Final Multiple Regression to Predict PTS Symptoms on 1-Year in Initial PTSDs

Variable	B	β	t	p	R	R^2	Change in R^2	Sig. of F for change
Alcohol abuse at time of initial assessment	85.53	.476	4.97	.000	.563	.317	—	—
Sum of initial CAPS								
Hyperarousal symptoms	1.06	.347	3.62	.0008	.712	.506	.189	.0001
Pre-MVA Axis II disorder	18.07	.275	2.91	.0056	.770	.593	.087	.0039
Sum of initial CAPS								
Avoidance symptoms	1.12	.223	2.29	.0268	.798	.637	.044	.0268
Constant	−11.64		−1.51	.1394				

Note: Sig. = significance. From "One-Year Prospective Follow-Up of Motor Vehicle Accident Victims," by E. B. Blanchard , E. J. Hickling, K. A. Barton, A. E. Taylor, W. R. Loos, and J. Jones-Alexander, 1996, *Behaviour Research and Therapy, 34,* 775–786. Copyright 1996 by Elsevier Science. Adapted with permission.

Thus, whereas 50% of those with initial PTSD will remit within 6 months, only about 25% of those who still have PTSD at 6 to 8 months will remit over the next 6 months. Moreover, for those with PTSD at a year after the MVA, less than 10% will remit over the following 6 months.

MVA survivors who still meet the criteria for PTSD 6 months or more after the MVA should clearly be given focused specific treatment—a topic to which we devote the last four chapters of this book.

Long-Term Psychosocial Effects of MVAs

In chapter 5 we documented the initial psychosocial impact MVAs can have on individuals, showing that those who met the criteria for PTSD had more subjective distress and were more role impaired than MVA survivors who did not meet the full PTSD criteria. In this section, we present the data on these same variables from the 12-month follow-up assessment. We have restricted this to those with initial PTSD because the others were not especially impaired. We have also subdivided the initial PTSD group into individuals who had remitted entirely or in part (12-month classification of non-PTSD or subsyndromal PTSD) and those who continued to meet the full criteria for PTSD at 12 months.

Table 7-12 summarizes the indicators of subjective distress (our psychological test scores), and Table 7-13 summarizes the indicators of role impairment. All were subjected to a two-way repeated measures multivariate ANOVA (MANOVA) followed up with univariate ANOVAs on each variable.

Examination of Table 7-12 shows that the initial PTSDs who remitted were less distressed on each measure than the initial PTSDs who did not remit within the 12 months (all $ps = .002$ or better). On the IES, both subgroups of initial PTSDs showed a decline in IES score over 12 months ($p = .002$). There was a very interesting pattern of results on trait anxiety. Those who did not remit showed an increase over time, whereas those who did remit showed a slight decrease (interaction $F = 12.46, p = .001$). For the Beck Depression Inventory (BDI), those who did not remit showed no decrease in depressive symptoms, whereas those who did showed a slight decline.

Table 7-12

Psychological Test Scores for Participants With Initial PTSD Based on 12-Month Clinical Status

Measure	12-month diagnosis	Initial assessment M	SD	12 month assessment M	SD	Group F	p	Time F	p	Group × Time F	p	Within group t	p
Beck Depression Inventory	PTSD (n = 16)	20.6	11.4	20.3	10.5	12.71	.001	1.34	.253	0.89	ns	0.10	ns
	Sub + Non (n = 32)	13.1	2.2	9.9	7.2							2.21	.034
Impact of Event Scale	PTSD	41.7	14.2	39.5	17.4	17.00	<.001	18.77	<.001	11.15	.002	0.65	ns
	Sub + Non	31.6	16.2	14.6	9.7							6.38	<.001
State Anxiety	PTSD	75.0	18.3	77.1	16.0	19.4	<.001	0.80	ns	2.63	.112	-0.44	ns
	Sub + Non	59.7	18.6	52.5	18.8							2.12	.042
Trait Anxiety	PTSD	64.4	18.6	76.3	16.3	11.41	.002	5.09	.029	12.46	.001	-3.89	.002
	Sub + Non	57.7	9.1	55.1	12.5							1.06	ns
Global Assessment Scale	PTSD	57.0	8.9	56.8	11.6	3.23	ns	8.97	.004	9.54	.003	0.06	ns
	Sub + Non	55.0	13.2	63.0	7.1							-4.98	<.001

Table 7-13

Ratings of Role Performance Variables for Participants With Initial PTSD Based on 12-Month Clinical Status

Measure	12-month diagnosis	Initial assessment M	SD	12 month assessment M	SD	Group F	p	Time F	p	Group × Time F	p	Within group t	p
Major role function[a] (work, school, homemaking)	PTSD	3.4	1.2	2.8	1.7	2.77	.103	7.05	.011	0.26	ns	1.62	
	Sub + Non	2.9	1.6	2.0	0.8							2.65	.013
Relations with family[b] (Average of all first degree relatives plus spouse/partner)	PTSD	2.3	.8	2.5	0.7	0.50	ns	0.14	ns	2.90	.096	−1.71	.11
	Sub + Non	2.3	1.0	2.1	0.6							1.07	ns
Relations with friends	PTSD	2.1	1.3	2.7	1.4	0.40	ns	0.24	ns	3.66	.062	1.13	ns
	Sub + Non	2.4	1.6	2.0	1.1							1.51	ns
Recreation participation	PTSD	3.9	0.8	3.3	1.2	8.33	.006	10.6	.002	0.06	ns	2.03	.06
	Sub + Non	3.0	1.9	2.3	1.3							3.06	.005

[a]Ratings: 1 = no impairment, high level of performance; 3 = mild impairment ; 5 = severe impairment.   [b]Ratings: 1 = very good, very close emotional relationship; 3 = fair, believes relationship needs to be closer; 5 = very poor, no emotional closeness, avoids family member.

In Table 7-13 the results show improvement over the year in performance of major role function ($p = .011$) and in participation in recreation ($p = .002$) for both subgroups. For both of these variables, the two subgroups were about one whole scale unit apart—difference between satisfactory performance with no impairment (remitters) and somewhat impaired performance (nonremitters).

Interestingly, relationships with friends deteriorated for those who continued to meet the criteria for PTSD but improved slightly for the remitters (interaction $F = 3.66$, $p = .06$). It could be that the feelings of estrangement in those with PTSD become reality as these individuals withdraw over time from friends and social activities. Relationships with close family members remain stable at a generally good level.

Total CAPS scores for these two PTSD subgroups are revealing: For those who did not remit the initial and 12-month CAPS scores were 69.2 and 55.6, respectively. This represents a significant ($p = .008$) decline. For the remitters, there was a highly significant decrease in total CAPS score, from 55.0 to 15.7, $t(31) = 11.3$, $p < .0001$. The subgroup that had not remitted continued to be a very symptomatic, distressed, and impaired group of individuals who were clearly in need of psychological treatment.

Effects on Travel Behavior

Our last point in this chapter on follow-up is an examination of travel behavior. In chapter 5 (Table 5-18) we noted a large initial effect of the MVA on travel behavior, especially for MVA survivors who were initially diagnosed with PTSD. Table 7-14 presents a summary of these effects for individuals initially diagnosed with PTSD who were re-assessed at 12 months.

Of the initial nine individuals with PTSD who met our criteria for driving phobia, eight were followed up at 12 months. The two whose PTSD had not remitted were still not driving, whereas all of the remitters had returned to driving. As Table 7-14 shows, there was still some travel reluctance in a sizable minority (40.6%) of the initial PTSDs who had remitted. For those still meeting the full criteria for PTSD, there had been some decrease

Table 7-14

Travel Behavior Effects at 1-Year Follow-Up for MVA Survivors Initially Diagnosed with PTSD

12-month diagnosis	Initial		12-month		Within-group p
	M	SD	M	SD	
Driving phobia					
PTSD ($n = 16$)	2	12.5%	2	12.5%	ns
Remitted ($n = 32$)	6	18.8%	0		.0313
Any travel reluctance					
PTSD	14	87.5%	11	68.8%	ns
Remitted	29	90.6%	13	40.6%	< .001

in travel reluctance but not to a significant degree. Again, it is clear that there is a substantial subset of MVA survivors greatly in need of psychological help, even a year after their accidents.

Longer Term Follow-Up by Mail

In chapter 4 we described our final follow-up, a mail survey using the PTSD Checklist (PCL). A set of questionnaires, including the PCL, IES, BDI, and the State-Trait Anxiety Inventory (STAI), and a set of questions about new MVAs and other new personal traumas and about mental health treatment for symptoms related to the original MVA were mailed to all participants, including those who had dropped out at the 6-month or 12-month follow-up time point. For individuals who did not respond to the first mailing, and for whom the envelope was not returned by the postal service as "addressee unknown," a second mail request was sent. Included in the request for answers was an offer of $5 for returning the completed questionnaires in the stamped return envelope.

We received 100 replies, 98 of which were complete, for an overall return rate of 62% (of the 158 original MVA survivors). These 98 represented 75% of those available at the 12-month follow-up.

Thus, any conclusions have to be tempered with knowledge that there may be a bias due to nonrespondents. The results represent the status of these MVA survivors 18 to 30 months after their initial assessment or almost 2 years post-accident.

Diagnoses were on the basis of responses to the PCL, utilizing both the locally derived total PCL score of 45 or greater, and also an inspection of individual symptom scores to see whether the *DSM-III-R* (APA, 1987) pattern of symptoms requirements were met. The overall diagnostic results are reported in Table 7-15.

From Table 7-15 one can see that we were able to collect data on 72.5% of the initial non-PTSDs, 60.0% of the initial subsyndromal PTSDs, but only 54.8% of those originally diagnosed with PTSD. These findings mirror the results in Table 4-5, which showed relatively poorer retention among those with an initial diagnosis of PTSD, beginning at the 6-month follow-up.

Of those originally diagnosed with PTSD, 8 (23.5%) were still noticeably symptomatic more than 2 years after their MVA, with an average PCL score of 55. The other psychological tests reflect the subjective distress these individuals still acknowledge. Other information, including data on new MVAs, from this longer term follow-up are summarized in Table 7-16, wherein one can see that 7 individuals had had new MVAs since their last contact with us, an interval ranging from 6 to 24 months (average interval since index MVA was 26.4 months), whereas in 9 other cases, a close family member had had an MVA. This finding echoes Norris's (1992) finding of a high rate of MVAs in the American population.

Of those initially diagnosed with PTSD, in particular, one finds that only 2 had new MVAs, whereas 14 acknowledged other new trauma. Of the 34 initial PTSDs 12 had some form of mental health treatment during the follow-up interval, including half ($n = 3$) of those who still met criteria for full PTSD.

Fortunately, many of the most seriously affected MVA survivors, those initially diagnosed with PTSD, remitted over the first 6 to 8 months after the MVA, and by 1 year at least 60% had remitted. Beyond that point, our prospective data tend to agree with the large scale retrospective results of Kessler et al. (1995): There is a sizable proportion of PTSDs from MVAs who have a very chronic course of the disorder with only minimal additional spontaneous remission.

Table 7-15

Results of Mail Survey of MVA Survivors

Initial diagnosis (CAPS)	Follow-up diagnosis (PCL)	Frequency	Interval from initial diagnosis to follow-up (months)		Follow-up PCL score		Follow-up IES score		Follow-up BDI score	
			M	SD	M	SD	M	SD	M	SD
PTSD	PTSD	6	26.0	3.1	62.0	15.4	42.8	22.4	36.0	13.7
	Sub-PTSD	2	28.4	4.6	35.0	5.7	46.0	33.9	4.0	0.0
	Non-PTSD	26	27.7	6.2	25.2	7.7	7.3	7.8	7.2	6.9
Sub-PTSD	Sub-PTSD	4	24.4	1.9	38.3	6.3	24.0	6.5	12.3	9.0
	Non-PTSD	23	25.4	7.7	19.8	4.3	4.2	7.2	4.6	6.2
Non-PTSD	Sub-PTSD	2	18.9	0.2	39.0	2.8	30.0	21.2	7.0	4.2
	Non-PTSD	35	26.8	6.0	0.1	5.8	4.5	8.6	4.5	5.0

Note: Totals are in bold.

Table 7-16

Other Results of Mail Survey of MVA Survivors

Initial diagnosis	Follow-up diagnosis	Frequency	Frequency of new MVAs in follow-up interval	Frequency of new family member MVA in follow-up	Frequency of new other trauma in follow-up	Frequency of receiving mental health services in follow-up
PTSD	PTSD	6	2	1	3	3
	Sub-PTSD	2	1	0	2	1
	Non-PTSD	26	4	6	11	16
Total for initial PTSD		**34**	**7**	**7**	**16**	**20**
Sub-PTSD	Sub-PTSD	4	0	1	0	3
	Non-PTSD	23	1	7	6	11
Total for initial Sub-PTSD		**27**	**1**	**8**	**6**	**14**
Non-PTSD	Sub-PTSD	2	1	0	1	0
	Non-PTSD	35	7	6	18	12
Total for initial Non-PTSD		**37**	**8**	**6**	**19**	**12**
Total sample		**98**	**16**	**21**	**41**	**46**

Note: Totals are in bold.

149

8

Delayed-Onset PTSD
From MVAs

It is well recognized that some individuals do not develop PTSD immediately following a trauma; instead, for reasons that are not clear at this time, the onset of full PTSD syndrome is delayed for some period of time. The *DSM–IV* recognizes this phenomenon officially and classifies PTSD with delayed onset as a subcategory of PTSD for which there is a delay of at least 6 months between the trauma and the individual's meeting the full diagnostic criteria. There is a very limited literature on this phenomenon among MVA survivors. Part of the reason for this situation is probably that the best way to identify these cases is by conducting a prospective follow-up of traumatized individuals to detect the onset of the delayed cases.

As was reported in chapter 3 (Table 3-2), Green et al. (1993), in their study of 24 Australian MVA survivors who were hospitalized because of injuries, found only one case of PTSD at the 1-month follow-up point. At the 18-month follow-up they found five more cases. All five delayed-onset cases had shown a subsyndromal form of PTSD (part of the total symptom complex but not enough symptoms to meet the full criteria) at the 1-month assessment. Other factors that identified those who would eventually show an onset of PTSD were high scores on the IES at the 1-month follow-up.

Mayou et al. (1993), in their prospective follow-up of British MVA survivors admitted to the emergency room, found 14 cases of PTSD among 174 assessed at a 3-month follow-up. At the

12-month follow-up, 5 of those cases had remitted; more important for this chapter, there were 6 new cases of PTSD, representing 3.4% of the total sample. Thus, these 6 cases are examples of delayed-onset PTSD. No explicit information was provided on the 6 cases.

In Epstein's (1993) prospective follow-up of 15 seriously injured (admitted to shock-trauma center) MVA survivors it was noted that 2 of his 6 eventual PTSD cases were not diagnosed until 3 to 6 months after the MVA. In both of these cases, the individuals had relatively high scores on the Avoidance subscale of the IES. Epstein noted that both patients initially denied reexperiencing symptoms. During the frequent follow-ups (interviews every 9 to 10 weeks), the intrusive memories finally emerged, leading to diagnoses of delayed-onset PTSD. Epstein stated that high initial levels of avoidance symptoms can interfere in the diagnosis, and he recommended frequent reassessments for seriously injured MVA survivors so that reexperiencing symptoms that may be masked by high levels of avoidance can be detected.

Bryant (1996) reported on two cases of seriously injured MVA survivors who had each suffered significant head injury and who eventually developed (delayed-onset) PTSD. In the first case, the individual suffered 5 weeks of post-traumatic amnesia (PTA). Approximately 10 months after the accident, the individual had begun lessons to learn to drive again. A near miss while he was a passenger triggered a prolonged (2-hour) dissociative episode. Over the next few days he acknowledged various reexperiencing symptoms triggered by pictures he had seen of his accident and accounts he had heard of it. Although he had no direct memory of the accident, he clearly developed PTSD.

The second case involved a man who had a 3-week period of PTA secondary to his head injury, an extensive subdural hematoma. Seventeen months after the MVA, a police report was released indicating that another person, who was killed in the crash, had probably been the driver instead of the participant. It is not clear whether accounts of the MVA he had been told led to his extreme reexperiencing and hyperarousal symptoms. In any event, he clearly met the criteria for delayed PTSD at this point.

Bryant's (1996) findings contradict the prevailing clinical wisdom that head-injured patients who suffer from PTA do not develop PTSD because of the absence of memory for the traumatic event (Middleboe, Andersen, Birket-Smith, & Friis, 1992). We would agree that vicarious experience of the accident from photographs and accounts of the MVA can be a sufficient basis for developing PTSD. In fact, the *DSM–IV* (APA, 1994) allows for vicarious traumatization to serve as the stressor. We have observed this in two cases. However, this "vicarious traumatization" is based on accounts and pictures the patient had viewed between the MVA and our initial assessment (1 to 4 months post-MVA) in our cases.

The literature on delayed-onset PTSD from other types of trauma yields one large and very carefully conducted study on this phenomenon: McFarlane's (1988) prospective follow-up of Australian fire fighters following a severe outbreak of bush fires. He assessed a large sample (469 fire fighters) with the IES and the GHQ on three occasions: 4 months post-trauma, 11 months post-trauma, and 29 months post-trauma (Goldberg, 1972). The latter is alleged to be a good (valid and sensitive) measure of psychiatric "caseness" among Australians. A total of 315 individuals responded on all three occasions.

Within this latter sample, he found 62 cases of delayed-onset PTSD: absent at 4 months, present at 11 months ($n = 17$, 5.4% of total sample); absent at 4 months, present at 29 months ($n = 35$, 11.1%); or absent at 4 months, and present at both 11 months and 29 months ($n = 10$, 3.2%). McFarlane found noticeably higher levels of avoidance (as measured by the initial IES) among those who developed delayed-onset PTSD, a finding similar to that of Epstein (1993) with MVA survivors. There were no data on delayed-onset PTSD in the large scale epidemiologic surveys (NCS; Kessler et al., 1995; Norris, 1992).

The Albany MVA Project

Because of the use of the LIFE-type (Keller et al., 1988) interviews focusing on the 17 specific symptoms of PTSD at each of the follow-up interviews (6 months and 12 months), it became possible to track all 17 symptoms on a weekly basis. From this analysis, we identified 7 individuals who met the criteria for delayed-onset PTSD (4.4% of the original sample and 7.3% of MVA survivors who were initially negative for full PTSD). A detailed report of these findings can be found in Buckley, Blanchard, and Hickling (1996). We should note that these 7 participants continue to meet the criteria for PTSD if *DSM–IV* (APA, 1994) criteria are applied or if the scoring for CAPS items is shifted from our "rule of 3" to the more stringent "rule of 4." There was one other case in which onset of full PTSD occurred after our initial assessment, but the total interval between trauma and onset was only 4 months.

Detailed demographic and other assessment information on these 7 MVA survivors is presented in Table 8-1. As can be noted in Table 8-1, all 7 of these individuals received a diagnosis of subsyndromal PTSD at the initial assessment. Thus, our results are similar to those of Green et al. (1993) in their Australian study: Those with delayed-onset PTSD are not initially unscathed; instead they are symptomatic, but not symptomatic enough to meet the full criteria for PTSD. The delayed-onset sample was entirely Caucasian and predominantly female (86%, whereas 67% of participants were female in the initial sample), with an average age of 42.9 years, slightly older than our original sample's average age of 35.4 years.

Clinical Hint

It is of interest that not one MVA survivor classified as non-PTSD developed delayed-onset PTSD. (These individuals did not have any significant reexperiencing symptoms but may have had some avoidance or hyperarousal symptoms; see chapter 4, Table 4-5.) Whether this finding is idiosyncratic to our MVA sample or holds for all trauma victims is unclear. We believe a clinician can be fairly confident that an individual who escapes the trauma of an MVA without developing at least subsyndromal PTSD is extremely unlikely to develop PTSD later.

In three of the cases presented in Table 8-1 there was a proximal (within 4 weeks of when the individual met full PTSD criteria) traumatic event, but not in the other four. This finding lends support to the utility of the diagnosis of subsyndromal PTSD in

Table 8-1

Demographics for the Delayed Onset PTSD Subgroup

Case no.	Age	Gender	Ethnicity	Initial CAPS score	Proximal stressor	Interval from MVA to meeting DSM–III–R criteria for PTSD (days)
123	37	Female	Caucasian	41	Onset of agoraphobia and social phobia, relapse of opiod use	228
175	50	Male	Caucasian	36	No	273
178	41	Female	Caucasian	40	No	347
190	56	Female	Caucasian	25	No	291
209	36	Female	Caucasian	60	No	307
261	42	Female	Caucasian	28	New legal suit filed against subject	288
285	38	Female	Caucasian	41	Loss of medical benefits	251

our experience because 15.6% of the latter individuals deteriorated sufficiently over the course of a year to meet the full
criteria for PTSD.

To categorize MVA survivors with delayed-onset PTSD,
we compared them with delayed onset with the 38 other individuals initially diagnosed with subsyndromal PTSD who did
not deteriorate on three sets of variables: pre-MVA variables,
accident-related variables, and follow-up variables. For those
variables that were significantly different, we then compared
the delayed-onset PTSD cases with the acute onset PTSD cases
($n = 62$).

Delayed-Onset Versus Nondeteriorating Subsyndromals

We have compared the two groups on three clusters of variables:
demographic, pre-MVA variables, and variables related to the
accident and its immediate consequences. There were no differences amomg the demographic variables of gender, age, ethnicity, education, and marital status.

The pre-MVA variable comparison is presented in Table 8-2.
This analysis shows that only two variables were significantly
different: The subsyndromals who did develop PTSD had significantly better average relationships with their first degree relatives. In fact, it was a whole scale unit (on a 5-point scale) better
(see description of the scale in chapter 3). The overall level of pre-
MVA functioning, as measured by the GAS, was lower for the
subsyndromals who developed delayed-onset PTSD.

Table 8-3 reports the comparisons on a number of variables
assessed at the initial assessment (thus, post-MVA). Four variables from the 11 examined were significantly different: total
CAPS score ($p = .004$); score on PTSD symptom 6, behavioral
avoidance ($p = .001$); post-MVA family relationships ($p = .005$);
and post-MVA major role functioning ($p = .046$). Variables of
note that were not different were extent of physical injury (AIS
score) and degree of depression as measured by the BDI. The
finding of higher avoidance scores is consistent with Epstein's
(1993) report. It appears that family relationships did not change
appreciably from before to after the accident; thus, it is not surprising that the pre-MVA difference continued.

Table 8-2
Pre-MVA Variable Analyses for Delayed-Onset PTSD From Motor Vehicle Accidents

Variable	Mean/frequency		Statistic	Probability
	Delayed onset PTSD	Controls[a]		
Pre-MVA relationships with first-degree relatives (social support)	2.9	1.9	$t(43) = 3.12$	.003
GAS rating	69.7	82.1	$t(43) = 3.09$	.004
Prior Axis II (no/yes)	5/2	35/3	Fisher's exact	.166
Prior Axis I (no/yes)	3/4	23/15	Fisher's exact	.433
Previous trauma (no/yes)	1/6	3/35	Fisher's exact	.505

Note: GAS = Global Assessment Scale. Adapted from "A Prospective Examination of Delayed-Onset PTSD Secondary to Motor Vehicle Accidents," by T. C. Buckley, E. B. Blanchard, and E. J. Hickling, 1996, *Journal of Abnormal Psychology, 105,* 617–625. Copyright 1996 by the American Psychological Association.
[a]Initial subsyndromal PTSDs who did not deteriorate.

Table 8-3

Comparison of Variables Related to MVA and Status at Initial Interview for Delayed-Onset PTSD

Variable	Mean/frequency						Statistic	Probability
	Delayed onset PTSD		Controls[a]					
	M	SD	M	SD				
Sx. 6 CAPS (Avoidance)	3.86	1.95	1.05	1.72			$t(43) = 3.88$	0.001
Initial CAPS (total score)	38.7	11.4	28.2	10.5			$t(43) = 3.09$	0.004
Post-MVA family relationship	2.9	1.1	1.9	0.7			$t(43) = 2.98$	0.005
Post-MVA role functioning	3.3	1.0	2.2	1.4			$t(43) = 2.05$	0.046
Post-MVA GAS rating	59.9	6.4	68.4	12.4			$t(43) = 1.77$	0.084
Litigation (no/yes)	2/5		25/13				Fisher's exact	0.098
Fear of death in MVA	0.0	0.00	14.8	31.60			$t(43) = 1.23$	0.225
Driver/passenger	7/0		29/9				Fisher's exact	0.315
Beck Depression Inventory	9.0	5.6	7.4	6.6			$t(42) = .62$	0.538
AIS score	3.71	2.56	3.37	3.16			$t(43) = .27$	0.786
Current psychopathology (no/yes)	5/2		25/13				Fisher's exact	1.000

Note: Sx. 6 = symptom 6; GAS = Global Assessment Scale. Adapted from "A Prospective Examination of Delayed-Onset PTSD Secondary to Motor Vehicle Accidents," by T. C. Buckley, E. B. Blanchard, and E. J. Hickling, 1996, *Journal of Abnormal Psychology, 105,* 617–625. Copyright 1996 by the American Psychological Association.
[a]Initial subsyndromal PTSDs who do not deteriorate.

The accident clearly had a stronger effect on performance of major role functioning because those who develop delayed-onset PTSD were a full scale unit lower (slightly below fair performance with some impairment) than the subsyndromals who did not deteriorate (slightly below satisfactory performance with no impairment).

We also compared the two groups on variables that emerged during the follow-up. After identifying the mean month in which survivors with delayed-onset PTSD met criteria for PTSD (Month 7), we compared their physical injury quotients (PIQ), the variable quantifying relative degree of physical healing for Month 7: The delayed-onset group had a higher value (0.57) than the comparison subsyndromal group (0.22), $t = 2.83(39)$, $p = .007$. The two groups had not differed in initial AIS scores. It thus appears that the delayed-onset PTSD group was recovering physically at a slower pace.

The mean number of stressful events during the follow-up, defined as new MVAs, new legal issues, and any other events the participant identified as stressful, were compared. Individuals with delayed-onset PTSD had significantly more than the comparison group (2.9 vs. 1.1), $t(43) = 3.33$, $p = .002$.

Delayed-Onset PTSDs Versus Acute Onset PTSDs

We compared the 7 individuals with delayed-onset PTSD with the 62 MVA survivors with acute onset PTSD on all of the variables that reached significance in the earlier comparisons with subsyndromals who did not deteriorate. These comparisons are reported in Table 8-4.

We found two significant differences: Individuals with delayed-onset PTSD had more negative life events during the follow-up and they had poorer pre-MVA family relationships. There was also a trend ($p = .057$) for those with delayed-onset PTSD to have been functioning less well overall prior to the MVA.

Clinical Hint

Our clinical impression from these individuals is that MVA survivors who are fairly symptomatic but do not quite meet the

Table 8-4

Acute Onset PTSD Versus Delayed-Onset PTSD Group Comparisons

	Mean					
	Delayed onset PTSD		Acute onset PTSD			
Variable	M	SD	M	SD	t (67)	Probability
No. of negative life events during follow-up	2.9	2.0	1.3	1.6	2.36	.021
Pre-MVA family relationships	2.9	1.1	2.0	0.8	2.26	.027
Pre-MVA GAS rating	69.7	12.7	78.5	11.19	−1.94	.057
Post-MVA family relationships	2.9	1.1	2.3	0.9	1.48	.145
Physical Injury Score (Month 7)	0.51	0.30	0.37	0.26	1.28[a]	.207
Sx. 6 CAPS (Avoidance)	3.9	2.0	4.1	2.6	−0.24	.814

Note: GAS = Global Assessment Scale. Adapted from "A Prospective Examination of Delayed-Onset PTSD Secondary to Motor Vehicle Accidents," by T. C. Buckley, E. B. Blanchard, and E. J. Hickling, 1996, *Journal of Abnormal Psychology, 105,* Table 4. Copyright 1996 by the American Psychological Association.
[a] *df* = 53.

full criteria for PTSD are at risk for delayed-onset PTSD if they have relatively poor family relationships (low social support) and if they were functioning somewhat poorly before the MVA. These individuals constitute the subsyndromals most at risk to deteriorate.

Our other clinical impression, unsupported by our data analyses, is that new trauma, especially related to an MVA (a new MVA or even a relative's having an MVA), is likely to exacerbate new symptoms.

Longer Term Follow-Up

We were able to follow-up five of these individuals with delayed-onset PTSD at the 18-month point. Two had remitted in part (back to subsyndromal PTSD), and one was essentially symptom free. Thus, the overall time course for remission in this group was much like that of those with acute PTSD.

It is clear from the world's MVA survivor literature and from our own prospective follow-up data that delayed-onset PTSD is a real, and potentially sizable, problem that can easily be missed if one focuses only on the first 1 to 3 months after the MVA. It also seems to represent only incremental deterioration (i.e., in which an individual becomes positive for one additional symptom rather than the case in which someone who appeared psychologically unscathed suddenly develops noticeable symptoms). We do believe MVA survivors with noticeable reexperiencing and hyperarousal symptoms (our subsyndromal PTSDs) should be monitored periodically for possible deterioration to full PTSD.

Chapter

9

The Role of Physical Injury in the Development and Maintenance of PTSD Among MVA Survivors

In this chapter we examine our data to address two points that have received little attention in the literature: (a) What is the relation between extent of initial injury and the development of psychological symptoms, particularly PTSD and (b) What role does physical healing play in the maintenance of, or recovery from, psychological symptoms?

We know from chapter 2 (see Table 2-1) that most people who are involved in MVAs do not suffer notable physical injury; however, about 3 million Americans are injured in MVAs each year. For the most part, the MVA survivors we studied were physically injured. For example, a commality among all survivors who participated in the Albany MVA studies was that they had sought medical attention as a result of their accident. In fact, 94 were seen in the emergency room and released after examination and treatment, whereas 24 more were actually admitted to the hospital for periods ranging from 1 to 90 days. The other 42 participants sought medical attention on their own within 2 days of their MVA.

Most of the studies summarized in chapter 3 (see Tables 3-2 and 3-3) involved a physically injured MVA survivor population. Thus, investigators implicitly assume that there is likely to be a connection between physical injury and psychological difficulty or at least that one is more likely to find psychological problems in MVA survivors with some physical injury. To the best of our knowledge, this very reasonable assumption has never been examined empirically.

An examination of the reports presented in Tables 3-2 and 3-3 reveals details on the degree of injury assessed with the Abbreviated Injury Scale (AIS; American Automotive Medicine Institute, 1985) or a variant (Feinstein & Dolan, 1991; Green et al., 1993; Malt, 1988; Mayou et al., 1993). However, none of these reports any relationship between degree of injury and PTSD or extent of PTS symptoms. Bryant and Harvey (1995) explicitly pointed to nonsignificant relations between extent of injury and avoidance or intrusion symptoms.

A report from another area, criminal assaults of women, by Kilpatrick et al. (1989) found a clear effect of physical injury on PTS symptoms. Data were collapsed so that extent of physical injury was not graded. Presence of physical injury was a strong independent predictor ($r = .34$) of whether the assault victim developed PTSD.

The Albany MVA Study

As we mentioned in chapter 4, the initial physical injuries of our participants were scored using the AIS. This instrument provides scaled ratings from 1 to 6 for the injuries to each extremity, the trunk and the head. All six ratings are summed for the total AIS score. For example, a simple fracture of the fibia (leg) receives a score of 2, and a compound fracture, a score of 3, whereas crushing the lower leg would warrant a 4.

In a preliminary report (Blanchard, Hickling, Mitnick, Taylor, Loos, & Buckley, 1995), using the data on our first 98 MVA survivors, we found that AIS score was significantly correlated with extent of PTS symptoms as measured by the CAPS, $r(96) = .311$ ($p = < .017$), and with whether the individual developed full PTSD, $r(96) = .302$ ($p = < .017$). A multiple regression analysis revealed that both extent of injury and extent of fear of death at the time of the MVA were independent predictors of PTS symptoms ($R^2 = .349, p = .007$).

One can see from chapter 6 (Table 6-2) that the relationship continued to be present for the entire sample. The correlation of AIS and PTS symptoms (initial CAPS score) for the entire sample was .250 ($p < .01$). Similarly, the point-biserial correlation of AIS and whether a participant developed PTSD was .245 ($p < .01$).

Further confirmation of the importance of extent of physical injury in the development of psychological symptoms can be found in the multivariate prediction work summarized in Tables 6-3 and 6-4. In both the logistic regression to predict development of PTSD (Table 6-4) and the multiple regression to predict PTS symptoms (Table 6-3), initial AIS scores entered as significant independent predictors. It seems clear to us that the extent and severity of physical injuries play a significant role in the development of psychological symptoms; it is likewise clear that extent of physical injury predicts only a portion of the variance in the psychological outcome of an MVA. Thus, there is a mind–body (or body injury–mind injury) connection from the beginning.

The Role of Injury Recovery in PTS Symptoms

The second mind–body question is what role physical healing plays in mental recovery (and its converse, what role lack of healing plays in the prolongation of PTS symptoms). At our prospective follow-up interviews we assessed the participants' views of how well they had recovered from each of their physical injuries. For each separate injury participants were asked its status, and responses were scored on a 4-point scale: 3 = *unchanged;* 2 = *improved but still causes difficulty* (e.g., pain and lack of strength or flexibility); 1 = *much improved, but participant is still aware of injury with mild symptoms;* 0 = *completely healed, asymptomatic.* Then using the LIFE technique we traced the time course of change over the follow-up interval. From this we generated an injury rating for each separate injury for each month.

Our next data-reduction step was to calculate an average PIQ for each month in the following manner: For each separate injury, we divided the highest rating for that month by the rating at the time of the initial assessment (this value was typically 3, but could be 2 or 1). We then summed all of the individual PIQs (for one injury, two injuries, or more, such as broken ribs, broken arm, and whiplash injury with pain and reduced range of motion to the neck, shoulders, and upper back), and we calculated an average PIQ for the month. We repeated this for each month. For a participant who had shown essentially no recovery by the first month of follow-up, the PIQ score might be 1.0; by way of contrast, an individual with the abovementioned injuries who healed quickly and who had had good physical therapy might have a PIQ score of 0.11 by the sixth month of follow-up.

To examine the role of physical injury healing in psychological recovery for MVA survivors with an initial diagnosis of PTSD, we compared two subgroups, those who had shown partial remission (to subsyndromal PTSD) or full remission (to non-PTSD) by the 6-month follow-up ($n = 31$) and those who continued to meet the full PTSD criteria at 6 months ($n = 24$). The average PIQ scores of these two subgroups for each month are presented in Table 9-1.

We calculated a two-way repeated measures MANOVA (Subgroup × Time), which yielded a main effect of time, exact $F(5, 49) = 21.04$, $p < .001$ (Pillais corrected), and of subgroup, $F(6, 48) = 2.06$, $p = .075$, but no significant interaction. Between-group comparisons at each month revealed significant ($p < .05$) differences at Months 4 and 6, with trends ($p < .09$ or better at Months 2, 3, and 5).

From the mean PIQ scores reported in Table 9-1, it is apparent that the group who had remitted fully or in part recovered physically at a more rapid rate. Their PIQ scores dropped below 0.5 by Month 3, whereas those who did not improve psychologically were still above 0.5 even by Month 6.

We repeated this analysis on the sample ($n = 47$) available for the 12-month follow-up. The average monthly PIQs for Months 7 to 12 for each subgroup (for remitters, $n = 31$, vs. nonremitters, $n = 16$) are reported in Table 9-2.

The two-way repeated measures MANOVA revealed a significant main effect of time, exact $F(5, 41) = 2.52$, $p = .045$ (Pillais corrected), but no effect of subgroup or interaction. Moreover, none of the between-group comparisons at individual months were significant.

It is apparent from the mean PIQ scores presented in Table 9-2 that our subgroup of individuals who continued to meet the criteria for full PTSD at 12 months plateaued with regards to remission of injuries. There was slight (3% to 4%) variation

Table 9-1

Average Physical Injury Quotients for Initial PTSDs on a Month-by-Month Basis Showing Full or Partial Remission Versus No Remission

Group	Month of follow-up					
	1	2'	3'	4*	5'	6*
PTSD at 6 months	.797	.731	.664	.634	.576	.571
Sub- or non-PTSD at 6 months	.716	.587	.526	.469	.435	.404

Note: Differences are significant at $p < .05$ (*) or $p < .09$ (').

month-by-month but no overall trend. The remitted group showed a gradual improvement, but even they did not reach zero. It is as if the physical injuries in those who continued to be symptomatic enough to qualify as full PTSD have ceased to improve. To some degree this factor mirrors the data in chapter 7 (see Figure 7-2) showing only slight continued psychological remission after 6 months in the group initially diagnosed with PTSD.

As a final way of examining the relationship to see how well it held on an individual case basis, we examined the 6-month PIQs for three subgroups of MVA survivors with initial PTSD: those who had not remitted (full PTSD, $n = 24$), those who partially remitted (subsyndromal PTSD, $n = 7$) and those who had fully remitted (non-PTSD, $n = 24$). This array is shown in Figure 9-1.

One can see that, although the array of PIQ scores for those who continued to meet the full criteria for PTSD span the full range of scores, for those initial PTSDs who remitted the array of scores is attenuated and clusters toward the recovery end of the axis (PIQ = 0). The few subsyndromals are scattered across the axis.

Table 9-2

Average Physical Injury Quotients for Initial PTSDs on Month-by-Month Basis Showing Full or Partial Remission Versus No Remission for Months 7–12

Group	Month of follow-up					
	7	8	9	10	11	12
PTSD at 6 months	.387	.387	.371	.387	.387	.348
Sub- or non-PTSD at 6 months	.355	.318	.281	.272	.282	.285

We also calculated correlation coefficients between individual 6-month PIQs and 6-month CAPS scores and change in CAPS scores from initial to 6 months. Whereas the correlation of 6-month CAPS and 6-month PIQ was significant, $r(53) = .301$, $p = .025$, the correlation between change in CAPS and PIQ at 6 months was not, $r(53) = -.204$, $p = 0.14$. The direction is correct, that is, the greater the change in the CAPS (representing more psychological improvement), the lower the PIQ score (representing more physical improvement). Clearly, there was no strong dose–response relationship. Despite our failure to find a dose–response relation, it seems clear from our data that there was a mind–body connection for MVA survivors and that the progress in psychological recovery or healing was tied in part to progress in physical healing. At an anecdotal level, many patients with noticeable PTS symptoms explained that the injuries, with the concomitant pain and restricted range of motion and other limitations, served as a frequent reminder of the MVA and its psychological impact. In fact, it was an unavoidable reminder that triggered arousal (and sometimes anger or

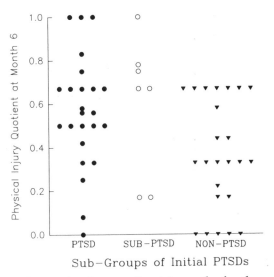

Figure 9.1. PIQ examination results at 6 months for three survivor subgroups with initial PTSD.

guilt). (Interestingly, this exposure did not seem to serve the therapeutic purpose of enforced exposure and subsequent extinction). Thus, long-lasting, nagging injuries, especially the soft tissue injuries of whiplash, seem to impede psychological recovery.[1] This is a topic area in need of more extensive research and of collaboration among orthopedists, physical therapists, and mental health professionals.

---

[1]We have assumed a causal direction, that physical injury and its healing influence psychological state. It is equally possible that the survivor's psychological state influences physical state and healing. For our measurement especially, the patient's estimate of the degree of healing and of his or her physical state, it could well be that overall psychological state influences the patient's perception of his or her physical state and thus leads to a spuriously high correlation.

10

The Role of Litigation in the Remission of MVA-Related PTSD

It is widely believed that litigation and its settlement play a large role in the natural history of psychological symptoms and disability among accident victims. Conventional clinical wisdom holds that individuals will continue their symptomatic complaints until after a suit is settled, ostensibly to enhance their chances of collecting a large settlement. A corollary is that once the suit is settled, one should expect to see a dramatic improvement, especially in psychological symptoms.

Much of modern thinking and conventional clinical wisdom on this subject seems to date from a presentation in 1961 by an eminent British neurologist, Henry Miller, that was subsequently published in the *British Medical Journal.* In his address, given at the Milroy Lecture and titled "Accident Neurosis," Miller (1961) presented data on 50 accident victims (31 from industrial accidents and 18 from MVAs) followed for 2 to 4 years after settlement of their compensation suits. The average interval from initial accident to settlement was 26 months. Miller had found evidence for "gross psychoneurosis" in this sample when individuals were examined prior to settlement, including an "unshakable conviction [on the part of the patient] of unfitness for work" and "an absolute refusal to admit any degree of symptomatic improvement" (p. 922). Predisposition to neurosis was supposedly evident in only 15 of the 50 cases. When these patients were examined after their claims were settled (either positively or negatively), 41 of 45 who had worked previously had returned to work. Only 2 had had psychiatric treatment for their symptoms.

These findings led Miller (1961) to conclude that "the cause of accident neurosis is not the result of physical injury" but arises (a) "when the accident is due to someone else's fault" and (b) "has occurred in circumstances where payment of financial compensation is potentially involved" (p. 992). Miller stated,

> In my opinion it [accident neurosis] is not a result of the accident but a concomitant of the compensation situation and a manifestation of the hope of financial gain. The condition is not encountered where this hope does not exist or where it has been finally satisfied or dissipated. (p. 994)

Almost all subsequent research and reviews disagree with Miller's (1961) conclusions. As noted in chapter 3, Mendelson (1982) followed 101 accident victims (42 from MVAs, 59 from industrial accidents) after their compensation claims were settled. Thirty-five (25 MVA, 10 industrial) accident victims had resumed work prior to settlement. Forty-four of the remaining 66 had not returned to work 16 months after claim settlement. Likewise, Thompson (1965), in a study of 500 accident victims with post-traumatic neurosis, usually anxiety states ($n = 406$) with possible superimposed neurotic depression ($n = 156$), found that "the effects of financial settlement on the course of the illness had negligible benefit" (p. 133).

Kelly and Smith (1981) sought to trace 100 accident victim patients seen by them whom they had diagnosed with post-traumatic syndrome to learn what happened after their compensation claims were settled. The average time from injury to settlement was 3.8 years. Fifty-one patients were located: 16 had returned to full-time work before the settlement; 4 had returned to work after the settlement; 22 were not working (but apparently able); 3 had incapacitating symptoms; 4 had died; and data were incomplete from 2.

In one of the more elegant studies, Tarsh and Royston (1985) followed 35 of 50 patients they had assessed on medicolegal referral because of gross somatic symptoms for which no adequate physical basis could be established. The average time from injury to settlement was 5 years. Two patients never left work; 2 others returned before settlement. After settlement, 4 (of 31) returned to the same work, and 4 others, to lighter duty work. These 8 returns ranged from 1 to 5 years postsettlement (with 5 within 2 years). Thus, the majority (two thirds) never returned to work.

Weighill (1983) was dismayed by the methodological problems plaguing this "settlement" literature but seemed to agree that most of the published evidence disagreed with Miller's (1961) conclusions concerning the absence of return to work before settlement and relative high rate of return to work with settlement. He also called for studies of psychiatric patients with and without compensation cases and for prospective study of compensation cases.

More recently, Mayou and colleagues (Mayou, 1995; Mayou, in press; Mayou et al., 1993), in the course of conducting a prospective follow-up of 200 MVA victims seen in an emergency room in Oxford, England, addressed the role of litigation and compensation among MVA victims. At a 3-year follow-up, Mayou (1995) found 96 individuals had filed claims, whereas 75 had not. Of the 96, 56 were settled by the 3-year point. Mayou pointed out that there were no effects of initiating nor settling litigation:

> Overall, there was no evidence that there were significant differences in any aspect of outcome between those who sought compensation and those who did not; furthermore, there was no evident difference between those who settled early and those who settled late. (p. 795)

However, Mayou continued on to note,

> This information [on individuals who settled after 1 year but by the third year] suggests that the subjects did report some improvement at this follow-up point compared with those who had still not settled. (p. 795)

Unfortunately, no data to support these conclusions were presented in the articles.

The Albany MVA Project

From our project and the 1-year prospective follow-up we had data pertinent to the litigation issue from 132 MVA survivors: 18 who settled litigation within the first 12 months of the follow-up, 49 who had initiated litigation by the time of our initial assessment but who had not settled by the 12-month follow-up, and 65 MVA survivors who never initiated litigation.

These categorizations were determined from the structured interviews administered initially and at the 6- and 12-month follow-ups. Initially, participants were asked if they had contacted a lawyer; if they answered affirmatively, they were scored as involved in litigation. Status of the potential litigation was assessed at each follow-up, and dates of any settlements were obtained. Because New York has a "no fault" automobile insurance law, the bulk of a MVA survivor's medical bills are paid by his or her own insurance company. Thus, suits solely to recover medical expenses are relatively rare.

Demographic and diagnostic data on these three subgroups are presented in Table 10-1. We compared the three patient groups on the variables summarized in Table 10-1. These analyses revealed no significant differences among our three groups on age, gender, or the distribution of initial diagnoses. There was a significant difference on extent of initial injury (AIS score), $F(2, 129) = 7.02, p = .0013$; follow-up tests with Duncan's post hoc test revealed that the group that had settled the litigation within the 1-year follow-up was more severely injured than the other two groups that did not differ. There was also a significant difference in the extent of initial PTS symptoms as measured by the CAPS, $F(2, 129) = 8.44, p = .0004$. Follow-up tests revealed that the non-litigants had significantly ($p = .05$) lower PTS symptoms scores than the two litigant groups that did not differ.

It is of some interest to see that the presence of noticeable psychological distress, as indicated by a diagnosis of PTSD or subsyndromal PTSD, was not the sole (or even a primary) determinant of whether an MVA survivor became a litigant. Almost a one fourth of the litigants were initially diagnosed as non-PTSD.

Table 10-1

Group Mean Demographic and Diagnostic Data on Three Groups of MVA Victims

Demographic and diagnostic data	Litigation settled within 12 months ($n = 18$)	Litigation not settled within 12 months ($n = 49$)	Nonlitigants ($n = 65$)
Age (SD)	42.1 (13.8)	35.0 (11.1)	35.8 (13.7)
Gender (M/F)	7/11	15/34	21/44
Pre-MVA employment status			
Employed	13 (72%)	39 (80%)	44 (68%)
Unemployed	2 (11%)	0	2 (3%)
Homemaker	1 (6%)	3 (6%)	5 (8%)
Student	1 (6%)	3 (6%)	13 (20%)
Disabled	1 (6%)	2 (4%)	0
Retired	0	2 (4%)	1 (2%)
Initial diagnostic status			
PTSD	8 (44%)	23 (47%)	18 (28%)
Sub-PTSD	5 (28%)	15 (31%)	22 (34%)
Non-PTSD	5 (28%)	11 (22%)	25 (38%)
Initial CAPS score (SD)	40.7 (29.5)	43.7 (27.5)	25.6 (20.4)
Initial Abbreviated Injury Scale score (SD)	9.2 (11.3)	5.1 (4.3)	3.5 (4.2)

Note: CAPS = Clinician-Administered PTSD Scale. Row entry percentages on the basis of column totals are reported in parentheses.

Change in PTS Symptoms Over Time

Our primary indicator of psychological status over time was the CAPS interview. The mean CAPS score for each group at each point in time are given in Table 10-2. A repeated measures MANOVA revealed a main effect of group, $F(2, 129) = 8.68$, $p < .001$, and of time, $F(2, 128) = 60.2, p < .001$ (Pillais corrected), but no interaction between these two variables. Because of the slightly different slope between the 6- and 12-month follow-up points for the group for which litigation was settled in comparison to those of the other two groups, we reanalyzed the data for the two follow-up points, using the initial score as a covariate. Again, there was no interaction.

To explore further whether there were possibly litigation settlement effects among those who initially were more symptomatic, we repeated the analyses on only those members of the three groups who met criteria for PTSD and also for the combination of those who initially met criteria for PTSD and subsyndromal PTSD. These analyses yielded the same results, main effects of group and time, but no interaction.

A follow-up one-way ANOVA on CAPS scores at 12 months was significant, $F(2, 129) = 8.16$, $p = .0005$. Follow-up tests revealed that the nonlitigant group scored significantly ($p = .05$) lower than the group for which litigation was still pending; the group that had settled scored in between these two groups and did not differ from either. All three groups had significantly ($p = .01$) lower CAPS scores at the 12-month follow-up point than they had initially, including the litigants whose suits were pending. Thus, it seems clear that even those litigants with pending suits were significantly less symptomatic over time.

Other Measures of Subjective Distress

The psychological tests used in our study were additional measures of subjective distress. Some litigants settled prior to the 6-month follow-up assessment, whereas others settled after that time but prior to the 12-month assessment. The 6-month follow-up assessment values for the litigation-settled group were thus partially confounded. To avoid this confound, and to detect possible settlement effects, we analyzed the data from the uncon-

Table 10-2

Mean CAPS Scores for Initial Assessment and Follow-Up Points
for All Litigation Groups

Group	Initial M	Initial SD	6-month follow-up M	6-month follow-up SD	12-month follow-up M	12-month follow-up SD
Nonlitigant	25.6	20.4	12.7	23.6	8.2	15.0
Litigation settled by 12 months	40.7	29.5	22.6	22.2	15.3	19.6
Litigation not settled	43.7	27.5	26.5	24.1	23.4	24.9

founded points, those from the initial assessment and from the 12-month assessment. Values for these two points for each group for each test are summarized in Table 10-3.

These were subjected to an overall Group × Time MANOVA, followed by tests on each of the individual variables. Results of the individual tests are also presented in Table 10-3. The overall MANOVA yielded a main effect of group, approximate $F(8, 326)$ = 3.65, $p < .001$, and of time, exact $F(4, 117) = 6.04$, $p < .001$, but no interaction.

If one examines Table 10-3 one can see that for three variables BDI, State Anxiety, and IES, there were main effects of group and time but no interaction. In each of these instances, follow-up analyses revealed that the nonlitigants were less distressed than the two litigant groups that did not differ at the initial assessment. At the 12-month assessment for three of the measures (State Anxiety, Trait Anxiety, and IES), the same pattern of results obtained: the nonlitigant group scored significantly ($p = .05$) lower than either of the two litigant groups that did not differ. For the BDI, however, the group with the litigation pending was significantly ($p = .05$) more depressed than the nonlitigant group, whereas those whose litigation was settled were intermediate and not different from either of the other two groups.

Table 10-3

Values for All Litigation Groups at Initial and 12-Month Assessments on Each Psychological Test

Measure	Group	Initial assessment		12-month assessment		F and p values		
		M	SD	M	SD	Group	Time	Group × Time
Beck Depression Inventory	Nonlitigant	7.7	7.5	5.1	8.1	4.87, .009	8.29, .005	1.03, ns
	Lit. settled	10.7	6.0	7.6	7.8			
	Lit. pending	11.5	9.9	10.4	10.0			
STAI State Anxiety	Nonlitigant	49.8	16.0	44.4	13.0	4.97, .008	3.54, .06	1.17, ns
	Lit. settled	57.1	20.4	54.8	17.7			
	Lit. pending	56.6	19.9	56.0	21.9			
STAI Trait Anxiety	Nonlitigant	50.8	13.4	46.2	14.6	1.82, ns	0.35, ns	3.16, .046
	Lit. settled	52.3	15.7	54.5	16.4			
	Lit. pending	53.4	16.4	54.3	20.8			
Impact of Event Scale	Nonlitigant	14.0	15.7	7.4	10.9	12.84 < .001	19.25, < .001	.19, ns
	Lit. settled	24.9	19.6	19.8	20.9			
	Lit. pending	28.6	17.3	20.1	17.8			

Note: STAI = State–Trait Anxiety Inventory. Lit. = litigation.

For Trait Anxiety, there were no main effects, only the interaction. Whereas the nonlitigants scored lower at follow-up, the two litigant groups increased slightly. The two litigant groups did not differ at either assessment.

Role-Functioning Variables

Table 10-4 reports the values for the variables assessed with the LIFE-Base and LIFE related to role functioning. We present three points in time, pre-MVA, initial assessment (post-MVA), and 12-month follow-ups for the three groups of accident victims. For the reasons mentioned earlier with the psychological tests, the analyses did not use the 6-month assessment values.

As noted in chapter 4, we remind the reader that our variable, major role function, was derived hierarchically—in line with the varying status of participants shown in Table 10-1. If the participant was working 30 hours per week or more, then rating values for work were used; if the participant was a full-time student, then ratings for school performance were used; finally, if the participant did not work outside of the home, then the rating values for homemaking were used. For relationship with family, we averaged the individual ratings for all first-degree relatives and spouse or partner. All variables were rated on 1 to 5 scales, with 1 indicating best and 5 indicating worst; the scales are defined in chapters 4 and 5.

These variables, which define role functioning and role impairment, were subjected to an overall repreated measures MANOVA (Group × Time), followed by analyses on each variable separately and then follow-up tests. The overall MANOVA yielded a main effect of group, approximate $F(8, 252) = 4.69$, $p < .001$; a main effect of time, exact $F(4, 125) = 11.97, p < .001$; and an interaction of Group × Time, approximate $F(8, 252) = 1.95$, $p = .05$.

An examination of Table 10-4 reveals that there were no significant effects of litigation status (group) or the passage of time (or settlement of litigation) on average relationships with family. The average overall relationship was rated as *good* across all points in time.

Table 10-4

Role-Functioning Variables for All Litigation MVA Victim Groups at All Assessment Points

Variable	Group	Pre-MVA	Initial assessment (Post-MVA)	12-month follow-up	Time	Group	Group × Time
Major role functioning (work, school, homemaking)	Nonlitigant		2.2	1.6	24.5, < .001	6.20, .003	3.50, .003
	Lit. settled		2.3	1.8			
	Lit. pending		3.2	1.9			
Family relationships	Nonlitigant	2.1	2.1	2.0	1.02, ns	.03, ns	0.0, ns
	Lit. settled	2.1	2.2	2.1			
	Lit. pending	2.0	2.1	2.1			
Relationship with friends	Non-litigant	1.6	1.6	1.6	5.17, .025	6.76, .002	3.19, .045
	Lit. settled	1.9	2.6	1.8			
	Lit. pending	1.8	2.1	2.1			
Participation in recreation	Nonlitigant	1.6	2.2	1.7	31.4, < .001	11.76, < .001	1.25, ns
	Lit. settled	1.8	2.9	1.9			
	Lit. pending	1.6	3.2	2.6			

Note: Lit. = litigation.

For the performance of major role function and relationships with friends, however, there were main effects of group and of time as well as significant interactions for each variable ($p. < .05$ or better). Follow-up analyses revealed, for relationship with friends, no difference among the groups before the MVA, with a significant difference at the initial assessment between litigants versus the nonlitigants (.05). At the 12-month follow-up, the non-litigants had significantly ($p < .05$) better relations with friends than those whose suits were still pending. Those litigants whose suits were settled scored in between and did not differ from either of the two groups.

For performance on major role function at the initial assessment, those litigants who had not settled their suits within the first 12 months performed noticeably poorer ($p = .05$) than either the nonlitigants or the litigants who settled. In fact, the difference was a whole scale unit (between satisfactory performance with no impairment and fair performance with mild impairment). At the 12-month assessment, the three groups functioned significantly better, with no difference in functioning among them. Thus, those litigants whose suits were still pending had improved markedly (average of 1.3 scale units) over the year.

For participation in recreation, the nonlitigants were significantly more involved at the time of the initial assessment than the litigant groups that did not differ. At the 12-month follow-up, the nonlitigant group and those whose litigation was still pending were significantly different; litigants who had settled were intermediate but not significantly different from either of the other two groups.

Return to Work

The frequencies of each group that was working full time or part time at the time of the MVA (96 of 132, 72.7%) and their employment status at the 12-month follow-up are reported in Table 10-5.

We compared the status of individuals from each group who had been working full time prior to the MVA as to whether they were working at all (full time or part time) at the 12-month follow-up. The chi-square (2, $N = 85$) = 5.95, $p = .05$, was significant; those whose suits were still pending were less likely to be

Table 10-5

*Twelve-Month Employment Status of Members of All Litigation
Groups Who Were Employed at the Time of the Accident*

Group	Employed Full time	Part time	Unemployed	Disabled
Nonlitigant (N = 44)				
Full time (n = 38)	34	3	1	—
Part time (n = 6)	1	3	2	—
Litigation pending (N = 39)				
Full time (n = 36)	24	6	3	3
Part time (n = 3)	2	1	—	—
Litigation settled (N = 13)				
Full time (n = 11)	9	2	—	—
Part time (n = 2)	—	—	—	2

working at the 12-month follow-up, partially supportive of
Miller's (1961) position.

Initial Differences Between Litigant Versus Nonlitigant MVA Victims

One question to ask about this topic is whether litigants at the initial assessment point were different from the nonlitigants. The
answer is generally in the affirmative. Litigants had higher PTS
symptom scores as measured by the CAPS; they showed higher
levels of subjective distress as indicated on the standardized psychological tests; and their role performance was more impaired
with regard to major role function, relationships with friends,
and use of leisure time as indicated by participation in recreational activities. Average relationships with family members
were not different. They also had more severe physical injuries as
measured by AIS scores.

Unfortunately, one cannot determine the direction of causality
from these data. It could be that, because of greater subjective

distress, greater role impairment, and a higher level of PTS symptoms, these MVA survivors decided to seek compensation through litigation. Alternatively, it could be that having decided to initiate litigation, these litigating MVA survivors portrayed themselves at the assessment (which occurred after litigation had been initiated) in a more distressed and impaired light.

Support for the former interpretation comes from the greater average degree of physical injury, as measured by AIS scores, for the litigating group. In fact, it could be that the extent of injury was the causal variable; that is, those who were more injured were more likely to initiate litigation, even though their health care was to be paid by the no fault insurance trust.

Follow-Up Differences Between Litigants Who Settle Versus Litigants Whose Cases Are Still Pending

Miller's (1961) prediction on this point is fairly clear: Individuals with litigation still pending should be more distressed and more impaired. Although the direction of the group means in our data generally support Miller's viewpoint (i.e., the group mean scores show less distress and impairment for litigants who settled versus litigants whose suits were still pending), in no instance was this effect statistically significant. Thus, on balance, we did not find differences at follow-up between litigants who settled versus those whose suits were still pending.

At the 12-month follow-up, the general finding was that the values for the litigants who settled were not different from those who never initiated litigation on role-functioning variables and degree of PTS symptoms. However, on other measures of psychological distress, State and Trait Anxiety, and the IES scores, the litigants who settled remained more distressed than those who never initiated litigation.

More important, litigants whose suits were still pending at 12 months showed consistently more psychological distress and role impairment, as well as higher PTS symptom scores, than those who never initiated litigation. Again, this is consistent with Miller's (1961) view that such individuals continue to be symptomatic until after their suits are settled.

Improvement Over the Follow-Up Interval

For the most part, all three MVA victim groups improved over the 12-month follow-up interval: The two exceptions were in relationships with family members (which did not deteriorate after the MVA and thus remained at the *good* level throughout) and Trait Anxiety scores.

When we examined the specific within-group change for each group from the initial assessment to the 12-month follow-up point, we found that nonlitigants improved significantly on all variables except family relationships. Likewise the litigants whose suits were settled improved significantly on all role-functioning variables except family relationships but had no significant change on any psychological distress measures. For the crucial group, those litigants whose suits had not been settled by 12 months, we found significant reduction in measures of PTS symptoms, that is, CAPS scores, IES scores (which were highly correlated), and major role function and participation in recreation. However, relationships with friends did not improve nor did the measures of psychological distress, BDI, State Anxiety, or Trait Anxiety.

These latter results are thus partially supportive of Miller's (1961) contention in that on some variables there was no improvement prior to settlement, whereas on other variables there was significant improvement. In fact, on the most crucial variables, impairment in major role function (e.g., work performance) and presence of PTS symptoms, litigants whose suits were still pending showed significant improvement over the year. It is only on other measures of generalized psychological distress that no improvement was shown.

On the crucial functional variable of return to work for those who were employed full time at the time of the accident, 83% of individuals whose legal suits were still pending were back at work full time ($n = 24$, 66.7%) or part time ($n = 6$, 16.7%). These data clearly contradict Miller's (1961) assertion that such individuals do not return to work until after the suit is settled. We found that 100% of those who had been employed full time at the time of the MVA and whose suits had been settled were back to work.

The only finding partially supportive of Miller's (1961) contentions is that significantly fewer individuals whose suits were still pending and who had been working full time at the time of the MVA had returned to work. Thus, although he expected none to return, we found a majority had returned to full-time employment. However, the fraction of this group that had not returned to work was less than the fraction found in the other two groups.

Overall, our data are consistent with most of the work since Miller's (1961) article, that is, work not supporting his view about accident neurosis. Those who had suits pending were generally back to work either full time (67%) or part time (16%) and generally had substantially reduced levels of PTS symptoms and of role impairment. However, trends in our data were supportive of the notion that individuals with pending suits did more poorly than those who never filed suits or those who had settled suits. Those with pending suits were consistently more distressed and functioned less well than those who never filed suits and showed nonsignificant differences from those whose suits were settled. It could be that, with larger samples, those differences might reach significance.

Speculation

There are two final points related to litigation on which we would like to speculate, on the basis of anecdotal, rather than systematic, data. The first point is that the process of litigation can result in retraumatization and that such an ongoing process can account for the trend for those who were still in litigation to be less well. Pitman et al. (1996) and Napier (1991) have pointed out that the potential impact that the process of litigation may have on the perpetuation and exacerbation of symptoms. Pitman et al. (1996) suggested that the very act of litigation may affect PTSD symptoms through what was described as "retraumatization." They stated that the need to confront the traumatic history through interviews with attorneys, depositions, and courtroom testimony thwarts the victim's characteristic efforts at avoidance and predictably results in the resurgence of intrusive ideation and increased arousal. Furthermore, this is done in a system many view as adversarial, in which the plaintiff is pitted against the defendant, who, through the occurrence of the traumatic event, may already be seen as the "enemy." Patients as participants in the process may come to see that although they perceive themselves as victims, they are now the one placed on trial, exacerbating any sense of vulnerability and victimization. In addition, whereas the MVA survivor may have already suffered a major loss financially as a result of the traumatic event, pursuit of litigation necessitates further financial risk and anxiety because the positive outcome is not assured. Pitman (1996) found that accident survivors, in filing law suits, are seeking understanding (and justice) more than financial gain.

Our own unsystematic observations are that formal contact with the litigation process, especially giving depositions and appearing in court, lead to increases in PTS symptoms. (To some extent this is to the MVA survivor's advantage because the nonverbal communication of distress is heightened.)

Malingering

The second point on which we wish to speculate is the broad one of *malingering*. It is always possible for the clever individual with the appropriate MVA and physical injury history to give biased (in terms of portraying more distress than is present) or even false answers to us and to everyone else involved in the litigation process.

We made no effort to check on the veracity of our research participants' reports, either details of the accident or reports of their psychological symptoms at any point in the follow-up. The interviewers were all experienced clinicians and probed when answers were inconsistent or when the nonverbal behavior was inconsistent with verbal content. We had no instances in which we felt we had been misled.

However, when serious financial rewards are at stake, it is possible that individuals will not tell the truth but instead may malinger. Unfortunately, we have no ready guidelines on how to detect this phenomenon and are thankful that it is probably rare.

11

Acute Stress Disorder Among MVA Survivors

In this chapter we examine acute stress disorder (ASD) as experienced by survivors of serious MVAs and distinguish this disorder from PTSD. We also provide detailed analyses of 14 cases of ASD from among 62 initial cases of PTSD in the Albany MVA Project. We explore pre-MVA variables, initial assessment variables, and follow-up data.

The reintroduction of the PTSD diagnostic category in *DSM–III* (APA, 1980) provides a category with which to diagnose and code individuals who have been exposed to a traumatic event and who then experienced avoidance, numbing, hyperarousal, and reexperiencing symptoms over the next month or more. Prior to the 1-month point, individuals who were clearly distressed and symptomatic could be diagnosed and coded only with adjustment disorder.

The latter diagnosis seemed an understatement for rape survivors and others who were acutely distressed in the days following the trauma up until they crossed the temporal threshold that allowed a formal diagnosis of PTSD. The publication of the *DSM–IV* (APA, 1994) and its inclusion of a new diagnostic category, ASD, was in part an attempt to remedy this diagnostic situation and to provide a more meaningful diagnostic label for

We acknowledge Kristine Barton's crucial role in the research reported in this chapter.

distressed trauma victims during the days immediately following the trauma. Moreover, the introduction of ASD provides a
category to highlight the frequent occurrence of dissociative
symptoms as part of the acute response to trauma.

There is great overlap in the diagnostic criteria for ASD and
PTSD; however, there are some important differences. Exhibit
11-1 presents a comparison of the diagnostic criteria. From examining the two disorders we see that the differences are the necessity of dissociative symptoms in ASD (but not in PTSD), fewer
avoidance and numbing symptoms in ASD than in PTSD, and
the temporal difference (2 days to 4 weeks for ASD vs. at least 1
month for PTSD).

There is little literature on ASD, per se. Cardena and Spiegel
(1989) reported the presence of dissociative symptoms in 34% to
57% of trauma victims. Marmar et al. (1994) and also Holen
(1993) reported that higher levels of dissociation acutely are associated with higher levels of PTSD symptoms in long-term follow-
up of trauma victims.

Bryant and Harvey (1995) studied acute stress responses
among two groups of MVA survivors, 38 who had had a mild
head injury (Glasgow Coma Scale scores of 13 to 15 and post-
traumatic amnesia of less than 24 hours) and 38 non-head-
injured MVA survivors. Survivors were assessed 1 to 15 days
post-MVA. Although the participants were given a structured
interview used to diagnose PTSD (the PTSD-I of Watson, Juba,
Manifold, Kucala, & Anderson, 1991), no formal diagnostic judg-
ments were presented.

Comparisons of the two groups revealed greater subjective
fear, higher levels of PTSD symptoms, and higher total IES scores
and IES intrusion scores among the non-head-injured group than
those with mild head injury. No assessment of dissociative symptoms was reported. It is clear that the non-head-injured were
very acutely distressed, having an average IES score of 25.7 and
a State Anxiety score of 46.6. It is not clear what a PTSD-I scale
score of 45 might mean.

A more recent report from the Australian research team
Harvey and Bryant (1996) assessed 171 acute admissions to a
regional trauma center who were MVA survivors. Among them
were 92 individuals who had no head injury and 79 who had

Exhibit 11-1

Comparison of DSM–IV *Diagnostic Criteria for Acute Stress Disorder and Post-Traumatic Stress Disorder*

Acute stress disorder	Post-traumatic stress disorder
A. Person exposed to traumatic event in which . . . 1. Person is exposed to actual or threatened death or serious injury for self or others 2. Person's response involved intense fear, helplessness, or horror B. Either while experiencing traumatic event or after the event, person has three or more dissociative symptoms: 1. Sense of numbing, detachment, absence of emotional responsiveness 2. Reducing in awareness ("being in a daze") 3. Derealization 4. Depersonalization 5. Dissociative amnesia	A. Person exposed to traumatic event in which . . . 1. Person is exposed to actual or threatened death or serious injury for self or others 2. Person's response involved intense fear, helplessness, or horror
C. At least one reexperiencing symptom	At least one reexperiencing symptom
D. Marked avoidance of stimuli that remind person of trauma	At least three avoidance or psychic numbing symptoms
E. Marked hyperarousal symptoms	At least two hyperarousal symptoms
F. Marked distress or role impairment	Marked distress or role impairment
G. Disturbance lasts for 2 days to 4 weeks	Disturbance lasts for at least 1 month

suffered a head injury resulting in post-traumatic amnesia (PTA) of 5 minutes to 48 hours (mean PTA = 12.7 hours). The non-head-injured group comprised 61 men and 31 women who ranged in age from 17 to 63 (M = 33.3) and who were hospitalized for an average of 7.6 days. The head-injured group contained 55 men and 24 women, with an average age of 29 years. Their average hospital stay was 11.6 days. All participants were assessed from 2 to 24 days after the MVA with questions on how badly hurt they were in the MVA, a structured interview for diagnosing ASD, and several psychological tests.

Among the non-head-injured group, 13% (n = 12) met the full *DSM–IV* criteria for ASD, whereas another 20.7% met all but one criteria and were seen as subclinical ASD. For the head-injured group, 5.1% (n = 4) met full criteria for ASD and 12.7% for subclinical ASD. Separate regression analyses to predict ASD severity (the sum of the number of ASD symptoms present) for the two groups of patients were conducted and revealed that the level of depression as measured by the BDI and prior history of PTSD loaded significantly for both groups. For the non-head-injured group, prior psychiatric history and previous MVA loaded. For the head-injured group, age and extent of physical injury loaded. Sixty-one percent of the variance in ASD severity was explained for the non-head-injured group and 72% for the head-injured group.

We suspect, on the basis of conversations with A. Harvey (personal communication, August 1996) that this research team is continuing to conduct more research on ASD and MVAs. What is very crucial is whether the formal diagnosis of ASD is predictive of the course of recovery, an indicator of what form of treatment would be more advantageous, or both.

Albany MVA Project

Because of the detailed records of the participants' reactions to their MVAs, we were able, after the fact by chart review, to identify 14 cases of ASD from among our 62 initial cases of PTSD. A graduate research assistant reviewed all of the records for descriptions of dissociative phenomena in the patient's account of the accident and its immediate aftermath. Those cases that were potentially positive were reviewed by one of the senior clinician–interviewers to confirm the presence of dissociative symptoms. Examples of dissociative phenomena were the following: time distortion (feeling as if everything is happening in slow motion), depersonalization (feeling as if the MVA survivor is watching the accident occur from a removed position), and mental confusion (being dazed without head injury).

These data are reported in detail by Barton, Blanchard, and Hickling (1996). To examine the 14 ASD cases, we randomly selected 2 other PTSD cases, thus controlling for diagnosis and overall PTS symptom severity, matched for gender and age (within 5 years) to the ASD cases. We then compared the 14 cases of ASD with 28 matched cases of PTSD on several families of variables, similar to the comparisons in chapter 8 on delayed onset PTSD. We made comparisons on (a) pre-MVA variables including preexisting psychopathology; (b) post-MVA comorbidity and psychosocial functioning, as well as psychological test scores; and (c) 6-month follow-up data.

Pre-MVA Variables

Table 11-1 presents the values for the ASD group and the PTSD comparison group on psychiatric variables that were present before the MVA. Consistent with Spiegel and Cardena's (1991) findings, and those of Harvey and Bryant (1996), we found higher levels of previous trauma and previous PTSD among our MVA survivors who met the criteria for ASD. We also found that individuals with ASD were more likely to meet criteria for prior mood disorders other than major depression, again consistent with Harvey and Bryant (1996). Finally, over one third of our ASD subgroup met the criteria for one or more personality disorders.

Initial Assessment Variables

The next set of comparisons were made on variables assessed after the MVA at our initial assessment (1 to 4 months post-MVA). The tabulations for them are reported in Table 11-2. From examining the large array of variables in Table 11-2, one finds no

Table 11-1

*Comparison of MVA Survivors With ASDs With PTSDs on
Preexisting Conditions and Past Psychopathology*

Variable	ASD (n = 14)	PTSD (n = 28)	p
Previous trauma	12 (85.7%)	18 (64.3%)	.14
No. of previous traumas	2.00	1.07	.02
Past PTSD	6 (42.9%)	3 (10.7%)	.02
Past anxiety disorder (Other than PTSD)	6 (42.9%)	6 (21.4%)	.15
Past mood disorder (other than MDD)	4 (28.6%)	0	.003
Past alcohol/substance abuse or dependence	2 (14.3%)	1 (3.6%)	.20
Any past AXIS-II disorder	5 (35.7%)	1 (3.6%)	.005

Note: MDD = major depressive episode. From "Antecedents and Consequences of Acute Stress Disorder Among Motor Vehicle Accident Victims," by K. A. Barton, E. B. Blanchard, and E. J. Hickling, 1996, *Behaviour Research and Therapy, 34,* Table 2. Copyright 1996 by Elsevier Science. Adapted with permission.

significant differences between MVA survivors with PTSD who earlier met criteria for ASD and similar MVA survivors with PTSD who did not meet criteria for ASD. From our data, meeting criteria early on for ASD did not seem to lead to a better or worse psychological picture 1 to 4 months postaccident.

Follow-Up Data

One of the primary reasons for noting the appearance of ASD and its associated dissociative symptoms is the observation (after the fact or retrospectively) by Marmar et al. (1994) that individuals

Table 11-2

*Comparison of MVA Survivors With ASD to PTSDs on Initial
Psychiatric Psychological and Psychosocial Data*

Measure	ASD (*n* = 14)	PTSD (*n* = 28)	*p*
Beck Depression Inventory	17.2	15.8	.58
State Anxiety	65.1	66.4	.82
Trait Anxiety	67.2	59.7	.10
Impact of Events	41.1	34.8	.26
CAPS	66.1	58.3	.26
GAS	56.2	57.6	.69
Individual's estimate of present functioning	64.6	53.2	.42
Individual's satisfaction with recreational activities	3.7	3.0	.23
Individual's overall life satisfaction	3.4	3.3	.82
Major role functioning impairment	3.3	3.1	.65
Current major depression	9 (64.3%)	15 (53.6%)	.51
Current mood disorder other than MDD	1 (7.1%)	1 (3.6%)	.61
Any current Axis I	9 (64.3%)	17 (60.7%)	.82

Note: CAPS = Clinician Administered PTSD Scale; GAS = Global
Assessment Scale.

with PTSD and dissociative symptoms tend to have a poorer
outcome than those with PTSD and who have no dissociative
symptoms.

Table 11-3 presents the primary measures on the two samples
(ASD and PTSD controls) from the 6-month follow-up assessment. (Details on this follow-up are discussed in chapters 4 and
7.) One can see that the two groups showed very similar rates of

Table 11-3

Six-Month Follow-Up Data on ASD MVA Survivors

Diagnostic measure	ASD (n = 11)	PTSD (n = 25)	p
PTSD at 6 months	5 (45.5%)	12 (48%)	.89
Dropout rate	3 (21.4%)	3 (10.7%)	.35
6-month CAPS scores	45.7 (34.2%)	41.9 (32.1%)	.75

Note: Row entry percentage for each column are reported in parentheses. From "Antecedents and Consequences of Acute Stress Disorder Among Motor Vehicle Accident Victims," by K. A. Barton, E. B. Blanchard, and E. J. Hickling, 1996, *Behaviour Research and Therapy, 34,* Table 5. Copyright 1996 by Elsevier Science. Adapted with permission.

remission and very similar average CAPS scores at the 6-month follow-up. Thus, on the primary variables of interest, meeting the criteria for early ASD made no apparent difference at 6 months.

Comparisons on all of the other variables assessed at the 6-month follow-up point are presented in Table 11-4. As with the initial assessment data, the 6-month follow-up revealed no significant differences on any of the variables in Table 11-4 between those with ASD and the PTSD comparison group. Thus, we found no follow-up effects of initially meeting the criteria for ASD compared with a matched group of MVA survivors.

We cannot speak, within our analyses, of whether initial dissociative symptoms predict later PTSD. Our initial assessment was not attuned to that question. (Work by Harvey and Bryant in Australia is likely to shed light on this issue.) It is also possible that we missed some cases of ASD among our sample, again, because of the nature of the initial interview. We did not focus explicitly on the presence of dissociative symptoms during or after the MVA. Thus, we might have missed some cases. We do

Table 11-4

Six-Month Follow-Up Data on Psychological, Psychiatric and Psychosocial Variables for MVA Survivors With ASD

Variable	ASD (n = 11)	PTSD (n = 25)	p
Beck Depression Inventory	18.0	15.4	.56
State Anxiety	62.4	64.1	.84
Trait Anxiety	67.2	63.6	.56
GAS	63.4	61.2	.66
IES	33.9	28.2	.46
Individual's satisfaction with recreational activities	2.5	2.6	.86
Major role function impairment	2.6	2.4	.75
Current major depression	3 (27.3%)	9 (36%)	.61
Current mood disorder other than MDD	2 (18.2%)	1 (4%)	.16
Current alcohol/substance abuse or dependence	1 (9.1%)	0	.13
Current Axis I disorder	7 (63.6%)	13 (52%)	.52

Note: GAS = Global Assessment Scale; IES = Impact of Event Scale; MDD = Major depressive disorder. From "Antecedents and Consequences of Acute Stress Disorder Among Motor Vehicle Accident Victims," by K. A. Barton, E. B. Blanchard, and E. J. Hickling, 1996, *Behaviour Research and Therapy, 34,* Table 4. Copyright 1996 by Elsevier Science. Adapted with permission.

believe, however, that the cases we identified were positive for ASD because the dissociative symptoms were pronounced enough for the participant to mention them.

On the basis of our small, retrospectively identified sample, we do not believe that meeting the criteria for ASD within the month following the MVA is at all predictive of short-term (6 month) outcome. Individuals who are involved in serious MVAs, and who are likely to have the dissociative symptoms necessary to warrant the diagnosis of ASD, are different in some ways before the accident than MVA victims who develop PTSD but do not develop ASD.

Future research, such as that ongoing by the Australian team of Bryant and Harvey, may show that ASD does have prognostic significance. For now, we do not find that it is important.

12

Psychophysiological Assessment With MVA Survivors

This chapter examines psychophysiological assessment of MVA survivors. We begin by reviewing three published reports of this population. Next, we consider the results of the Albany MVA Project, in which we used such testing as an integral part of our overall assessment of MVA survivors.

Since the pioneering studies by Blanchard, Kolb, Pallmeyer, and Gerardi (1982) and Malloy, Fairbank, and Keane (1983), psychophysiological assessment has been an integral part of research on PTSD in Vietnam veterans. A large-scale multisite study of the potential role of psychophysiological assessments in the overall evaluation of Vietnam veterans (Veterans Administration Cooperative Study No. 334; Kolb & Keane, 1988) is in the final stages.

What seems clear from that research is that individuals with PTSD show a distinctive pattern of probably sympathetically mediated arousal when they are exposed to cues reminiscent of the trauma. This finding appears robust enough with heart rate (HR), and perhaps electrodermal activity (EDA), to have usefulness at the level of the individual.

Research with other traumatized populations, such as sexual assault victims (Forneris, Blanchard, & Jonay, 1996) and civilian populations exposed to mixed trauma (Shalev, Orr, & Pitman, 1993), have replicated the general findings that emerged from the Vietnam veteran research.

Studies of MVA Survivors

At least three published reports have used psychophysiological assessments with MVA survivors. In an early report from our center, we (Blanchard, Hickling, & Taylor, 1991) assessed 4 MVA survivors (1 male and 3 female) with PTSD on HR, systolic and diastolic blood pressure (SBP and DBP), and skin resistance level as a measure of EDA. Procedures included exposing participants to three stressors: mental arithmetic and two idiosyncratic scenes reminiscent of their own MVA, separated by 5 minute baselines. The scripts for the scenes were similar to the procedure used by Pitman, Orr, Forgue, de Jong, and Claiborn (1987).

Participants showed HR increases to each of the MVA descriptions ($n = 8$) averaging eight beats per minute (BPM). On five of the eight trials (and at least once for each participant) there was an SBP increase. Only 2 of 4 participants showed EDA responses. These data support the value of the HR response to idiosyncratic descriptions of participants' own MVAs as a useful assessment tool for assessing PTSD in MVA survivors.

Shalev et al. (1993) assessed an Israeli civilian population ($n = 26$) that had experienced various traumas, including 10 MVAs. (Unfortunately, for our purposes, separate data on MVA survivors were not available.) Half ($n = 13$) of the sample met the *DSM-III-R* (APA, 1987) criteria for PTSD, half did not. Average age was 35 for the PTSD group and 28 for the non-PTSD group. Average time since the trauma was 4.3 years for the PTSD group and 5.6 years for the non-PTSD group. Among the MVA survivors, 4 met criteria for PTSD and 6 did not.

The research team used Pitman et al.'s (1987) idiosyncratic scripts procedure. Results from between-group comparisons of individuals with PTSD and those without it during the personal traumatic imagery revealed significant differences on HR (13.9 BPM increase for PTSDs vs. 2.0 BPM increase for non-PTSDs, $p = .003$) and on frontal EMG ($p = .01$) but not on skin conductance, although there was a baseline difference ($p = .04$) between the groups on this measure. The HR finding is consistent with much of the research on Vietnam veterans with PTSD.

Bryant, Harvey, Gordon, and Barry (1995) assessed initial eye fixations and orienting responses (EDA) of MVA survivors

(n = 10) with PTSD compared with age and gender-matched controls. Those with PTSD satisfied *DSM–IV* (APA, 1994) criteria on the basis of a structured interview and the IES. Mean time since the MVA was 38.6 months. Participants were asked to look at four words (in quadrants around a fixation point) that on certain trials included "threat words" (e.g., *blood, ambulance*) or neutral words. Only half of the PTSDs were used in the EDA. The remaining 5 PTSDs showed more orienting responses overall than the controls but did not respond differentially to the threat words. Thus, in terms of psychophysiological responding, the MVA survivors with PTSD were more responsive, but the responsivity was not necessarily to cues reminiscent of the trauma.

The Albany MVA Project

Psychophysiological testing was an integral part of the overall assessment of the MVA survivors in the Albany MVA Project. These results have been reported twice: the first study (Blanchard, Hickling, Taylor, Loos, & Gerardi, 1994) described the results for the first 50 MVA survivors and 40 non-MVA controls. The second study (Blanchard, Hickling, Buckley, Taylor, Vollmer, & Loos, 1996) reported on a replication of the initial results with an additional 105 MVA survivors and 54 additional controls. The second study also reported 1-year reassessment data on the whole MVA sample (n = 125) as well as some other analyses on the combined sample.

Psychophysiological Responses

In our initial report we included skin resistance level as a measure of EDA. It was dropped from the replication because of equipment difficulties and undetected electrode failure. It was measured from 1 cm silver/silver chloride electrodes filled with Beckman electrode paste and attached to the ventral surface of the index and middle finger, which had previously been cleaned with isopropanol. We used a Grass Model 7 polygraph and a 7-P1 preamplifier. The bridge circuit was calibrated to zero and the level of skin resistance read from the dials once per minute.

Clinical Hint

Although EDA has not proved to have the discriminating power of HR in our work with PTSD, on the basis of its value in other studies we recommend it be included as a second response (after HR) if one is going to use more than one response measure. If only one measure is to be taken, we strongly urge the use of HR.

We measured HR, SBP, and DBP with a Dinamapp Critikon 1990 that was programmed automatically to take readings of the responses once per minute. It uses an inflatable cuff and microphone over the brachial artery, at the level of the heart, to detect Korotkoff sounds for determining SBP (onset of K sounds) and DBP (offset of K sounds). The Dinamapp Critikon 1990 also measures interbeat interval during this period and converts that to HR in BPM. These values are displayed digitally.

Forehead electromyogram (EMG) was measured with Grass precious metal electrodes filled with Grass electrode paste. After cleaning the forehead with Brasivol and then isopropanol, the active sensors were attached to individuals' foreheads about 2 1/2 cm above the eyebrow, centered on the pupil. The ground was placed midway between them. The response was detected by a Grass 7-P3 preamplifier and integrated with a 7-P10. Forehead or frontal EMG has proven of little usefulness in this work and that of others working on the psychophysiology of PTSD. We do not recommend using it.

Assessment Procedures

All of our assessments were done with the participant comfortably seated in an upholstered chair with good support for the neck and head (a few assessments were done on individuals who were still in a wheelchair due to injuries). Participants' feet were on the floor. The room was dimly lit. The participant was alone in the room in voice contact with the technician over an intercom. (In Blanchard et al., 1991, the experimenter was in the room with the participant.)

The conditions and verbatim instructions are presented in Exhibit 12-1. As one can see, there were four stressors, each lasted about 3 minutes, separated by baseline phases of 5 minutes. The

Exhibit 12-1
Psychophysiological Test Conditions

Adaptation: 2–7 min
 Polygraph is calibrated
 Dynamapp is calibrated
 SUDS* rating is elicited
Baseline (BL): 5 min
 "Please sit quietly with your eyes closed."
 Data sampled = mean of 2–4 min.
Mental math: 3 min
 "Please count backwards by 7s starting at 250."
 SUDS, "How anxious do you feel right now?"
 Data sampled: Min 2
Return to BL 1: 5 min
 "Please sit quietly with your eyes closed."
 Data sampled = mean of 2–4 min
 (same pattern for return to BL 2 and 4)
Audiotape 1: 3 min
 "Please listen to this audiotape."
 SUDS, "How anxious do you feel?"
Return to BL 2: 5 min (same instructions as return to BL 1)
Audio 2: 3 min (same instructions as Audiotape 1)
Return to BL 3: 5 min return to BL 3: 5 min (see instructions as return
   to BL 1)
Eyes open: 2 min
 "Please sit quietly with your eyes open."
 Data sampled—mean Min 1 and 2 used in lieu of return to BL 3
Videotape: 3 min
 "Please watch this video"
 SUDS, "How anxious do you feel?"
 Data sample = Min 2
Return to BL 4: 5 min (same instructions as return to BL 1)
Relax: 2 min
 "Please take a deep breath and let yourself begin to relax. (Pause)
 And take a deep breath and let yourself sink more deeply into the
 chair. (Pause) Just let your muscles become more and more heavy as
 you sink more deeply into the chair. (Pause) As you become more
 and more relaxed I'd like you to imagine as vividly as you possibly
 can that your are" . . . (describe a specific scene elicited during
(continued)

Exhibit 12-1   *(Continued)*
Psychophysiological Test Conditions

set up. This is a scene describing a specific instance when individual was warm and relaxed. Examples include lying on beach, lying in a tub of warm water, fishing, or looking out over a mountain valley)
  Data sampled = mean min 1 and 2
Return to BL 5: 15 min
  "Please sit quietly with your eyes closed, enjoying your relaxed feelings."
  Data sampled = mean of 2–4 min

Note: SUDS = Subjective Units of Discomfort Scale. Ratings: 0–100, 0 = not at all anxious and 100 = the most can imagine. From "The Psychophysiology of Motor Vehicle Accident Related Post-Traumatic Stress Disorder," by E. B. Blanchard, E. J. Hickling, A. E. Taylor, W. R. Loos, and R. J. Gerardi, 1994, *Behavior Therapy, 25,* Table 1. Copyright 1994 by the Association for Advancement of Behavior Therapy. Adapted with permission.

mental math is seen as a standard stressor that elicits a pressor response (increased BP and HR) in most individuals.

We used the idiosyncratic audiotapes attempted to capture the participant's MVA as he or she described it at the initial assessment. There was a brief lead-in setting the date, time of day, and situation. Elements of the MVA were then described, including actions by the survivor, thoughts, feelings, and sensations, with special attention to emotional responses. Two slightly different descriptions were made by the assessor so that the survivor was asked to imagine his or her own MVA twice.

Exhibit 12-2 is a verbatim transcript of part of the idiosyncratic script used in the assessment. The final stressor was a 3-minute videotape, depicting several car crashes, some of which were viewed from inside the vehicle. There was little depiction of blood and serious injury. The videotape was a composite from available materials.

Exhibit 12-2

Idiosyncratic Script Used in Assessment

You are on your way home from work; you are in a hurry. As you are driving down a very familiar road, a road you have driven many times before, you come upon a car. This car is driving at about 40 mph. You want to pass this car and you begin to do so when you enter a passing zone. You are halfway passing this car; you notice that there is another car, an oncoming car, in your lane now. You have been taking your time to safely get around the car. You increase your speed, in part because the car you are passing has also increased speed. As you pull back in you oversteer; you begin to go off the road. You over correct, as you swerve you cross the yellow line, you over correct again; you swerve and you are coming back into the lane that you had been driving in. You are not able to keep the car on the road. You are traveling at about 60 mph. You go off the road. You hit a ditch. You go end-over-end. Next you are lying on the ground. You are taking your time to think about what has happened to you. You want to check your movement. You move your head. You move your arms, but you cannot move your legs.

We used a single fixed order of experimental conditions. With hindsight, we might have had a tighter study had the order of stressors been randomized or varied by a Latin square. This would have controlled for possible order effects.

Results for Heart Rate

By far the most consistent and most powerful results came from HR, with SBP a distant second. The interaction of Group (MVA survivors with PTSD, subsyndromal PTSD, and non-PTSD and non-MVA controls) × Condition (see Table 12-1) was significant for HR and SBP but not for DBP or EMG. The most valuable data came from HR response to the first audiotape. We calculated a reactivity or response score by subtracting the preceding baseline value from the value for the stressor.

Table 12-1

Initial Assessment HR Reactivity Scores: All Diagnostic Groups at All Four Stressors and Initial Basal Values

Stressor	PTSD M	PTSD SD	Subsyndromal PTSD M	Subsyndromal PTSD SD	Non-PTSD M	Non-PTSD SD	Non-MVA M	Non-MVA SD
Mental arithmetic	7.7	7.3	6.0	7.6	8.5	6.89	8.8	9.59
Audiotape 1	4.2[a]	6.7	0.3[b]	5.2	0.8[b]	5.30	−0.6[b]	4.29
Audiotape 2	1.9	3.9	1.1	4.3	1.2	3.34	0.3	3.17
Videotape	−1.6	6.6	−2.0	4.0	−2.8	3.52	−1.6	3.80
Baseline 1	73.0	10.7	71.0	9.3	70.0	10.7	70.3	10.9

Note: Means in a row that share a superscript are not different at the $p = .01$ level by Duncan's multiple-range test. Adpated from "Psychophysiology of Post-Traumatic Stress Disorder Related to Motor Vehicle Accidents: Replication and Extension," by E. B. Blanchard, E. J. Hickling, T. C. Buckley, A. E. Taylor, A. Vollmer, and W. R. Loos, 1996, *Journal of Clinical and Consulting Psychology, 64,* Table 2. Copyright 1996 by the American Psychological Association.

The average HR reactivity values for this condition for each of the four groups, along with the initial baseline HR value, are presented in Table 12-1. The one-way ANOVA across groups for the reactivity scores was highly significant ($p = .0003$). Post hoc comparisons (Duncan's multiple-range test at $p = .01$) showed that the PTSDs had a greater response than any of the other groups, which did not differ.

The baseline HR values did not differ, contradicting the finding reported by Blanchard (1990) in his review of the Vietnam veteran literature that veterans with PTSD have higher resting HRs (by about 5 to 10 BPM) than other comparison groups of veterans.

The combined individual subject data from our two reports are shown in Figure 12-1. From examining these combined data, we

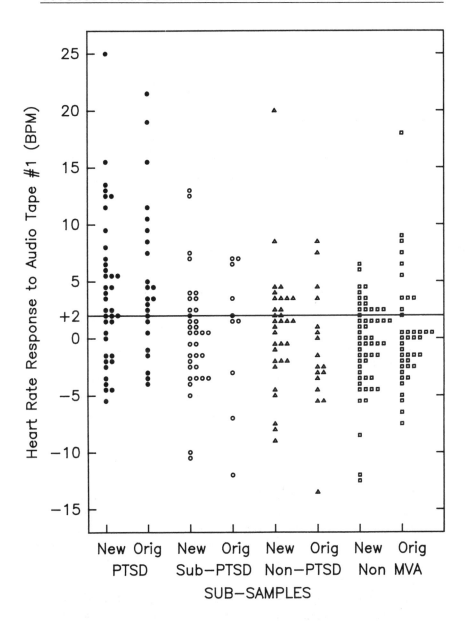

Figure 12-1.   Individual subject data for heart rate response to Audiotape # in beats-per-minute for original MVA sample (Blanchard et al., 1994b) and new sample (Blanchard et al., 1996) combined.

found that a cutoff score of +2BPM, that is, an increase in HR from return to Baseline 1 to Audiotape 1, of 2 BPM or greater discriminates among the groups (PTSD and other: sub-PTSD, non-PTSD, and non-MVA) fairly well with a sensitivity of 65.6, a specificity of 68.6, and a diagnostic efficiency of 67.9.

Clinical Hint

We believe this level of separation on a single measure has clinical utility at the level of the individual MVA survivor. Group mean differences are useful for hypothesis testing but one needs a simple, convenient measure, instead of a complex multivariate discriminate function, to have clinical utility.

Nonresponders

While correctly classifying two thirds of the PTSDs among MVA survivors is useful, one might ask if there are differences between those correctly classified (HR responders) and those not identified (HR nonresponders). We compared these two groups on anxiety, depression, total CAPS score, and CAPS score on the physiological reactivity item. These values are presented in Table 12-2. The only between-group difference was on State Anxiety with the HR responders reporting more anxiety ($p = .040$) and scoring about 8 units higher (67.3 vs. 58.9).

Follow-Up Results

As mentioned earlier, we were able to reassess 125 MVA survivors at the 1-year follow-up, including 45 who had initially been diagnosed with PTSD. Of the 45 initial PTSDs, 15 still met the criteria for PTSD, whereas 30 did not. Analyses of their psychophysiological data (especially HR) showed a decrease in reactivity for all participants for all stressors; however, those who did not remit (remained full PTSD at 1-year follow-up) continued to show a positive HR response to Audiotape 1.

Table 12-2

Psychological Test Scores of MVA Survivors With PTSD Who Showed or Did Not Show Heart Rate Response to Audiotape 1

Test	HR responders ($n = 40$)		HR nonresponders ($n = 21$)		
	M	SD	M	SD	p
Total CAPS score	61.5	23.3	55.4	17.8	ns
CAPS score for Item 17					
(physiological reactivity)	4.2	2.0	3.3	2.3	.066
Beck Depression Inventory	16.5	10.4	13.5	4.0	ns
STAI Trait	61.9	13.6	57.0	13.3	.096
STAI State	67.3	17.2	58.9	18.4	.040

Note: Adapted from "Psychophysiology of Post-Traumatic Stress Disorder Related to Motor Vehicle Accidents: Replication and Extension," by E. B. Blanchard, E. J. Hickling, T. C. Buckley, A. E. Taylor, A. Vollmer, and W. R. Loos, 1996, *Journal of Clinical and Consulting Psychology, 64*, Table 4. Copyright 1996 by the American Psychological Association.

Can Initial Psychophysiological Data Predict 12-Month Clinical Status?

The final question we asked was whether initial psychophysiological data predict 12-month clinical status. We had initial psychophysiological data on 48 PTSDs who were assessed at the 12-month follow-up (3 refused the follow-up psychophysiological assessment). Among this group, 16 still met the criteria for full PTSD, 7 for subsyndromal PTSD, and 25 for non-PTSD (essentially full remission).

For these HR data, we used a transformation that we previously used with Vietnam veterans: from the Audiotape 1 reactivity score (our best discriminating condition) we subtracted the reactivity to mental arithmetic as a way of correcting for overall tendency to respond to stressors with an increase in HR. The group mean values for this transformed response were 2.2 for PTSDs, -6.5 for subsyndromal PTSDs, and -5.2 for non-PTSD. The PTSDs scored significantly greater on this parameter ($p = .027$) than the other two groups (full or partial remitters) combined.

When we examined the individual participant results, using a cutoff of 0 (equal response to mental arithmetic and Audiotape 1), we correctly identified 11 of 16 initial PTSDs who had not remitted and 26 of 32 remitters, for a total correct classification (diagnostic efficiency) of 37 of 48 (77.1%). This represents an improvement on base rates of 66.7%.

It thus appears that psychophysiological assessment results obtained 1 to 4 months after an MVA have clinical utility not only initially help to confirm the diagnosis but also predict how the patient will function 12 months later. For these reasons, we believe that psychophysiological assessment has a truly useful role in assessing MVA survivors.

Our speculation is that the finding of greater psychophysiological reactivity among nonremitters with initial PTSD could represent a stronger conditioned emotional response (à la Keane et al.'s, 1985, behavioral model of PTSD) or a more entrenched cognitive fear structure (as postulated by Foa et al.'s, 1989, cognitive model of PTSD).

The use of psychophysiological responses in identifying MVA survivors with PTSD could present a partial answer to the issue raised in chapter 10 about detection of malingering. We say partial answer for two reasons. First, without current psychophysiological work described in this chapter, we found positive responses in about two thirds of all cases (overall diagnostic efficiency of 67.9%), which means we misdiagnosed almost a third of all cases. That level of potential error would probably not stand up in a legal setting. Second, at this point we do not know how well an MVA victim without PTSD can simulate the psychophysiological profile of an MVA survivor with PTSD. New research is needed to answer this question.

Despite these shortcomings, we believe psychophysiological responses, because they are a non-self-report measure and thus not as readily faked, potentially have a strong role to play in the comprehensive assessment of MVA survivors.

Treatment for Survivors

13

The Psychological Treatment of PTSD: An Overview and Review

A lthough the psychological disorder now known as PTSD has been identified for decades, little is known empirically regarding effective treatments for the disorder. This is not because there is a lack of opinion or of ideas regarding psychological treatment. Quite the opposite is, in fact, the case. This chapter presents a brief overview of the considerable literature found on the treatment of PTSD. Herein, we describe Solomon, Gerrity, and Muff's (1992) review, focusing particular detail on the psychological treatments. Recent reviews by Meichenbaum (1994) and Van der Kolk, McFarlane, and Hart (1996) are also selectively discussed. Finally, we review the concerns regarding psychological treatments developed for other populations of PTSD sufferers, and we present applications of techniques relevant to MVAs.

Solomon et al.'s (1992) Review

In their 1992 review of PTSD treatment, Solomon et al. (1992) found 255 English language reports that described the efficacy of various treatments for the psychological effects of exposure to traumatic events. They added that the vast majority (244) of the reports described case histories and, far less frequently, open trials.

This review limits itself to nonpharmacological approaches to treatment, other than to mention that a separate literature exists for the biological aspects of PTSD, and subsequent pharmacological interventions (see Solomon et al., 1992, and others listed in that review article). As Solomon et al. pointed out, practically every form of psychotherapy has been tried on individuals suffering from PTSD. Whereas most of the studies point out treatment efficacy, few have been subjected to systematic tests.

In their review, Solomon et al. (1992) selected studies that treated PTSD and met the following criteria: (a) inclusion criteria of participants on the basis of exposure to a traumatic event and assessed according to *DSM–III* (APA, 1980) or *DSM–III–R* (APA, 1987) criteria and (b) random assignment to the treatment of interest and either an alternative treatment or a no-treatment (or wait list) control group. Eleven studies met these criteria for inclusion, including drug treatment studies. This summary focuses on the results of the psychological treatment studies they reviewed.

Behavior Therapy

The behavioral treatments for PTSD have been based on the learning theory conceptualization of the development of PTSD. This, simply put, involves the pairing of a neutral stimulus with an extremely frightening stimuli (e.g., a traumatic event). The previously neutral stimulus through classical conditioning becomes aversive and capable of producing higher order conditioning, whereby many stimulus (e.g., words, thoughts, physical states, and images) also come to produce anxiety or fear. The conditioning is followed by the development of an avoidance response, through operant conditioning in that avoidance temporarily decreases the anxiety now associated with the conditioned stimulus.

Interventions then are designed to reduce the impact of the conditioning and the avoidant behavior. This is accomplished by having exposure to the feared situation (stimulus) either repeated or prolonged by either imaginal or in vivo exposure. Techniques can use either systematic desensitization (i.e., gradually increasing the intensity of the feared stimulus) or flooding (i.e., extended exposure to high-intensity stimulus). Solomon et al. (1992) reported on six studies that used behavioral techniques and met their criteria.

Systematic Desensitization

In the first study reviewed, Peniston (1986) reported on a treatment for PTSD that used relaxation training and 48 30-minute sessions of biofeedback-assisted, imaginal desensitization. Peniston reported that the treatment group, compared with a no-treatment control group, reported fewer nightmares, flashbacks, muscle tension, and hospital re-admissions. Treatment effects reportedly held for up to a 2-year follow-up evaluation. Brom et al. (1989) compared patients receiving systematic desensitization with those receiving hypnotherapy, those receiving psychodynamic therapy, and a wait-list control group. The results were that all patients in the treatment groups showed more improvements than those in the wait-list control group 3 months after treatment, as measured by a drop in symptoms reported on several questionnaires, with no difference among the three active treatment conditions.

Flooding

Of the four controlled studies that used flooding as a treatment paradigm, three were conducted on a veteran population. Keane et al. (1989) reported that individuals given implosive therapy reported reduced fear, depression, state anxiety, and intrusive symptoms as compared with a wait-list control group. Cooper and Clum (1989) reported in their study that individuals who received flooding, compared with a control group, reported reductions in sleep disturbance and in "psychoticlike" symptoms. Finally, Boudewyns and Hyer (1990) found that patients who received flooding showed significantly greater improvement than patients who received a program of individual counseling on a measure of Veterans' adjustment 3 months after treatment ended.

Foa et al. (1991) in an elegant study of different cognitive behavioral procedures, compared Meichenbaum's stress inoculation training (SIT) with prolonged exposure (PE), supportive counseling, and a wait-list control condition for rape survivors with chronic PTSD (average time since assault was 6.2 years). Foa et al. used a global outcome measure as well as symptom cluster specific measures of PTSD. At post-treatment the SIT condition was superior to the supportive counseling and the wait-list conditions overall and on the reduction of avoidance symptoms in particular. SIT was not statistically superior to the PE condition at post-treatment. At a 3.5 month follow-up, the SIT and PE groups were not statistically superior to the supportive counseling control group overall or on any symptom cluster. However, whereas the PE group showed continued improvement over the follow-up interval, those in the SIT group showed a nonsignificant loss of treatment gains. In the PE condition, the patients intensely relived the trauma experience by repeatedly describing the event during therapy sessions, listening to an audiotape recording of the description each day, and through in vivo exposure to feared and avoided situations. Solomon et al. reported that, whereas flooding is effective for reducing the symptoms of intrusive recollections of PTSD, it does little to reduce symptoms that relate to emotional numbing and avoidance.

Some concerns about the use of flooding have been reported, including exacerbations in case studies where there was an increase in alcohol use, depression, and precipitation of panic attacks. Pitman et al. (1991) raised cautions about the limits of flooding, particularly when symptoms are from conditions other than anxiety. They added that because PTSD patients may also suffer from anger, guilt, and depression, other forms of therapy may be warranted because these emotions are not believed to extinguish in the same fashion as anxiety.

Cognitive Therapy

As Solomon et al. (1992) pointed out, although still untested, behavioral techniques may prove to be more effective when combined with cognitive therapy. They described the behavioral techniques as methods to activate fear and promote habituation, whereas cognitive therapies have been developed to reduce anxiety by providing the patient with skills to control their fear.

One of the most developed cognitive therapies for PTSD is SIT (Veronen & Kilpatrick, 1983). SIT as described by Veronen and Kilpatrick is actually a combination of therapies that include muscle relaxation, thought stopping, breathing control, communication skills, and guided self-dialogue consisting of cognitive restructuring (i.e., modifying the patient's thinking and underlying beliefs about self, world, and future) and stress inoculation (SI; i.e., discussing the patient's reaction to stressful situations, rehearsing coping skills, and testing the skills under stressful conditions).

To our knowledge, only one randomized, controlled investigation of cognitive therapy for PTSD has been conducted, the Foa et al. study (1991). This study found SIT to be the most effective therapy for reducing symptoms of PTSD when measured at the conclusion of treatment. However, at the time of follow-up, 3.5 months later, the pattern had changed such that prolonged exposure demonstrated the greatest efficacy in reducing PTSD symptoms. Foa et al. explained this shift by suggesting that SIT provides immediate anxiety relief but that patients may not have continued the techniques after the end of treatment, which is thought necessary for continued improvement. In contrast, PE is expected to produce temporary, heightened anxiety with its introduction, but this is thought to lead to more permanent change in the memory of the trauma and thereby more lasting gains.

Psychodynamic Treatment and Hypnotherapy

Solomon et al. (1992) summarized the intent of psychodynamic therapies as helping the traumatized individual integrate the traumatic event into his or her understanding of the meaning of life, self-concept, and world image. The emotional reactions are thought to be the reaction of the traumatized person's dealing with discrepancies between internal and external information. The discrepancies serve to create motives for defense and control, as shown in PTSD by the symptom clusters of intrusion and avoidance. Similar to that of psychodynamic theory, the main goal of hypnotherapy is to allow the traumatized individual to release unconscious material (e.g., memories, thoughts, and feelings) and to integrate the traumatic event.

Solomon et al. (1992) reported that, to date, there has only been one controlled study of either psychodynamic or hypnotherapy approaches to the treatment of PTSD. This is the study mentioned earlier by Brom et al. (1993), who compared patients receiving psychodynamic therapy, hypnotherapy, and systematic desensitization with a wait-list control group. All three treatment groups showed significantly greater improvement than the wait-list control group. The psychodynamic group was reported to show the greatest reduction in avoidance symptoms, with less change in intrusion symptoms. The hypnotherapy and desensitization groups showed the opposite trend, with a greater reduction in intrusion symptoms and less change in avoidance symptoms.

Meichenbaum's Review

In an encyclopedic effort, Meichenbaum (1994) produced a clinical handbook/practical therapist manual for assessing and treating PTSD. Meichenbaum pointed out two characteristics of the treatment literature to date: (a) Clinicians have been extremely creative in using almost any type of intervention with PTSD survivors, and (b) there is a remarkable limitation of good outcome data in the treatment literature reviewed to date. He cautioned that at this time there is not sufficient evidence to suggest the superiority of any one form of treatment over any other or is there an appreciation of how various treatment components can be combined most effectively.

To illustrate the breadth of topics for treatments of PTSD, Meichenbaum (1994) provided the following list:

> Pharmacological interventions, crisis intervention, individual and group psychodynamic therapies, individual therapy, time-limited dynamic therapies, time-limited trauma therapy,

individual behavior therapy, systematic desensitization and EMG biofeedback, eye movement desensitization and reprocessing therapy, guided imagery based intervention, individual and group cognitive–behavioral stress inoculation therapy, dialectical behavior therapy and problem solving, marathon therapy group, cognitive restructuring or cognitive processing therapy, inpatient treatment programs, eclectic inpatient program, multifaceted outpatient intervention, second generation inpatient program, readjustment counseling services, partial hospitalization and day treatment programs, outpatient group programs for women veterans, gestalt techniques, marital and family therapy, hypnosis and hypnotherapy, solution focused and strategic therapy, reauthoring therapy, transcendental meditation, abreactive treatments, post-traumatic therapy, reintegration therapy, general skills multimodal therapy, group psychotherapy, community-wide and school-based interventions, outpatient clinic, family based interventions, ritualistic approaches, art and movement therapies, relapse prevention programs, cross cultural counseling, integrative biopsychosocial approach, pastoral care and twelve step program, self-help audiotapes, outward bound programs. (pp. 287–294)

As one can see from Meichenbaum's list, the approaches to PTSD treatment have varied considerably. The treatments, according to Meichenbaum, have varied for several reasons: (a) because of the techniques being used and (b) because of the population they are trying to reach. Meichenbaum stated, regarding the types of treatment used for PTSD, "You name it and it seems to have been tried with PTSD clients" (p. 284). He went on to note, "There is not sufficient evidence to suggest the superiority of one form of treatment over any other, nor any appreciation of how the various treatment components can be combined most efficiently" (p. 284).

Van der Kolk, McFarlane, and Hart (1996), in describing a general approach to the treatment of PTSD, offered the following suggestions for a phase-focused, treatment model. First, they suggest that treatment of PTSD should focus on the stabilization of the patient's symptoms. This includes education about the disorder and identification of feelings through verbalizing about the somatic states experienced. Second, they suggest treatment should focus on the reconditioning of the traumatic memories and responses. Learning to tolerate and accept the memories of the intense emotional experience of the trauma, rather than avoiding the distress, is thought to be a crucial part of recovery. Third, treatment should focus on a restructuring of the traumatic schemes. The personal meaning of the trauma, both conscious and unconscious, needs to be organized and integrated.

Adaptation to the stressful experience is thought to consist of a modification of the self-view and the worldview. Fourth, there needs to be a re-establishment of a secure social connection and interpersonal efficacy. The role of social support is thought to be critical to the resiliency and recovery of trauma survivors. Finally, treatment should address the accumulation of restitutive emotional experiences. By this they mean that, for survivors to recover fully, they should expose themselves to situations that lead to feelings of mastery and pleasure.

Although there are other articles that provide an overview of PTSD treatment, these recent reviews were selected to set the stage for treatment of MVA-related PTSD. Before we directly discuss research on that population, we touch on selected factors found in the general treatment of PTSD literature that have added to our understanding of MVA treatment.

First, is the concern that the literature describing treatment of veterans with PTSD may have less contribution to our treatment problem than literature dealing with more acute problems. One issue central to our review of relevant literature is the concern that the treatment literature with chronic PTSD, such as that found in the Vietnam veteran population, is not particularly encouraging. Moreover, it is not at all clear to us that treatment efforts, developed and tested on a population that has had PTSD for 15 to 25 years, are especially relevant to the treatment of MVA survivors who have been symptomatic for a considerably shorter period of time. With this focus, the treatment of rape survivors and other assault survivors with PTSD who are relatively acute would seem more relevant (e.g., Foa et al., 1991).

Specialized Techniques of Interest

Harber and Pennebaker (1992), in discussing how to overcome traumatic memories, shared several treatment techniques of interest. They discussed a series of studies termed *trauma confession studies*, in which individuals were brought to a laboratory and then randomly assigned to write (or talk) about either deeply traumatic experiences or superficial topics. Depending on the study, participants may write for 15 to 20 minutes each day for 3 to 4 days or talk about the traumatic event and the superficial event both on the same day for 3 to 7 minutes. Harber and Pennebaker summarized the studies as showing that the effect of disclosure is remarkably powerful. In the studies where the participants talk only about their trauma for a few minutes, a quarter of them cried. The writing samples portray horror and tragedy. Corresponding with the writing samples is an improvement in the health of the participants as measured by fewer visits to the health center. According to Harber and Pennebaker, one of the most robust findings of their studies is that confronting traumas through writing reverses inhibitory stresses. They describe the act of writing as an active coping mechanism and as the construction of a narrative in which one finds meaning in the organizing of a coherent structure. By putting the trauma into written description, the authors conclude that trauma survivors begin the reconstructive process of trauma assimilation. Speech and written expression permits the articulation of the trauma's private, and seemingly ineffable, qualities. Concurrently, the structure of language restricts the emotional flow, guided by channels formed by the organizational rules of grammar. It is through the evoking of memories that carry an emotional content, yet controlled and structured by language, that the process of traumatic assimilation occurs. Gidron, Peri, Connolly, and Shalev (1996) caution, however, that written disclosure of a traumatic experience, without the provision of coping skills, may actually contribute to an increase in health visits and avoidance symptoms, as found to be the case in a sample of 14 trauma victims with PTSD compared with a control condition.

Ochberg (1991), in his description of post-traumatic therapy, also discussed the importance of letting the patient tell the trauma story. He notes the individual's search for meaning in the catastrophic situation. Techniques used within treatment include education (e.g., reading the *DSM–III* [APA, 1980] together, the impact of law and the legal system on the patient, the role of psychobiology) and the promotion of holistic health, nutrition, exercise, humor, and spirituality. Social integration and the role of family therapy are also discussed, as well as the potential role of groups.

Summary and Implications for MVA Survivors

As is abundantly clear by now, researchers have made a considerable effort to describe treatment approaches for PTSD. As Solomon et al. (1992) reported, over 250 treatment articles were found in 1992. By now, even more are present. Yet there is little in the way of controlled investigations to guide us. Relatedly, the treatments reported are often developed for a veteran population, whose experience with PTSD spans one and a half to two decades as a chronic condition. Our survivors have a different traumatic experience and have endured the condition for a significantly shorter period of time. With this overview as a backdrop, the next chapter reviews the studies that have directly dealt with survivors of MVAs and the subsequent psychological sequalae.

14

The Treatment of MVA-Related PTSD: A Review of the Literature

This chapter reviews the literature on accident phobias and the controversy over such a diagnosis when the survivor is also diagnosed with PTSD. The limited literature on the treatment of MVA survivors is reviewed both for the treatment of accident phobia and for PTSD.

Although there is a growing body of research exploring the psychological consequences of MVAs, there has been little reported literature on the treatment of PTSD following an MVA. The earliest mention of psychological consequences of MVAs, rather than addressing PTSD treatment, focused on a post-traumatic phobic response, typically to driving. Whether any of these cases may have, in fact, been a case of PTSD is impossible to determine from a retrospective review of the literature. The earlier cases actually could not have been diagnosed as PTSD as per the *DSM–III* (APA, 1980) because codification of the disorder did not become uniform until its publication. However, as a matter of historical interest, and as a way to gain perspective on today's conceptualization of treatment issues, selected examples are offered as part of this literature review.

Accident Phobia

Taylor and Koch (1995) in their review of anxiety disorders following MVAs described the history of accident phobia. As they pointed out, many terms have been used to describe MVA-related phobias, including *driving phobia* and *travel phobia*, but they reserve the term *accident phobia* to describe phobias arising from MVAs. They correctly point out that accident phobia is not only limited to the drivers of vehicles but can also afflict passengers, pedestrians, motorcyclists, or anyone involved in motor vehicle collisions.

The differential diagnosis between accident phobia and PTSD is important for several reasons, perhaps the most central of which is to establish a model on which to base treatment. Kuch et al. (1991, 1994) defined *accident phobia* as comprising three main features: (a) It is consistent with *DSM–III–R* (APA, 1987) or *DSM–IV* (APA, 1994) diagnostic criteria for simple phobia (called specific phobia in *DSM–IV*), (b) onset and content of the phobia are related to an MVA, and (c) anxiety symptoms and avoidance center around excessive fears of repetition of the accident. According to the *DSM–IV*, one cannot diagnose a simple or specific phobia if the patient also meets criteria for PTSD (see p. 411). It is, in fact, a hallmark of the PTSD patient that he or she by definition should be avoidant and fearful of the situation that was traumatic and life threatening.

Although we deal with assessment in earlier chapters in this book (e.g., chapters 3, 4, and 5), the issue becomes important when viewing earlier research. Because PTSD did not become codified in the *DSM* until its revision in 1980 it is certainly possible that earlier conditions may have been conceptualized and treated as a phobic response when they may in fact have been cases of PTSD. With the nosology changing over time, the critical issue becomes whether the treatment methodology used in those cases adds to an understanding of how to help MVA survivors.

The Treatment of Accident Phobia

The earliest report we could find on the treatment of accident phobia in our literature searches was that of Wolpe (1962). His work and the work of Kraft and Al-Issa (1965) both reportedly used systematic desensitization for the treatment of MVA-related phobia. Inspection of the studies, however, suggests that more complex intervention, in fact, occurred.

The nature of the MVAs for the two survivors was quite different. The MVA survivor treated by Wolpe (1962) was involved in an accident in which her car was struck by a truck while she was driving through an intersection, which rendered her unconscious. She was subsequently transported to a hospital by ambulance. She spent 1 week in the hospital for injuries to the knee and neck. It was discovered on the way home from the hospital that she became "unaccountably frightened." She reported heightened anxiety when driving, which worsened when a car approached her from either side. Prior traumatic experiences included involvement in an MVA at age 10 when a tractor crushed a side of the car in which she was a passenger. She was in London during World War II during the air blitz. During World War II she lost her fiancee, a pilot who was killed. Treatment was based on conditioning theories using prolonged exposure, in the belief that imaginal or in vivo exposure should reduce perceived anxiety and phobic avoidance. The earlier treatments combined relaxation training and used graded imaginal exposure as well as in vivo exposure. Wolpe, in fact, conducted over 57 desensitization sessions and used hypnosis in the treatment session as part of the imaginal desensitization procedure. The patients reportedly became completely at ease in all normal traffic situations and in two near misses while driving, and had no lasting emotional consequence.

Kraft and Al-Issa (1965) treated a 37-year-old man who had experienced two accidents as a road worker. The first accident occurred at age 30, the second at age 35. There was a prior history of a medical discharge from the army at age 17 for complaints of headaches and dizziness and a marriage from age 24 to 29 with reported sexual maladjustment. Following his second MVA he was unemployed for a period of 9 months and then admitted to a psychiatric hospital for 6 weeks. He tried a number of medications without resolution of the phobic response. Kraft and Al-Issa used 3 sessions of hypnotherapy, 22 sessions of desensitization (1.5 hours each), and 10 follow-up sessions. A follow-up at 6 months showed the patient to be free of symptoms. Kraft and Al-Issa also noted that the patient's symptoms remitted prior to a legal settlement, lowering the consideration of secondary gain from monetary compensation. The desensitization sessions took place over a 3-month period. More recently, Quirk (1985), using similar techniques, showed a reduction in MVA-related anxiety.

As Taylor and Koch (1995) pointed out, systematic desensitization and other methods of imaginal exposure have been found useful for exposing patients to aspects of the MVA that cannot be reproduced through in vivo exposure. Recent studies have treated accident phobia with a combination of imaginal exposure and in vivo exposure. Blonstein (1988) treated an accident phobic over 33 sessions, using 22 weeks of imaginal exposure followed by 11 weeks of graduated in vivo exposure. Treatment was conducted by the therapist directing 5 of the imaginal sessions, with much of the remaining sessions completed as directed homework assignments. The imaginal exposure exercise involved 30 to 45 repetitions of a 1-minute, endless loop audiocassette description of anxiety-provoking driving scenarios. In vivo exposure involved frequent exposure to the scene of the MVA. The patient drove past the scene 7 to 13 times per exposure episode (taking between 15 to 60 minutes, 3 days per week) for 11 consecutive weeks. Fear and avoidance were reportedly significantly reduced as measured by self-report rating scales. Several other case studies have also used similar approaches, including Horne (1993), Levine and Wolpe (1980), and Rovetto (1983). The latter two cases used in vivo desensitization through radio contact, with Rovetto telemonitoring psychophysiological responsiveness as well as getting verbal reports of subjective functioning from the individual.

An extremely dangerous startle reaction was treated by Fairbank, DeGood, and Jenkins (1981) for an MVA victim who was also described as having a driving phobia. The startle response was so dramatic as to cause a potentially dangerous driving situation, wherein at the sight of an approaching vehicle in the left lane the patient would become highly anxious and abruptly jerk the steering wheel to the right. Following her MVA, the patient had swerved off the road several times as a result of this involuntary startle response. The patient was treated first with three sessions of progressive muscle relaxation and autogenic training, which was followed by 2 weeks of daily in vivo exposure. In vivo exposure consisted of the patient driving twice per day along a mile-long segment of heavily traveled two-lane highway. As measured by self-reports of anxiety and frequency of startle response, the patient improved significantly, with gains being reportedly maintained at a 6-month follow-up visit.

Treatment of PTSD

In one of the earliest reports of the treatment of accident-related PTSD, McCaffrey and Fairbank (1985) used a broad spectrum assessment and treatment package for two individuals who met *DSM–III* (APA, 1980) criteria for PTSD secondary to transportation accidents. One of the survivors had two traumatic accidents related to helicopter crashes. The second individual was a 28-year-old woman who presented with a host of PTSD-related symptoms following four automobile accidents over a 14-month period.

Treatment consisted of three components: relaxation training, flooding in imagination (implosive therapy; IT) to fearful stimulus, and self-directed in vivo exposure to the feared stimulus. The first 2 weeks of treatment involved relaxation with homework practice followed by IT, which was preceded by and ended with therapist-led relaxation exercises. IT entails having each patient describe (using all five sensory modalities) the physical characteristics (i.e., symptom-contingent cues) associated with his or her trauma. Subsequent IT sessions were focused on a combination of symptom-contingent cue presentations and the use of hypothetical cues associated with the traumatic events (viz., fear of bodily injury, dying, aggressive behavior, rejection, and punishment for wrongdoing). The first individual was treated with four IT sessions, each approximately 2 hours in length. Sessions were focused on the individual's guilt about a friend who had died in the crash and fear he too would die in a similar crash. The patient was then seen for four additional sessions during which other aspects of the trauma were presented in imagination and a graded series of imagined events was portrayed. The patient was also encouraged to engage in as much self-directed in vivo exposure as possible.

The second individual, who had experienced multiple MVAs, was treated with a combination of symptom-contingent cues (e.g., the patient being responsible for the accidents) and hypothetical cues (e.g., fear of causing the death of an innocent person and her own death) during the first four IT sessions. At that point she reported a slight reduction in anxiety during the sessions but little decrease in the associated symptoms of PTSD, and reported a worsening of her sleep difficulties. The authors reported a change in treatment strategies at that point because the patient mentioned that her mother, who had been extremely upset with the patient because of the accidents, had deserted the family for over 3 years when the patient was 10 years old. Reportedly, the stepfather told the patient that the reason the mother left was because the patient was a "bad child." The treatment also focused on issues related to the mother and the patient's relationship with her. Treatment also included three IT sessions dealing with the same contingent cues and the hypothetical cues related to fear and guilt about perceived responsibility. Gains as measured by self-report of symptoms related to PTSD were shown for both patients and reported to be sustained at the 12-month follow-up.

Kuch et al. (1985, 1987) at about the same time reported on his experience with the assessment and treatment of PTSD after car accidents. Kuch et al. (1985) studied 30 people (22 women and 8 men), with 12 being treated, whereas the remaining 18 were assessed for medicolegal opinion. The 12 treatment participants were provided 4 to 12 hours of imaginal flooding, with images of their accident and in vivo exposure to driving or being driven for no less than 1 hour, and up to 3 hours, per session for four sessions. Six of the 12 participants were reported to have marked improvement, with 4 others improving on their ability to drive following the provision of lorazepam or diazepam in declining dosages during exposure and after receiving several hours of cognitively oriented therapy. Two individuals experienced no benefit and remained unable to drive. Although the study was uncontrolled, the authors suggested that treatment could be offered with effectiveness, despite the fact that litigation might be ongoing.

In a later article, Kuch (1989) shared his impression that a conditioning paradigm guides his work with accident survivors, particularly with the occurrence of post-traumatic phobia. He further reported how "worries" about illness may obscure specific phobias and become the presenting complaint, particularly with whiplash survivors. Kuch also reported on the common occurrence of anger in survivors and how many survivors feel "victimized by the system." Treatment reportedly used primarily an exposure-based intervention, with patients first being desensitized to the role of passenger and then to the role of driver. Kuch reported a preference for in vivo over imaginal exposure but added the two may successfully be used in combination. Kuch concluded by expressing concern that chronic pain may inter-act with the presentation of PTSD, with pain often remitting as driving-related anxiety decreases in reported intensity.

Muse (1986) also reported anecdotal cases of PTSD and the effect of chronic pain. He reportedly treated three cases of MVA-related PTSD in which individuals also suffered injuries resulting in lingering pain. Patients were treated with a pain-management program (which included physical exercise, biofeedback, supportive counseling, and medication). Although this program was somewhat effective in reducing the level of the patients' pain, there appeared to be little impact on the symptoms of PTSD. The patients were then treated with between 11 and 16 sessions of systematic desensitization followed by 2 sessions of in vivo exposure. At that point symptoms of PTSD began to decline, with treatment gains continuing 4 to 7 months later, as assessed during follow-up evaluations.

In an earlier work, Hickling et al. (1992) treated 20 post-traumatic headache patients, 10 of whom had PTSD as a co-morbid condition to the post-traumatic headache. Whereas both groups responded equally well to the combination of treatments provided (cognitive–behavioral, relaxation, biofeedback, and exposure), those with PTSD required considerably more time ($p < .05$) to show treatment results (26 vs. 11 sessions on average). Moreover, treatment did not show positive results for the headaches until symptoms for PTSD had been addressed.

McMillan (1991) reported on the unusual presentation of a case of PTSD, wherein the patient had a severe head injury but no recollection of the MVA. The patient reportedly had been unconscious for 3 to 4 days following the accident and suffered post-traumatic amnesia for 6 weeks. A close friend of the MVA survivor had been killed in the MVA. During recovery from the accident, the patient experienced increasingly intrusive thoughts of the friend who had been killed. Treatment for the PTSD began 14 months after the MVA. Treatment consisted of weekly sessions, lasting over 4 months in total, and included imaginal exposure using both verbal and written material and in vivo exposure to contingent cues of the MVA including visits to the friend's grave. Treatment used therapist-assisted exposure, self-directed exposure, and development of a close relationship with a friend or confidante outside of the treatment sessions. Symptoms of PTSD were reduced according to self-report and lasted through at least a 4-month follow-up period.

Horton (1993) also reported a case study of an MVA victim who suffered PTSD and mild neuropsychological impairment. Treatment consisted of 12 weekly sessions of behavior therapy, which used systematic desensitization and self-directed exposure. Treatment again was found to be positive, as measured by a decrease on the Willoughby Questionnaire (Wolpe, 1982) and by self-reported PTSD symptoms.

Horne (1993) reported on three case studies, all of which involved individuals with psychological problems that lasted more than 6 months after the MVA. Treatment included imaginal exposure to a hierarchy of car travel scenes, in vivo exposure, relaxation training, cognitive–behavioral therapy, and contact with significant others. Treatment length ranged from 14 sessions to more than 30 sessions (> 1 year in time, for the two cases for which length of treatment was reported). Positive treatment results were reported for each case, although it is important to note that, although formal treatment had ended, there were still considerable residual problems reported by Horne for the treated survivors.

Lyons and Scotti (1995) reported on a case of direct therapeutic exposure (DTE), illustrating a treatment methodology using both imaginal and in vivo flooding, and implosive therapy. Their study describes the clinical application of DTE in detail as a case study example of application to the larger clinical problem of MVA survivors. As their case illustrates, the patient showed reduced anxiety and depressive symptoms, reexperiencing (e.g., intrusive thoughts and images, flashbacks, and nightmares), physiological arousal, and lessened avoidance. The case illustrated how depression, substance abuse, anger, and aggression were not exacerbated during the provision of DTE and reappeared and returned to baseline level when outpatient sessions were not held regularly. The authors speak to the importance of adjunctive treatment methods, including problem solving, communication, anger control, marital or family therapy, and other treatments to attend to the individualized needs of this clinical population. Finally, they comment on the importance of the therapeutic relationship as developed by the therapist listening to the patient's report of the trauma. They believe an empathic response to the often horrific material is one of the keys to rapport building and conceptualize treatment as attending to distorted or repressed memories, delusions regarding guilt and fear of punishment, and even hallucinatory behavior, all of which are treatment issues traditionally thought to extend beyond the realm of behavior therapy at first glance. For their illustrative case, they also see the factors of pharmacotherapy, problem solving, and relaxation training as important adjuncts to DTE. The case, in summary, appears to incorporate many cognitive, supportive, and interpretative elements besides a strictly behavioral approach to the treatment.

Best and Ribbe (1995) also recently shared their approach to treatment for survivors of accidental injury using the illustrative case of a 23-year-old man who had been in a serious MVA 6 months prior to seeking treatment. Their overview of treatment techniques included attention to physical, cognitive, and behavioral fear responses. Effective treatment they believe should include a combination of relaxation training (e.g., Jacobsonian deep-muscle relaxation, controlled breathing), cognitive interventions (e.g., thought stopping, activation-belief-consequences; ABC training), rational emotive therapy, and behavioral techniques (i.e., role playing, exposure therapy, stress inoculation therapy). They further commented on "special issues" for therapy with accident survivors that include perceived life threat, the extent of physical injury and its lasting impact on the patient, differences in when patients present to treatment (immediately after the trauma vs. years later), and the role of the therapist as advocate for the patient.

Miller (1994) in his review of civilian PTSD shared his own considerable work in this area and commented on how in "virtually every case of significant trauma, the patient struggles with shattered fantasies about fairness, justice, security and the meaning of life" (p. 662). Some patients are therefore forced to view their own mortality and vulnerability, coming to perceive themselves as different from the rest of the world as a result of the trauma. Existential struggles with the search for meaning, rather than alleviation of symptoms, may be a productive direction for treatment. Miller's (1989) own work includes anecdotal reports or the positive anecdotal outcome of treatment through antidepressant medications and traditional psychotherapy and behavioral therapy.

Koch and Taylor (1995) also reported their ideas on assessment and treatment of PTSD following an MVA. In a recent article they use anecdotes to support their belief in the provision of cognitive and behavioral interventions, primarily in vivo exposure and cognitive beliefs about driving phobia. They see the overprediction of danger and underprediction of safety as important targets for cognitive restructuring. In their article, they discuss what they view as important issues regarding the sequencing of treatment (i.e., which co-morbid psychological disorder or pain disorder to treat first). Although in general they suggest treatment of pain prior to treatment of phobia, they do not see this as a hard and fast rule.

Burstein (1986) in an earlier study compared treatment characteristics of patients with PTSD who were successfully treated within a short period of time (3 months or less) with the treatment characteristics of those who had been in treatment for greater than 12 months. Although both groups had a wide range of traumatic stressors, 7 out of 13 in the short-term group and 9 out of 15 in the long-term group had an MVA as their traumatic stressor for PTSD. All of the patients received medication (usually an antidepressant, imipramine or an MAOI, or phenelzine) and individual supportive psychotherapy. Goals of treatment were to decrease phobic avoidance and facilitate confrontation of the phobic situation in vivo. Ancillary issues, such as preexisting PTSD-precipitated marital issues, were treated in the individual sessions. The patients were selected in a retrospective review of

84 records. Inclusion within the study was based on a successful outcome as determined by the absence or near absence of PTSD during a 2-week period of no treatment. Patients who had terminated prematurely or who were still active in treatment were not used in the study. There did not appear to be any significant differences reported for the type of stressor, reported symptom distress, possible compensation factors, or time from trauma to intervention. The long-term treatment group was reported to require higher daily dosages of a tricyclic.

In perhaps the only controlled intervention study attempted to date for survivors of traffic accidents, Brom, Kleber, and Hofman (1993) studied the effectiveness of a psychological package designed to stimulate healthy coping following an MVA. They saw the reactions and needs of survivors as ranging from (a) normal responses that do not require any assistance from professionals to (b) survivors helped by the support of trained victim assistants who may help survivors or diminish the number of persons who develop disorders to (c) counseling and crisis intervention for the serious life event.

The treatment package they developed included the following: (a) practical help and information (i.e., general information about reactions after a serious life event, symptom patterns one may experience, attempts to place reactions in the context of normal coping, and practical matters such as medical or financial matters); (b) support (i.e., a safe and quiet environment to reassure the victim that the event is really over), meant as a structured experience whereby the victim can label their emotions and mobilize their own social network; and (c) reality testing, wherein the intervention attempts to facilitate coping through confrontation. Coping is thought of by Brom et al. as a process of forgetting and retrieving. Confrontation and reality testing regarding the symptoms the survivors are experiencing may help the symptoms become less frightening. Interventions are to occur over several sessions, at least 2 to 3 months following the accident. The intervention was designed to aid in the early recognition of any psychological disorders and make appropriate referral to trained professionals.

Individuals were drawn from a police registry of MVA survivors in The Netherlands. The initial sample was gathered from a list compiled over a 1-year period. The accident was judged by five independent raters to be from moderately serious to serious, on the basis of registration forms and then by rating the severity of the accident. Interrater reliability of accident severity was somewhat poor, ranging from .51 to .71.

The police then informed the survivors about the project. One group of individuals received a letter asking them to participate in a research project, whereas the other group received a written invitation to participate in a secondary prevention program. The selection to either group was random. The sample consisted of 83 participants (30 women and 53 men) in the monitoring group and 68 participants (32 women and 36 men) in the intervention group. Letters were mailed to 738 persons, with a response rate of 36 % for the monitoring group and only 13% for the intervention group. Mean age was 39 and 36 years, respectively. At the time of follow-up, the dropout rate was 24% in the monitoring group and 16% in the intervention group. Outcome measures included the IES (Horowitz et al., 1979), using a Dutch translation; the Trauma Symptom Inventory, which is a selection of the SCL-90 (Arendell & Ettema, 1981) consisting of 29 items that are thought to reflect negative emotional experiences, tensions, sleep disturbances, and lack of interest in the external world; and the Evaluation Questionnaire, which is a short questionnaire given only to the intervention group that asked them their degree of satisfaction with the elements of the treatment program. Treatment was carried out by two experienced therapists and consisted of three sessions that could be extended to six sessions.

The study found that 1 month after an MVA, about half of the survivors showed moderate to severe symptoms of intrusion and avoidance. By 6 months after the MVA, these symptoms had improved, although 8% of individuals were still rated as severe, whereas another 10% to 17% showed moderate symptoms. About 90% of the intervention group indicated that they were content or very content with the intervention. Importantly, there was no significant difference in the degree of improvement on the IES between the intervention group and the monitoring control group. Thus, Brom et al. (1993) were not able to prove the effectiveness of their intervention or that their intervention had more effectiveness than the passage of time.

Finally, Mayou (1994, personal communication) described another very brief intervention for survivors of MVAs. Here the intervention was a session in the hospital, accompanied by a booklet, advice for seeking further help and booklet, and advice on management to general practitioners. Again the impression was that treatment was not effective. Mayou concluded that it may have been overly ambitious to expect that such a brief intervention so soon after an accident would be effective, but it was hoped that the experience would help make future interventions acceptable and provide ideas about the timing of interventions for those who truly need treatment. Table 14-1 presents a summary of treatment studies.

Conclusion

To date there has been only one controlled investigation of treatment of PTS symptoms among survivors of MVAs. Brom et al.'s (1993) study did not show a differential (as measured by the IES) to impact on PTS symptoms in MVA survivors assigned to a brief treatment versus a monitoring control condition. Case study reports on the treatment of PTSD following MVAs are encouraging and in general follow a cognitive behavioral model.

As we reviewed in chapter 13, there is a relatively large literature on the treatment of PTSD. Solomon et al. (1992) in their review of PTSD treatment identified 255 English language reports at that time. Much of the investigation has dealt with veterans, and it is not at all clear that treatments that had been developed and tested on a population that had PTSD for over 15 years is especially relevant to the survivors of MVAs who had been symptomatic for less than a year. The literature on the treatment of rape survivors and assault survivors, who had relatively acute symptoms, appears to be relevant to our work with MVA survivors, but this work is typically on assault survivors 5 to 6 years post-trauma and has been limited to female participants.

The case studies reported in this chapter have in general followed a similar model of cognitive–behavioral treatment. Behavioral treatment using imaginal and in vivo exposure has

Table 14-1
Treatment Studies of MVA-Related PTSD

Author	Description of study	No. of sessions	Results
McCaffrey & Fairbank (1985)	2 Accident-related survivors; 1 with MVA. Tx. for MVA consisted of relaxation training, imaginal and in vivo exposure, relationship training, imaginal and in vivo exposure, relationship issues with mother	15	Drop in symptoms for PTSD. Continued ratings of fear, drop in skin conduction with exposure post-treatment.
Kuch, Swinson, & Kirby (1985)	12 MVA survivors received treatment consisting of 4–12 hr of imaginal and in vivo exposure	N/R	6 of 12 showed marked improvement. 4 additionally improved with medication and cognitive therapy.
Muse (1986)	3 MVA survivors who suffered PTSD and chronic pain; treatment included (a) pain treatment (exercise, biofeedback, supportive counseling, and medications) and (b) systematic desensitization and in vivo exposure	11–16 for PTSD Treatment	Pain, no treatment effect for PTSD; with exposure, drop in PTSD symptoms.

234

Table 14-1 *(continued)*
Treatment Studies of MVA-Related PTSD

Author	Description of study	No. of sessions	Results
Hickling, Blanchard, Schwarz, & Silverman (1986)	8 of 12 MVA survivors with PTSD and post-concessive headache; all received treatment consisting of relaxation training, cognitive–behavioral treatment, and supportive counseling; one case used antidepressant medication	8–40	Patients with PTSD required almost 2.5 times as much treatment as those without PTSD.
Burstein (1986)	28 survivors of civilian trauma reviewed retrospectively to determine differences between short- and long-term treatment variables. 16 of 28 were MVA survivors	N/R	Long-term patients required antidepressant medication treatment. Type of psychological treatment was not readily discernible.
Burstein et al. (1988)	2 case examples illustrating differences between chronic Vietnam PTSD and acute civilian PTSD	N/R	N/R

(Table 14-1 continues)

235

Table 14-1 *(continued)*
Treatment Studies of MVA-Related PTSD

Author	Description of study	No. of sessions	Results
McMillan (1991)	1 MVA survivor; case study treating PTSD involved no recollection of MVA; treatment used imaginal and in vivo exposure and social involvement	16	Drop in PTSD symptoms
Horton (1993)	1 MVA survivor; case study of mild head injury and MVA-related PTSD; treatment consisted of behavior therapy, systematic desensitization, and self-directed in vivo exposure	12	Drop in PTSD symptoms
Brom, Kleber, & Hofman (1993)	112 persons who suffered serious trauma (bereavement, acts of violence, and MVAs). Treatment consisted of (a) trauma desensitization, (b) hynotherapy, and (c) psychodynamic therapy; all compared with a wait-list control group	Mean length a = 15.0 b = 14.4 c = 18.8	Improvement in PTSD symptoms in 60% of treated patients as compared with 26% of the untreated group

Table 14-1 (continued)
Treatment Studies of MVA-Related PTSD

Author	Description of study	No. of sessions	Results
Horne (1993)	3 MVA survivors treated with imaginal and in vivo exposure, relaxation training, and cognitive–behavioral treatment; collateral therapy occurred at least once with each survivor	14–30	Positive gains overall; however, residual problems were still reported
Mayou (1994)	1 session of intervention in hospital, consisting of booklet and advice on management of potential symptom; sample size unknown	1	Subjective impression was that treatment was not effective
Lyons & Scotti (1995)	1 MVA case study illustrating direct therapeutic exposure (DTE); DTE may involve imaginal and in vivo exposure, problem solving, anger management, relaxation therapy, use of medication, relapse prevention, and cognitive scenes; audiotape homework of DTE scenes; case involved 13 inpatient DTE scenes and 4 as outpatient; case prematurely terminated due to distance	17 (DTE)	Case closed prematurely because of failure to report to treatment

237

(Table 14-1 continues)

Table 14-1 (*continued*)
Treatment Studies of MVA-Related PTSD

Author	Description of study	No. of sessions	Results
Best & Ribbe (1995)	2 case examples illustrating treatment and assessment issues of MVA-related PTSD; treatment included relaxation, cue-controlled breathing, imagery, RET, cognitive restructuring, SIT, thought stopping, role playing, and exposure therapy; issues of life-threat and physical injury were discussed	N/R	N/R
Koch & Taylor (1995)	3 case examples; treatment used exposure and cognitive therapy	N/R	N/R
Hickling, Loos, Blanchard, & Taylor (1997)	12 MVA survivors treated with cognitive–behavioral approach; treatment used in vivo and imaginal exposure, relaxation training, and cognitive techniques	Tx. Length $M = 20$	Improvement in CAPS scores on 11 of 12 individuals at 6 months, 10 of 12 by 12 months
Hickling & Blanchard (1997)	10 MVA survivors treated with manualized treatment protocol using cognitive–behavioral techniques	9–12	Significant drops in CAPS scores for all 10 individuals

Note: N/R = not readily available; RET = rational emotive therapy; SIT = stress inoculation therapy.

been reported for over a decade. Cognitive models suggest using a variety of techniques, including thought stopping, cognitive reappraisal, and reframing, although special issues of driving phobia, mortality, and impact of pain and lingering physical injury also are thought to complicate the clinical picture.

Comprehensive treatment models, such as those of Best and Ribbe (1995) and Lyons and Scotti (1995), have been proposed. Treatments that sound very limited (e.g., systematic desensitization) on review, in fact, seem to hold several elements that again speak to a comprehensive treatment package (e.g., Best & Ribbe, 1995; McCaffrey & Fairbank, 1985). It is of interest that, although treatment, even in behavioral models, addresses the implications of one's life's meaning and the interpretation of events that there does not yet appear to be anecdotal material reflecting these treatment approaches for MVA survivors. The literature certainly is available for PTSD treatment in other populations (e.g., rape and physical assault).

15

The Albany MVA
Treatment Project

This chapter begins with a description of the thinking under-lying our approach to treatment. The treatment is guided and driven by these theoretical understandings. We provide the description of our pilot studies in detail to illustrate the results that led to our current approach in treatment. Where it is useful, we provide clinical examples and anecdotes.

Albany Treatment of MVA Survivors

The assessment studies completed in Albany led to an interest in trying to apply our data to the treatment of PTSD. However, our approach to treatment was not solely based on the available research. As one is now aware, the treatment literature is, in fact, quite sparse on the effects of MVAs.

Our treatment of MVA survivors with PTSD was developed from both our clinical experience in the treatment of PTSD and the knowledge gained in our MVA assessment study. As discussed in chapters 13 and 14, there has been little formal investigation of the treatment of MVA-related PTSD to date to guide clinicians. Studying the survivors with PTSD from MVAs has helped our understanding of the disorder and formulations on treatment in several ways.

Treatment Rationale

DSM–III–R (APA, 1987) and *DSM–IV* (APA, 1994) criteria for PTSD, in addition to the experience of the traumatic event (generally thought to be outside the range of usual human experiences; Criterion A) describe three clusters of symptoms that make up PTSD: (a) reexperiencing of the traumatic event (Criterion B), (b) persistent avoidance of stimuli associated with the trauma and/or numbing or decrease in general responsiveness (Criterion C), and (c) persistent symptoms of increased arousal that was not present prior to the trauma (Criterion D). However, because not all survivors of MVAs present identically (Blanchard et al., 1994; Kuch et al., 1985) and because the need for treatment may vary across these survivors, we have come to believe that it might be more useful to conceptualize PTSD after an MVA as comprising four interrelated sets of symptoms and clinical problems. These four symptom clusters are (a) reexperiencing, (b) avoidance, (c) psychic numbing, and (d) hyperarousal. These symptom clusters as outlined below appear to lead to distinct, well-defined treatment interventions, the focus of which may need to shift considerably across survivors of the accident. This is a critical component of our treatment rationale in that each intervention has a defined purpose and logic for its application to MVA survivors with PTSD.

Reexperiencing

One of the hallmark symptoms of PTSD is the presence of intrusive thoughts, recollections, and dreams of the crash, perhaps most graphically demonstrated by dissociative or flashback experiences or distress when the individual is exposed to situations that resemble the crash (trauma) or some particular aspect of the MVA.

MVA survivors in American culture are likely to be faced with a multitude of driving situations potentially leading to distress: by exposure to driving experiences, when riding as a passenger in a car, watching the nightly news, or reading descriptions of local MVAs. One patient shared her experience of going home and seeing her very own accident graphically displayed on the 6:00 news.

We agree with other research and clinical reports (e.g., Foa et al., 1989) that vicarious exposure and forced reexperiencing of the trauma, coupled with some education and cognitive therapy designed to reinterpret the event and its outcome, is reasonable and in our opinion indicated, given our current understanding of treatment effectiveness. This follows in part from the conceptualization of trauma memory and the reexperiencing of symptoms in terms of emotional processing (Foa et al., 1989). The trauma memory is then placed in the position of "reexperiencing with new understanding" and, it is hoped, lessens anxiety because the exposure without negative consequence should limit the potency of the stimulus with repeated pairings.

One focus of intervention with this symptom cluster is to try to help the patient understand that some reexperiencing symptoms are an expected and "normal" part of the reaction to a significant trauma. Vicarious exposure can then occur by having the patient either verbally or in writing confront their personalized description of the MVA and their emotional reaction to the description. Again, because of the variety of MVA experiences (e.g., lying in a car trapped overnight, being extracted with the jaws of life, seeing a truck speeding closer, or sliding out of control on an icy road surface), it is thought critical and consistent with earlier research (Pitman, 1991) that the description for exposure be personalized. The focus here is to try to help the patient access, and thereby confront, as many parts of the cognitive network of difficult memories as possible, making the memories conscious and salient, rather than allowing the patient to avoid them. This is done in a supportive, therapeutic environment, with the negative consequences acknowledged but reinterpreted in as positive a fashion as possible.

Avoidance Symptoms

There is considerable evidence that avoidance symptoms can be approached through education, graded exposure homework, applied relaxation (to assist in coping with the negative arousal that exposure will initially elicit), and cognitive techniques to aid in the reinterpretation of the experiences (e.g., Burstein, 1989; Foa et al., 1986; Horne, 1993). Existing behavioral treatments for

PTSD have used graded exposure (e.g., Munjack, 1984), whereas cognitive therapy has been well recognized as a therapy for phobic avoidance (e.g., Meichenbaum, 1977). Treatment may involve education to explain the development of a trauma reaction, using Mowrer's (1947) two-factor theory as Keane (1985) did in his formulation of PTSD. This rationale helps in the therapist's repeated requests to the patient for systematic exposure that may occur for graded in vivo exposure tasks or for in-office imaginal desensitization. When a significant other or spouse is enlisted to help with in vivo exposure (or to at least minimally tolerate and understand the PTSD reaction that is occurring with his or her partner), the provision of a rationale and conceptualization of why the reaction has occurred is found to be of great benefit. This has most often occurred in our experience when many MVA survivors express feeling particularly uncomfortable or avoid riding in a car as a passenger. Instead, often the MVA victim prefers to drive the vehicle himself or herself, ostensibly for the sense of control this provides. The perceived loss of control when riding as a passenger, at some point in the patient's psychological treatment, often requires an exposure-based treatment. Significant others can be of central importance in the completion of this assignment. Their understanding and acceptance of the thinking behind the development of this symptom in their partners, and their own role in the perpetuation and amelioration of the problem, at times can be critically important in the context of even a largely individualized treatment model. Applied relaxation is also often used to assist the patient in dealing with the heightened overarousal that an exposure task may bring (e.g., Hickling, Sison, & Vanderploeg, 1986).

Psychic Numbing and Estrangement Symptoms

As Litz (1992) noted, the symptoms of psychic numbing and estrangement are the least studied and understood cluster of symptoms that make up PTSD. Litz has proposed that the symptoms might represent a selective emotional-processing deficit, whereas Keane (1985) conceptualized emotional numbing as an avoidance behavior representing an attempt to suppress all strong affect because it has become viewed as dangerous and as a reminder of the trauma.

We have viewed the cluster of symptoms making up psychic numbing—inability to recall an important aspect of the trauma, markedly diminished interest or participation in significant activities, feelings of detachment or estrangement from others, restricted range of affect (e.g., unable to have loving feelings), and a sense of foreshortened future—as closely resembling depression (e.g., feelings of sadness or emptiness; decreased concentration; irritability; markedly diminished interest or pleasure in all or almost all activities; feelings of worthlessness; recurrent thoughts of death; and symptoms causing distress or impairment in social, occupational, or other important areas of functioning; see Table 15-1).

Subsequently, behavioral techniques such as pleasant event scheduling (Lewinson & Graf, 1973) appeared logically applicable. Pleasant event scheduling involves increased activity (within physical limitations of any sustained injuries) and an encouragement of increased interpersonal involvement with people who patients might have been close to (but now feel estranged from) prior to the MVA. This appeared to be a reasonable and rationally based intervention, in an area where there was little to guide current treatment efforts (e.g., Van Der Kolk, McFarlane, & Hart, 1996).

Next, the use of cognitive techniques with underlying depressive schema and with irrational beliefs (to be challenged as appropriate) was viewed as important. Our research and clinical observations support the presence of these cognitions, because of both the high incidence of depression coexisting with PTSD and, as we think of the symptom cluster, the apparent similarity in symptom presentation.

Hyperarousal

Patients with PTSD by definition present with hyperarousal symptoms, both in general and for specific situations reminiscent of their MVA. Relaxation has been shown to be an effective technique in helping to counter these symptoms in both a veteran (Hickling et al., 1986) and an MVA population. For individuals

Table 15-1

Similar Symptoms of PTSD and Depression

PTSD	Depression
Psychic numbing 1. Markedly diminished interest or participation in significant activities	1. Markedly diminished interest or pleasure in all or almost all activities most of the day, nearly every day, as indicated by either subjective account or observation made by others
2. Restricted range of affect (e.g., unable to have loving feelings)	2. Depressed mood most of the day, nearly every day, as indicated by either subjective report (e.g., feels sad or empty) or observation made by others (e.g., appears tearful)
3. Difficulty concentrating	3. Diminished ability to think or concentrate, or indecisiveness, nearly every day (either by subjective account or as observed by others)
4. Difficulty falling or staying asleep	4. Insomnia or hypersomnia nearly every day.
5. Sense of foreshortened future (e.g., does not expect to have a career, marriage, children, or a normal life span)	5. Recurrent thoughts of death (not just fear of dying); recurrent suicidal ideation without a specific plan, or a suicide attempt or a specific plan for committing suicide
6. Irritability or outbursts of anger	6. Psychomotor agitation or retardation nearly ever day (observed by others, not merely subjective feelings of restlessness or being slowed down) *Note:* In children or adolescents, can be irritable mood

7. Inability to recall important aspects of the trauma	7. Diminished ability to think or concentrate, or indecisiveness, nearly every day (either by subjective account or as observed by others)
8. Hypervigilance	8. Psychomotor agitation or retardation nearly every day (observed by others, not merely subjective feelings of restlessness or being slowed down)

who require it, application of biofeedback techniques has also been used to facilitate the training of a reliable relaxation response.

In addition, monitoring of cognitions that occur during the exposure tasks is suggested to attend to any self-defeating or catastrophic thoughts that may be contributing to the elicitation or continuation of anxiety symptoms and subsequent avoidance. Cognitive treatment for trauma survivors has been reviewed by Foa et al. (1989) and Meichenbaum (1994).

An important and related psychological sequelae of the MVA is the subsequent impact it can have on driving. In Western culture it is often very difficult to get around without the use of motor vehicle transportation. As we have discussed, this reexposure to a stimulus that reminds the victim of the trauma is often experienced with discomfort or avoided as much as possible. Many people will endure requisite driving (e.g., to the store or to work) but will avoid any optional exposure to either driving or riding in a car. The *DSM–IV* (APA, 1994), when strictly used, makes it difficult to accurately diagnose a specific phobia for driving because (a) the anxiety can be accounted for by another mental disorder (i.e., PTSD), and (b) the anxiety may not invariably provoke an immediate anxiety response. There may also be occasions when the driving does not expose the individual to the specific triggers necessary for a phobic response. Finally, the response may not be seen so much as a fear than as a situation that triggers uncomfortable memories, affect, and anxiety. As discussed in the previous chapter, driving phobia has a solid research base for intervention, beginning with Wolpe's (1973) study.

However, given the often central role driving can play in MVA survivors' lives, we have struggled with various descriptions to explain what we believe to be often critically important aspects of the treatment effort. We currently use the term *driving phobia* as a rather narrow way of describing a situation wherein the individual avoids all driving or endures the driving (or riding) with a great deal of subjective discomfort. We also used the term *driving reluctance* to describe a less powerful form of avoidance wherein the individual avoids all or most discretionary driving (e.g., pleasure trips) or rides and avoids the site of the accident or driving situations related to their own MVA (e.g., rainy or snowy weather or high speeds). Obviously, these are different points on a continuum of discomfort but important issues when given the task of trying to describe the focus of treatment.

Patients with MVA-related PTSD typically present with varying combinations of these four symptom clusters, with some elements from each cluster present to meet the diagnostic criteria. Treatment would then logically include procedures to help counter all four symptom clusters with relatively more emphasis on one versus the other, depending on the patient's idiosyncratic set of symptoms.

Treatment Study 1

As part of NIMH's funded research project investigating the psychological effects of MVA, we obtained systematic data (described earlier in this book) on 158 MVA survivors. As part of our ethical responsibilities in conducting this study, all MVA survivors who were found to have psychological problems were referred for treatment. A referral list of local providers willing and experienced in the treatment of trauma survivors had been prepared prior to the initiation of the research project. Two of the providers included psychologists who also were involved in the NIMH study, one as a co-principal investigator and one as an assessor of MVA survivors.

The provision of treatment for MVA survivors by psychologists associated with the research study provided a unique opportunity to measure the change in symptoms across 6-month time periods, by evaluators independent of the treating psychologist, yet allowed access to chart notes describing the interventions used in treatment. In addition, although the treatment had been individually tailored for each participant, the overall treatment rationale of the two treating psychologists was primarily cognitive–behavioral, allowing for comparison of treatment commonalities and differences across cases with similar primary diagnoses, but with great attention to the intricacies of individual case material. This group of treated MVA survivors became our first pilot investigation of the treatment of PTSD as part of the Albany MVA Project. (Much of the material in Treatment Study 1 is summarized by Hickling et al., 1996.)

Research Participants

Research participants were 2 men and 10 women, with a mean age of 31.9 years for the women and 33.0 years for the men who had been part of the Albany MVA Project. Payment for psychological treatment was through no-fault insurance in New York state.

Procedure

As a participant in the MVA Project, each individual underwent a comprehensive psychological evaluation by one of the four experienced doctoral-level psychologists, as described in chapter 3. A complete written report of all findings was made to each research participant at the conclusion of the initial assessment. At that time treatment recommendations and explicit referrals were made. A listing of local mental health practitioners who reportedly were familiar with PTSD and its treatment was then shared with the research participants.

Diagnosis of PTSD

PTSD was diagnosed using criteria outlined in the *DSM–III–R* (APA, 1987) and on the basis of the CAPS interview (see chapter

3). The diagnosis was reached independent of treatment and was in fact the basis for recommendation of treatment following the individual's initial interview as a participant in the MVA Research Project.

Results

A description of participants by age, sex, diagnosis, co-morbid diagnosis, and treatment procedures is presented in Table 15-2. Each of the participants was involved in a two-car MVA, with physical injury quotients (see chapter 9) ranging from .66 to 1.0, as reported in Table 15-3.

Table 15-4 presents a breakdown of the main area of change in this initial treatment study, the change in CAPS scores across 6-month periods. In addition to total CAPS score, a breakdown of scores by symptom cluster for each case is presented. As can be seen in Table 15-4, 10 patients improved on total CAPS scores, whereas 2 patients essentially remained unchanged or, in fact, showed a worsening of symptoms across treatment. The total number of treatment sessions that had taken place across that same period of time is also reported, as well as whether psychological treatment was in progress during the evaluation period or whether treatment had been concluded.

Table 15-5 presents the changes that occurred in psychological test scores across the same 6-month time periods. As one can see, psychological test scores, as expected, paralleled changes in CAPS scores and end of treatment outcome. The reported changes in GAS scores for Patients 205 and 277 illustrates the worsening clinical picture for both patients.

Table 15-6 presents reported change in psychosocial functioning. GAS scores, as one would predict, paralleled changes in CAPS scores. The changes in psychosocial functioning were consistent with reported improvement as psychological gains were realized.

Commonalities in Treatment

This first study of psychological treatment allowed us to look at the types of treatment interventions that arose from experienced

Table 15-2

Participant Demographics and Diagnoses

Participant no.	Age	Sex	Diagnosis 1	Diagnosis 2	Treatment procedures
102	43	F	PTSD		In vivo and imaginal exposure, EMG biofeedback
103	32	M	PTSD	Major depression, OCD, social phobia	Imaginal exposure, driving hierarchy, and graded exposure
125	46	F	PTSD	Major depression	Desensitization, driving, graded exposure
129	19	F	PTSD		Imaginal exposure, desensitization
151	34	M	PTSD		Grief work, past trauma history, anger expression, social skills building, imaginal exposure
198	31	F	PTSD	Major depression	Anger management, social skills training, fear of death
200	24	F	PTSD		In vivo exposure, past trauma, assertiveness training, fear of death, couples treatment, grief work
203	24	F	Sub-PTSD		Anger management, past trauma, graded exposure
205	23	F	PTSD		In vivo exposure, fear of death, anger management
239	57	F	PTSD		Social skills training, assertiveness, anger management
277	22	F	PTSD		Imaginal and in vivo exposure, driving hierarchy
278	41	F	PTSD		Past traumatic losses, social skills training

Note: OCD = obsessive–compulsive disorder.

Table 15-3

Physical Injury Quotient (PIQ)

Participant no.	Initial PIQ	6-mo. PIQ	12-mo. PIQ
102	1.00	0.75	0.66
103	1.00	0.66	DO
125	0.83	0.50	0.33
129	0.66	0.00	0.00
151	0.88	0.44	0.66
198	1.00	0.66	0.50
200	0.66	0.66	0.83
203	0.88	0.88	0.88
205	1.00	0.75	0.83
239	1.00	0.66	0.66
277	0.92	0.50	0.83
278	1.00	0.66	0.75

Note: DO = dropout from assessment study.

clinicians and the frequency with which they were reportedly used for this limited population. It is of interest, but not surprising, that cognitive techniques were used as part of all 12 treatment cases. Although each psychologist operated independently in the treatment of his or her case, the overall orientation was eclectic and problem focused. All 12 patients received some type of exposure-based treatment, either in-office imaginal exposure, graded in vivo exposure, or both. All of the treatment patients also received relaxation training. Treatment for driving-related reluctance or phobia secondary to the MVA was part of treatment in 11 of the 12 cases. Driving reluctance was described as avoiding the accident area, restricting the driving speed, driving only on local roads, and being reluctant to be a passenger when others are driving.

Table 15-4

Change of CAPS Scores and Symptom Clusters Across 6-Month Intervals

Participant no.	Total CAPS scores					Symptom Cluster B			Symptom Cluster C			Symptom Cluster D		
	Total CAPS Initial	No. Tx. sessions between Initial and 6 mo.	Total CAPS 6 mo.	No. Tx. sessions between 6 mo. and 12 mo.	Total CAPS 12 Mo.	Initial	6 Mo.	12 Mo.	Initial	6 mo.	12 mo.	Initial	6 mo.	12 mo.
102	41	7	35	2	4	8	10	0	12	9	0	21	16	4
103	87	7	37	11	DO	20	10	DO	34	0	DO	33	27	DO
125	99	2	34	0	12	28	8	3	39	10	2	32	16	8
129	32	1	9	0	10	6	3	0	15	6	6	11	0	4
151	38	8	0	0	0	16	0	0	15	0	0	7	0	0
198	29	11	18	16	13	5	3	2	12	12	9	12	3	2
200	54	16	23	15	35	23	7	7	16	13	11	15	3	17
203	29	4	7	15	13	11	2	3	11	0	0	7	5	10
205	35	17	38	22	56	17	10	14	4	15	25	14	13	17
239	57	12	44	18	31	6	5	6	35	30	19	16	9	6
277	104	17	90	8	128	28	25	32	45	32	53	31	33	43
278	57	24	15	0	23	25	0	7	29	8	10	3	7	6
M	55.17	10.5	29.17	8.92	32.20	16.08	6.92	6.73	22.25	11.25	12.27	16.83	11.00	10.64

Note: DO = dropout from assessment study.

Table 15-5

Change in Psychological Test Scores Across 6-Month Time Intervals

Participant no.	Impact of Event Scale			Beck Depression Inventory			STAI State			STAI Trait			P Inventory		
	Initial	6 mo.	12 mo.	Initial	6 mo.	12 mo.	Initial	6 mo.	12 mo.	Initial	6 mo.	12 mo.	Initial	6 mo.	12 mo.
102	3	28	—	8	18	—	44	94	—	38	68	—	0	14	—
103	58	45	DO	24	13	DO	86	65	DO	69	66	DO	33	30	DO
125	59	—	42	17	—	20	100	—	57	44	—	62	—	—	4
129	29	7	7	7	8	2	73	52	62	66	52	61	14	—	18
151	27	18	7	8	15	26	73	73	59	58	62	48	1	3	0
198	7	41	7	17	21	25	43	72	53	63	84	74	12	20	16
200	47	9	32	12	1	4	38	47	98	31	45	86	9	19	23
203	39	42	16	6	8	13	57	61	42	45	59	43	0	2	5
205	29	—	43	10	—	20	64	—	55	45	—	69	9	14	13
239	37	—	28	22	—	—	95	—	96	80	—	80	23	—	20
277	51	59	70	33	39	50	85	79	91	77	83	105	30	39	44
278	8	38	20	13	11	16	45	58	45	66	62	62	25	16	22
M	32.8	31.9	22.4	12.3	14.9	15.8	66.9	66.7	63.0	56.8	64.5	65.0	14.2	17.4	13.4

Note: DO = drop out from assessment study. Dashes indicate results not available. STAI = State–Trait Anxiety Inventory.

Table 15-6

Change in Psychosocial Functioning Across 6-Month Intervals

Participant no.	GAS scores			Work/school			Family			Friends		
	Initial	6 mo.	12 mo.	Initial	6 mo.	12 mo.	Initial	6 mo.	12 mo.	Initial	6 mo.	12 mo.
102	61	75	85	2.5	0	0	1.00	2.00	1.33	1.0	1.0	2.0
103	45	65	DO	2.5	3	DO	2.83	2.00	DO	4.0	3.0	DO
125	41	60	61	2.5	2.0	1.0	3.00	1.00	1.00	5.0	1.0	1.0
129	60	70	71	1.0	1.0	1.0	1.50	1.67	1.67	2.0	1.0	1.0
151	50	91	95	0	1.0	1.0	1.00	1.00	1.00	1.0	1.0	1.0
198	60	51	50	2.0	3.0	6.0	1.50	2.50	2.50	3.0	2.0	2.0
200	51	55	61	1.0	2.0	2.0	2.20	2.00	2.00	2.0	3.0	3.0
203	55	50	75	0	0	0	1.00	1.50	1.00	1.0	1.0	1.0
205	60	55	40	1.5	3.0	2.0	1.00	2.40	2.00	1.0	2.0	4.0
239	50	59	50	1.5	2.0	1.0	3.00	2.50	3.25	1.0	3.0	3.0
277	40	40	40	2.5	0	4.0	2.00	2.00	2.50	1.0	3.0	2.0
278	41	60	50	1.0	2.0	3.0	1.00	1.00	2.00	1.0	2.0	4.0
M	51.6	61.0	69.7									

Note. GAS = Global Assessment Scale; DO = dropout from assessment study.

Cognitive techniques of some kind were used in all of the treatment cases. Cognitive techniques included thought stopping, guided self-dialogue (with preparation for the event), confrontation with the feared situation and management of the event, coping with feelings of becoming overwhelmed, reinforcement of the positive efforts and behaviors (Meichenbaum, 1977), cognitive restructuring (using an A-B-C-D paradigm for irrational thinking; Beck, Rush, Shaw, & Emery, 1979; Walen, DiGiuseppe, & Wessler, 1980), and modeling and role playing of the anxiety-provoking situations. Behavioral techniques to help manage the anxiety and subsequently to withstand any imagined or graded exposure were used and thought to be an integral part of the treatment.

Illustrative Cases

An illustration of one of the briefer courses of treatment (which actually took place in the hospital because the patient was immobilized because of multiple fractures) began with the patient's being instructed in the normal course of PTSD symptoms and their development as per the two-factor theory. The patient was requested to describe the accident in detail, which was used for imaginal exposure in subsequent sessions, emphasizing the emotionally laden words and perceptions she provided. Cognitive techniques, including cessation of negative self-talk, substitution of statement mastery itself, and challenging of irrational catastrophic beliefs, were used to help the patient counter the negative affect brought on by her accident, in which she had been trapped in her car overnight, off the road, believing that she would bleed to death or die from shock before she was found.

She was taught relaxation techniques, and these were used to counter any physiological discomfort brought on during imaginal desensitization and other moments of anxiety. Precipitants of anxiety were linked to negative cognitive schema and countered by the therapist with cognitive restructuring techniques challenging the irrational beliefs. These techniques were then demonstrated by the patient between sessions as a new learned way to challenge the anxiety and the thoughts related to the onset of anxiety (e.g., "I'm going to be trapped and die in a car"). Her thoughts about becoming trapped and dying in a car were challenged in the following manner. First, such an accident was presented as unlikely to occur. It was argued that she was much more likely to become a more cautious driver, having already purchased a car with air bags, and was therefore making it as unlikely as anyone could that she'd be in such a dire position again. It was acknowledged that she might have another accident, but that this was not a likely or predictable event for her to envision. Treatment was concluded before she could physically drive, but follow-up as part of the assessment study demonstrated that the later driving was performed without reported discomfort. One necessary component of treatment for this case was the attention to thoughts of mortality and the intense fear she had to endure until discovered by highway patrolmen. In a recent article (Blanchard et al., 1995), both extent of physical injury and perception of one's life threat (fear of dying) were found to independently predict the onset of PTSD in a sample of 98 MVA survivors.

A second case involved a patient who was seen for only two visits prior to her extended vacation out of the country. Because of the very limited time before her scheduled departure, a modified, cued desensitization technique was developed. Details of the patient's MVA were presented, reviewed, and discussed to determine which images provoked the greatest distress. Both her subjective discomfort (using the SUDS) and pain perception were assessed at various points throughout the narration. She was instructed in diaphragmatic breathing and visualization techniques for relaxation, during which her subjective discomfort and pain perception were assessed. A home desensitization procedure was introduced, with reported reduction in distress demonstrated by home practice and exposure as measured on rating sheets mailed over the time outside of treatment and by telephone contact.

Treatment Differences

The variety of MVAs, and the subsequent physical and psychological problems that develop, often necessitate idiosyncratic responses to treatment. As shown in Table 15-7, a few of the cases

Table 15-7

Description of Treatment Sample

Participant no.	Age	Sex	Weeks since MVA	Primary diagnosis	Co-morbid diagnosis	Initial CAPS	Physical injuries
301	45	F	131	PTSD	MDE GAD	65	Continuing muscle pain in the cervical, upper, and lower back region secondary to whiplash injury; loss of ROM in right arm with diminished grip strength; continuing sharp pains in both patient's wrists and ankles (in addition, patient was suffering from TMJ secondary to patient's MVA-related injuries)
302	36	F	36	PTSD	MDE	69	Continuing pain in her upper and lower back secondary to whiplash-type injury, which has also left patient with continuing cervical pain; parathesias in left hand and left foot; lost grip strength in left hand
304	63	F	23	PTSD	Driving phobia MDE GAD	85	Continuing neck, shoulder, and lower back pain from whiplash-type injury; noticeable headache problem since the accident
306	63	F	18	PTSD	MDE GAD	86	Continuing neck and shoulder pain in addition to chronic headaches
310	30	F	16	Sub-PTSD	Driving phobia	37	No continuing physical problems secondary to the accident

311	46	M	76	PTSD	GAD	46	Exacerbation of existing headache problem since the accident; cervical muscle stiffness; traumatic arthritis in the right thumb joint results in unremitting pain; loss of grip strength in the right hand (may have done some cartilage damage)
312	51	F	37	Sub-PTSD	MDE Specific phobia	46	Loss of strength in right arm secondary to soft tissue damage; continues to have chest pain secondary to a fractured sternum and headaches secondary to a concussion (did not suffer a blow to the head)
313	36	F	16	PTSD	GAD	65	No physical problems currently related to the MVA
316	54	F	85	PTSD	MDE	119	Two fractured vertebrate secondary to MVA (t-10, t-11) have left patient with considerable loss of strength and unremitting pain daily (at the time of initial interview the patient had one back surgery, which resulted in two supportive metal rods placed in patient's back to support patient's spine; injuries were severe enough to keep patient from returning to work)
324	32	F	82	PTSD	GAD	54	Continuing low back problems resulting in significant pain and loss of ROM; permanent deformity of nose; continuing dental restoration work (in addition, patient is suffering from loss of ROM and muscle strength in the right arm secondary to soft tissue damage sustained during the accident; combined with the back injuries, the injuries have been severe enough to keep patient out of work)

259

Note: MDE = major depressive episode; GAD = generalized anxiety disorder; ROM = range of motion; TMJ = temporal–mandibular joint dysfunction.

required attention to past traumas, in addition to the current MVA. Other cases dealt with anger management, whereas a few involved couples treatment.

Specific stimuli can also become uniquely tied to the particular MVA and cues associated with the memories and emotional responses. For instance, if an accident took place in a rainstorm, or during the autumn, these cues might provoke powerful emotional memories, which would require specific attention.

An illustration of this is the case of a patient who had done well in treatment and called for another appointment because of a resumption in her psychological distress. When inquiry as to the precipitants was made, it became apparent that seasonal cues (i.e., cooler temperature and barren trees in the northeastern United States during late autumn) had contributed to a return of intrusive thoughts and feelings related to the MVA. Imaginal exposure to the stimuli of trees against an evening sky and images of winter scenes reminiscent of her MVA, were presented in office imaginal exposure, paired with relaxation and cognitive restructuring of her response. Cognitive restructuring also occurred surrounding her heightened anxiety when thinking of her own mortality. We presented an implosive strategy in which the patient imagines the scene of her MVA and then subsequently paired it with deep relaxation. This experience led to the patient's association of her mother's death. She then was able to realize she had "lived well" following her MVA. Anxiety was noted to drop significantly after that point in her treatment. In vivo exposure then followed, again using cognitive techniques of coping or mastery self-statements and decatastrophizing the memory with current events. Associated with the fear of another MVA occurring was a fear of her own death that appeared related to memories of her mother's death.

In another case, the impact of earlier trauma, including the loss of a home because of fire and an attack and near rape as an adolescent had to be dealt with as a necessary component of treatment. The resultant fear was correlated with a worsening of physical pain from soft tissue damage in the shoulder and chest as a result of the seat belt that restrained the patient during her rear-end collision. The physical injury had limited her ability to draw and write. The injury, caused by a male driver, led the patient to associate her anger held toward the male assailants in her past and the vulnerability she now perceived as a part of her current level of functioning. This was illustrated by the requisite physical examination of her shoulder injury and the proximity of the examination to her breast and was associated with memories of sexual abuse. The memories, as well as memories of witnessing a suicide from a bridge reminiscent of the scene of the patient's MVA, were dealt with over the course of treatment. These anxiety-provoking memories were addressed with coping strategies and methods to assertively deal with the patient's own safety, which had in her perception been limited by the events of the MVA and the male driver who struck her car.

The above cases illustrate how even similar themes (e.g., mortality) can be tied to individually salient cognitions and memories. If specific cues are ignored or not responded to (e.g., trees in autumn or winter), powerful environmental stimuli can be missed and treatment rendered ineffective. Careful behavioral assessment and assessment of cognitive schema are essential if each individual is to have the optimal chance for improvement.

Thus, one is left with a picture that treatment can hold many commonalities that, in all likelihood, can be applied to almost every case. Yet, one needs to be aware of the powerful impact of idiosyncratic responses from the trauma (and its associations with past traumas) and to be able to provide a flexible, but theoretically driven, treatment intervention for each unique case.

Discussion

The treatment outcome data described herein support the notion that PTSD secondary to an MVA can be treated reasonably well. We think the cognitive–behavioral treatment model seems to have a great deal of promise, particularly if flexibly applied, and we believe that, although unintentional, the treatments seem to hold a core group of consistent interventions, yet the model allows the psychologists to attend to the needs of each unique presentation of difficulties. This, of course, is the model of private practice. Efficiency and rationally guided treatment was the model throughout the range of interventions.

Treatment length did vary considerably. This was not surprising given the myriad possible factors thought to contribute to the onset and continuation of PTSD. The varied treatment length was also consistent with the work of Burstein (1986), which showed that, whereas a significant number of MVA survivors improved in less than 3 months, a large number actually required prolonged treatment in excess of 1 year.

Finally, we were struck by how well the model of treatment led to a more systematic investigation of treatment of MVA-related PTSD. The methodology used in this initial study allowed an independent outcome to be assessed while the treatment was conducted with the flexibility that practicing clinicians use in everyday treatment efforts. However, the rigor of the research-scheduled evaluations of symptom change allowed for valid and reliable indices of outcome. The CAPS provided a useful measure to chronicle change in PTSD overall, as well as look at the symptom clusters we conceptually considered as areas of targeted improvement (see Table 15-4). In theory, we thought that, if it was determined that one symptom cluster did not improve, treatment could be reconsidered and newer interventions formulated and used. The study set the stage for a more rigorous, manual-based intervention.

Treatment Study 2

On the basis of the success of the nonsystematic initial intervention, a more formal, manual-based intervention was designed. To prepare for a controlled investigation of MVA-related PTSD treatment, a treatment manual incorporating the knowledge gained from the first study was used as an initial outline. We next constructed a treatment manual (Hickling & Blanchard, 1997) that designated session-by-session guidelines for a 10-session intervention (see Exhibit 15-1). Although the outline was for 10 sessions, the treatment allowed flexibility for a range of 9 to 12 sessions, on the basis of the symptoms presented and the judgment of the treating psychologist.

The second treatment study completed as part of the Albany MVA Project was a pilot study of the manual-based treatment.

Exhibit 15-1
Intensive Treatment Regimen for MVA-Related PTSD

Session 1
  Introduction; diagnostics reviewed; education—what is normal response to trauma; overview of treatment—different procedures to help with different symptom clusters; relaxation training—16-muscle group, instruction in home practice; verbal description of MVA and reactions by patient, instruction to write it out in detail for next visit; *patient expectancy questionnaire administered*

Session 2
  Read and elaborate description of MVA—instruction in home practice; relaxation training—16-muscle group, continued home practice; discussion of avoidance and idea of hierarchy of tasks; enlist significant other for next visit

Session 3
  Read patient's description of MVA reaction, discuss negative self-talk and begin substituting coping and mastery self-talk; avoidance hierarchy need for graduated approach behavior in vivo, significant other to assist, explain symptoms and treatments to spouse/partner; relaxation (8-muscle group); continue all homework

Session 4
  Reading exposure to MVA and consequences, add coping outcomes; relaxation 5-muscle group; approach behavior homework; check on self-talk and introduce coping and mastery self-dialogue

Session 5
  Reading exposure to MVA, with coping; relaxation by recall; approach behavior homework

Session 6
  Reading exposure to MVA, cue controlled relaxation as coping strategy; approach behavior homework; examination and correction of self-talk

Session 7
  Focus on psychic numbing, depression, and existential issues; remind patient to continue all previous homework; how to ask for help (to counter mind reading); pleasurable activity scheduling; explore for depressive schema and faulty logics; continue approach behavior homework and correction of self-talk

---

Exhibit 15-1 *(continued)*

Intensive Treatment Regimen for MVA-Related PTSD

Session 8
Pleasurable activity scheduling; explore depressive schema and faulty logic, cognitive restructuring; other home practice

Session 9
Same as Session 8

Session 10
Final visit. Review procedures, remind patient to continue practice at home, cognitive schema restructuring; make assessment appointment and schedule follow-up visit

---

This study was completed as part of the preparation for a grant application for a controlled investigation of psychological treatment of PTSD secondary to MVA (Hickling & Blanchard, 1997).

Participants

Recruitment of participants again used our physician referral network and advertisement in local newspapers. This resulted in approximately 110 telephone inquiries for possible treatment. Sixty-four MVA survivors were screened by telephone interview for possible PTSD or subsyndromal PTSD, using primarily the PCL (Weathers et al., 1993). From the telephone interviews, 25 MVA survivors were invited for further evaluation, with 21 keeping their appointment for in-depth assessment. (The assessment was the same as described in chapter 4.) Fourteen MVA survivors were then found eligible for, and were offered, treatment on the basis of the formal evaluation. Two of the participants declined the offer for treatment, one taking a referral to a private practitioner, with 12 agreeing to be treated with the manual-based intervention at no cost. Ten completed treatment and were then reassessed by independent evaluators at the completion of the treatment protocol. Two MVA survivors dropped out of treatment, 1 because of scheduling and transportation difficulties, and 1 because of re-injury, resulting in the patient's becoming bedridden and unable to drive and attend treatment.

The research participants for this pilot study of a manual-based treatment were subsequently 10 MVA survivors (9 female, 1 male) with a mean age of 45.6 (range 30 to 63 years). All participants were at least 18 years of age or older, had been involved in an MVA more than 6 months earlier than the time of the initial evaluation, and had sought medical attention for injuries related to the MVA within 72 hours of the accident. As we discussed in earlier chapters, the rationale for treating survivors who continued to demonstrate symptoms 6 months after the accident was to attempt to account for the significant percentage of survivors who show spontaneous improvement in PTSD symptoms over time without receiving treatment. The timetable for patient selection was determined from our studies of change in PTSD symptoms over time (Blanchard et al., 1995), in which it was found that, by 6 months, 50 % of patients who had initially met criteria for PTSD no longer met full criteria (see chapter 7). The rationale was that, if the victim was continuing to show noticeable, distressing symptoms 6 months after the accident, he or she was less likely to show improvement on his or her own. Subsequently, any change on criterion measures would be much more likely to reflect treatment effects rather than spontaneous improvement. Demographic and descriptive information for the MVA survivors who completed treatment is reported in Table 15-2. A brief description of any continuing physical problems is also shown (when present), as well as any other co-morbid Axis I diagnosis as per *DSM–IV* (APA, 1994) criteria.

Evaluation Methods

The initial diagnosis for PTSD was based on the CAPS (Blake et al., 1990), described in detail earlier. All interviews were taped and reviewed (by EBB). MVA survivors were diagnosed using *DSM–IV* (APA, 1994) criteria.

All participants in the study also completed the following psychological tests: the Beck Depression Inventory (BDI; Beck et al., 1961), the State–Trait Anxiety Inventory (STAI; Spielberger et al., 1970), the Impact of Event Scale (IES; Horowitz et al., 1979), and the PCL (Weathers et al., 1993) as a self-report measure of symptoms of PTSD.

The initial evaluation also used a locally constructed structured interview on the MVA and the survivors' reaction to the MVA (Appendix A). Evaluation of the pre-MVA and current psychosocial functioning of each victim was obtained through the use of the LIFE-Base (Keller et al., 1987). Four psychosocial functioning variables were obtained: (a) performance on major role function, either work (for those working 30 hours per week or more), school (for full-time students), or homemaking when the former categories did not apply; (b) quality of relationships with all primary relationships, including spouse or partner averaged across all family members who were rated; (c) quality of relationships with friends; and (d) participation and enjoyment of recreational activities. The variables were all rated on a 5-point scale where 1 indicated no impairment and high functioning or very good relationship and 5 indicated unsatisfactory performance or very poor relationship.

Follow-up evaluations were completed at the conclusion of treatment and at a 3-month post-treatment follow-up session and were conducted by independent evaluators (advanced doctoral students in clinical psychology). Each student had been trained in the use of the structured interviews and administration of the psychological tests.

Treatment

Treatment was provided by both EJH and EBB. Intervention was conducted using a symptom-focused, psychological treatment designed to address PTSD and subsyndromal PTSD found in MVA survivors. As outlined earlier, the treatment rationale was to attempt to intervene with the four interrelated symptom clusters we have conceptualized in PTSD: (a) reexperiencing symptoms, (b) avoidance symptoms, (c) psychic numbing, and (d) hyperarousal symptoms. The treatment manual (Hickling &

Blanchard, 1997) was written to address each of the symptom clusters as well as other problems commonly found to be present in PTSD following MVAs. The treatment methodology, although largely cognitive–behavioral in approach, tries to attend to the variability that can be found in individuals who have experienced traumatic events. Thus, attention to existential issues—mortality, anger, guilt, and so forth—was also provided using specified treatment interventions if necessary in the treatment manual.

Treatment Integrity

The pilot data were evaluated by graduate research assistants using the Therapist's Behavior Checklist (TBC), a locally constructed measure of in-session activities. Average interrater reliability on the TBC categories was satisfactory ($\kappa = .71, p < .05$).

Treatment integrity and therapist adherence to the treatment protocol was calculated by first tabulating the percentage of the specific therapist behaviors and procedures for a particular session (on the basis of the treatment manual) that actually occurred within the session. The overall average inclusion therapist adherence was 72%, with another 12% of specified therapist behaviors occurring at other points in the treatment. The frequency of interventions not specified in the treatment manual was then calculated, with the overall average being 1%. Thus, we believe the treatment integrity was adequate.

Results of Treatment

The pre-treatment, post-treatment, and 3-month follow-up CAPS scores for each participant, as well as any pre-treatment and follow-up primary and co-morbid Axis I diagnosis, are presented in Table 15-8. As each therapist had treated five of the cases, we analyzed the CAPS scores in a 2 (therapist) × 3 (assessments) repeated measures ANOVA, which yielded a main effect of assessments, exact $F(2, 7) = 10.4, p = .008$, Pillais, but no main effect of therapist or interaction of therapist and assessment.

Table 15-8
Results From Pilot Trial of Treatment of MVA Victims

Participant no.	Primary diagnosis	Co-morbid diagnosis (initial)	Initial CAPS (M = 67.2)	Post-CAPS (M = 21.6)	3-mo. FU CAPS (M = 18.4)	Primary diagnosis	Co-morbid diagnosis (3-mo. FU)
301	PTSD	MDE GAD	65	25	28	Non-PTSD	MDE
302	PTSD	MDE	69	37	44	Non-PTSD	MDE
304	PTSD	Driving phobia MDE GAD	83	40	15	Non-PTSD	None
306	PTSD	MDE GAD	86	7	2	Non-PTSD	None
310	Sub-PTSD	Driving phobia	37	10	3	Non-PTSD	None
311	PTSD	GAD	46	29	15	Non-PTSD	None
312	Sub-PTSD	MDE Specific phobia	46	23	31	Sub-PTSD	Specific phobia
313	PTSD	GAD	65	31	33	Sub-PTSD	Specific phobia
316	PTSD	MDE	119	0	3	Non-PTSD	None
324	PTSD	GAD	54	14	13	Non-PTSD	None

Note: GAD = generalized anxiety disorder; MDE = major depressive episode; FU = follow up.

Follow-up analyses of the assessment main effect with correlated t tests revealed a significant decrease in CAPS score from pre-treatment to post-treatment, $t(8) = 4.68$, $p = .001$, effect size (Cohen's $d = 1.480$) but no further significant improvement from post-treatment to follow-up. Analyses of each score of the four PTSD symptom clusters did show significant reduction on each symptom cluster ($p = .003$ or better).

Clinically, one would say all of the 10 patients had improved by the end of treatment. Five of the 8 who started with full PTSD were at a non-PTSD level by the end of treatment. The other 3 MVA survivors had decreased symptoms sufficiently to be diagnosed with subsyndromal PTSD. By the time of the 3-month follow-up, 2 of these 3 had, in fact, improved to non-PTSD. One of the 2 survivors who began with a diagnosis of subsyndromal PTSD was found to be non-PTSD by the end of treatment. A summary of each survivor's change in diagnosis and CAPS scores is presented in Table 15-8.

Psychological Tests

The group mean values for the five psychological tests administered at the three assessment periods are reported in Table 15-9. These data were analyzed using a one-way MANOVA, followed up with univariate ANOVAs and post-hoc tests.

The analyses of the psychological tests yielded a significant main effect for time, approximate $F(10, 22) = 3.25$, $p = .01$, Pillais. Univariate analyses revealed a significant decrease in symptoms on every measure used ($p = .008$ or better). All measures showed a significant decrease from pre-treatment to post-treatment. The only measure that continued to show an improvement from post-treatment to the 3-month evaluation period was State Anxiety.

Psychosocial Functioning

Ratings from the LIFE-Base and LIFE for psychosocial functioning were subjected to a repeated measures MANOVA, followed by univariate ANOVAs, corrected for sphericity because of the

Table 15-9

Summary of Psychological Distress Measures

Measure	Initial		Post-treatment		3-mo. follow-up			
	M	SD	M	SD	M	SD	F(29)	p
Beck Depression Inventory	16.9	9.0$_a$	8.61	5.6$_b$	5.9	5.0$_b$	8.21	.004
State Anxiety	70.2	21.4$_a$	57.1	13.8$_b$	48.5	10.5$_c$	9.86	.001
Trait Anxiety	67.3	17.1$_a$	54.0	13.9$_b$	47.9	8.4$_b$	6.65	.008
Impact of Event Scale	41.9	14.0$_a$	14.4	13.3$_b$	10.2	12.0$_b$	24.4	<.001
PTSD Checklist	56.0	12.0$_a$	34.4	10.1$_b$	32.7	11.5$_b$	17.3	<.001

Note: Means which share a subscript do not differ at .05 or greater.

270

Table 15-10

Summary of Role-Functioning Variables

Measure	Pre-MVA		Pre-Tx		Post-Tx		3-mo. FU		F	p^a
	M	SD	M	SD	M	SD	M	SD		
Major role function (work/school/homemaking)	1.6	0.5_a	2.9	1.1_b	2.1	1.1_b	—	2.2_b	1.84	.257
Relationship with first-degree relatives and spouse/partner	2.0	$0.7_{a,b}$	2.2	0.7_a	1.9	0.6_b	1.7	0.7_b	5.24	.033
Relationships with friends	2.2	0.8_a	2.7	1.3_a	2.1	1.1_a	1.6	0.7_b	3.44	.093
Recreational activity	1.5	0.7_a	3.4	1.0_b	2.4	1.2_c	2.4	1.0_c	13.77	.003

Note: Means which share a subscript do not differ at .05 or higher. FU = follow up; Tx = treatment.
[a] Probability for F test is corrected by Pillias for sphericity.

four time points and post-hoc tests (see Table 15-10). A similar pattern of scores was found for each variable, where the survivor was functioning at a poorer level (higher numerical score) than before the MVA. The decline in functioning was significant for both major role function and participation in recreational activity. There was a significant improvement by the end of treatment for family relationships and participation in recreation, and by 3-month follow-up for relationships with friends.

Major role function did not improve significantly. We conjecture this could be due to continued physical limitations (see Table 15-10), which were present for most of the survivors, and could very well be a function of patient selection from a pool of survivors who, to be eligible for treatment, needed to have sought care from a physician. It is of interest that the interpersonal relationship ratings showed improvement beyond the pre-MVA level by follow-up.

Summary

The changes in overall CAPS scores strongly suggest that this pilot investigation of a manual-based treatment protocol was effective in the reduction of symptoms of PTSD in survivors of MVAs. It is also suggestive that the symptom improvement can be delivered in a relatively short period of time and that results last for as long as 3 months. The results hold true for at least two psychologists who delivered the treatment and do not show differences in treatment outcome between therapists. Furthermore, the scores for psychological tests and LIFE-Base evaluations support the outcome of the pilot investigation.

The pilot study certainly contains many limiting factors. First, it was uncontrolled. However, data from a naturalistic follow-up of MVA survivors with PTSD found that from 6 months to 12 months only 5% of individuals who had PTSD at 6 months had fully remitted by 12 months and only another 5% showed some partial improvement spontaneously (Blanchard et al., 1997; see chapter 7). This pilot study would seem to suggest significantly greater improvement than one would have expected without an effective treatment being in place. As earlier studies (chapter 7) have demonstrated, the high spontaneous recovery rate for a portion of survivors with PTSD following MVAs, has made it difficult for interventions to demonstrate effectiveness within the first few months after the MVA. The rationale for providing a treatment at this time period was to attempt to address this outcome concern.

16

A Closer Look at Psychological Treatment: The Treatment Manual (and More)

A s one examines the initial treatment projects and the litera-ture on what has been learned in clinical practice, it becomes obvious that diagnosis for and treatment of MVA-related PTSD involve more than can be summarized in generalized statements and group data. Psychological treatment is a complex undertaking, with interwoven verbal and nonverbal exchanges occurring during each treatment session. Although we may focus on the theoretically based interventions that guide our treatment, the interactions of these variables, and the relationship that develops, contain much more than we can convey or share with our objective descriptions of the interventions used. The purpose of this section is to expand and elaborate on what occurs in treatment intervention. We do this in two manners. First, we describe the components of the treatment manual used within the second study. Second, we use case vignettes and examples to illustrate points drawn from the research studies and from clinical practice.

Session 1

The initial session of the study involved a review of the evaluation results with each patient. This included a description of their MVA, their reaction to the MVA, their symptoms of PTSD, and other Axis I diagnoses if applicable. This was a logical and important step in treatment for the following reasons: First, as the evaluation may have been done by someone other than the treating psychologist, this allowed the psychologist and patient to "get on the same page." Second, by sharing the evaluation results, a sense of understanding of the problem was communicated. Third, rapport was established, as any further clarification that "the patient had been heard" was shared by the evaluation results and sharing of the understanding describing their distress. It was demonstrated on a number of occasions that the recounting of the patient's story served as a powerful means of beginning the course of treatment and change.

In traditional practice, this same process occurs when a diagnosis is shared and the psychologist begins to outline a treatment plan and summary of his or her impression of the presenting problems. Subsequently, although we used this step as a rapid way of building the therapeutic alliance, in practice this begins in a more traditional fashion from the very referral process, a correct assessment of the problem, and then the outline of the psychological treatment.

A second major goal of the first session was to provide a discussion of a "normal reaction to trauma." By this we mean a rationale that trauma is experienced in a behavioral, cognitive, and emotional context. This is intended to reassure the patients that they are not "going crazy" or losing their mind, which often is expressed as one of their fears, but are having an expected reaction. This naturally leads to a discussion of our conceptualization of PTSD into four symptom clusters, all of which we address with a specific treatment.

In the initial session we discussed the diagnosis of PTSD, and what that means, as well as other populations of survivors with PTSD that they may be more familiar with. We also let them know that in our earlier work as many as 40% of MVA survivors who have sought medical treatment were diagnosed with either PTSD or a milder form of it shortly after the trauma.

The next major objective is to explain a theory of PTSD. We used Mowrer's (1947) and Keane's (1985) two-factor theory of PTSD. Although there are a number of other models that we could have used, we found this model easy to explain, and it lends itself to a ready explanation of the treatment we have outlined to help the survivors. It also normalizes why their avoid-

ance is understandable, while giving a rationale of why the exposure model will theoretically address the symptoms in that cluster that are disruptive to their functioning.

The last goal of the first session was the provision of relaxation
training. We used a 16-muscle-group relaxation initially because
it is easy to learn and demonstrate. The procedures are essentially consistent with those described in Bernstein and
Borkovec's *Progressive Relaxation Training Manual* (1973). We
explained to our MVA survivors that, because this is a skill that
takes some time to learn, we want to get started as early as possible. A description of the 16-muscle-group relaxation can be
found in Appendix C.

We concluded the first session with a request that patients provide, by the next session, a written description of their MVAs. We
stressed that we did not want a "police report" of the facts, but a
full description of the event as they remember it. The description
was to include what happened, where it happened, how and
why it occurred, and what memories, images, sights, sounds,
smells, or anything else they could recollect, even if it seemed
insignificant. We emphasized that this was not an "English
assignment" but a critical aspect of gathering the details to aid
with the treatment of their anxiety and intrusive thoughts. We
told them not to worry about the sentence structure or the grammar. Participants could discuss the events chronologically or in
fragments as they remembered the details. We reassured them
that this may be a hard assignment for them and reminded them
of the price of avoidance as per the two-factor theory of PTSD.
We also explained that this was a beginning step to taking charge
of the symptoms and confronting the memories perpetuating
their discomfort.

Last, any limits that were to be placed on treatment were
reviewed and agreed to by the patient and therapist. For example, if the treatment was not going to address dealing with
chronic pain or a marital problem, this would be specified. We
explicitly told patients with continuing pain and reduced mobil-
ity or range of motion that the treatment was not for their pain,
that we could not relieve their physical injuries. However, we
told them that, as treatment is successful, it may enable them to
cope with the pain better. The parameters of treatment in private

practice might involve the patient receiving medication from a treating physician or psychiatrist or attending group treatment or couples therapy elsewhere. In managed-care settings this might involve a behavioral contract around symptom reduction and then delineation of any limitations that might be done in the treatment planning at this time (e.g., "We will meet for 8–10 sessions and evaluate our progress at that time. If things are going as planned, we will proceed. If things are not proceeding as we anticipated we will reevaluate your treatment needs at that time.")

The patient is encouraged to practice the assigned relaxation training twice daily (a tape is provided for home practice, either made ahead of time or as they are instructed in PMR) and to write out a thorough description of their MVA.

Session 2

The second session begins with the patient reading and elaborating on his or her written description of the MVA. The therapist, as necessary, can ask questions or comment to elicit as thorough a response as the survivor can produce. The patient reads the description aloud, while the therapist looks to "round out" the scene. It is important to include details of the injuries, pain, and long-term consequences as the description is read. It is also important to note the patient's reaction to the scene, particularly where he or she exhibits discomfort. Remind the patient that it is normal to want to avoid aspects of the scene that can lead to discomfort and that this procedure will be of considerable importance to full recovery.

We find it helps to acknowledge that writing the description was probably very hard, especially because it reminded the patients of the MVA and made them think about and remember things they had been trying to avoid.

The patient is then asked, as part of homework, to read the description aloud three or more times per day. They are to add any new memories as they occur and to elaborate on the descriptions as the new memories occur. (We believe reading aloud engages more attention and focuses attention more on the memories.)

A discussion of avoidance and its place in the development and continuation of PTSD is offered. It is emphasized that avoidance is normal, that it does not signify weakness but is a normal effort at adaptation that unfortunately has the undesirable effect (as explained by learning theory) of worsening, rather than improving, the PTSD symptoms.

Relaxation training is repeated within the session, and it is explained to the patients that relaxation is an important skill, particularly as they begin to face anxiety-provoking thoughts and situations. Regular home practice is again stressed.

Session 3

At this time, a shift in treatment is begun. Overt instruction in cognitive therapy is initiated, and involvement with the significant other is planned. The review of the MVA description and reactions to any homework assignments between sessions are often the starting point of each subsequent therapy session.

In the third session, patients are introduced to coping self-statements and the process of trying to replace the negative thoughts and feelings that contribute to the anxiety and avoidance with more positive thoughts. As per Meichenbaum's (1985) SIT, the patients are instructed in ways they can use coping self-statements. These methods are (a) to help predict and prepare for potentially stressful situations (e.g., when they are to return to the scene of the MVA, ride in a car, or go to their lawyer's office for a deposition); (b) to help cope with stressful situations, for instance, by talking their way through them (e.g., as they're driving, watching a movie, seeing a friend who had been injured in the crash); and (c) to reward themselves after the stressful situation is over.

Patients are then asked to rank the feared or anxiety-provoking situations and are made aware of a graded exposure model, wherein they will be asked to approach the less stressful situations first in a planned, concerted effort to gain mastery over their reactions. A sample of coping statements specific for MVA survivors can be found in Exhibit 16-1.

Exhibit 16-1

Example of Coping Self-Statements

1. In preparation of stressful situations that you can predict will occur

    a. What is it I have to do?

    b. What plan can I develop with this?

    c. The situation is not impossible; I can handle this.

    d. Stop worrying; don't worry; worry isn't going to help anyway.

    e. I have a great many resources. I can put my mind to use.

    f. _____

    _____

    g. _____

    _____

2. During a stressful situation: Confrontation and coping

    a. I can deal with this situation, if I just do one step at a time.

    b. I've gotten through these situations before; they are not going to overwhelm me; it just *feels* that way at times.

    c. I can see this situation as a challenge or as an opportunity to improve rather than as viewing it negatively.

    d. These are the things I need to do to get through the situation (then list steps).

    e. Relax. I'm in control. Take a slow, deep breath.

    f. Keep the focus on the present; what do I have to do?

    g. _____

    h. _____

3. After the situation is over

    a. Whatever worked, pay attention to it.

    b. Don't punish self for being important but recognize all efforts and improvements, large or small.

Exhibit 16-1   *(Continued)*

Example of Coping Self-Statements

---

c. I made a good effort.

d. I'm learning how to deal with the situation more effectively.

e. I knew I could handle this; it takes time.

f. It wasn't as bad as I expected.

g. ———————————

An example of the use of coping self-statements follows: A patient expressed difficulty returning to the scene of her MVA. She knew she had to pass the scene of the MVA during a return visit home for the holidays. The MVA had occurred during a visit with her parents over Thanksgiving weekend. To help prepare for the trip, the patient tried to predict what the scene would be like. She knew it would be a faster highway because her parents lived on Long Island. She reminded herself that she had grown up in that region of the country and for many years had driven the highways. She developed a plan (similar to how she learned to drive the highways around her home) of staying in a particular lane, reminding herself of how long it was between exits, and using coping statements (e.g., that this was something she could handle). She told herself, "This [is] a difficult, but not impossible, situation. There is no need to worry before the event has even occurred."

To talk her way through the situation, she divided the necessary tasks into manageable steps. She reminded herself that she had managed high levels of anxiety before and now held newly developed skills (relaxation and coping self-statements) to talk her way through the time on the highway.

Finally, she was reminded that whatever happened would help her improvement overall. If all went well, she would gain confidence. The exposure would, in all likelihood, create anxiety,

Exhibit 16-2

Avoidance Hierarchy

SUDS rating   0 = *no discomfort;* 10 = *great discomfort*

SUDS rating		
_____	1.	_____
_____	2.	_____
_____	3.	_____
_____	4.	_____
_____	5.	_____
_____	6.	_____
_____	7.	_____
_____	8.	_____
_____	9.	_____
_____	10.	_____

Note: SUDS = Subjective Units of Discomfort Scale.

which would help her learn how to manage it better. The last reminder was to tell herself that this takes time and that by making this effort she would be furthering her overall improvement. We often have patients remind themselves that they are good, safe, and prudent drivers. Verbalizing this seems to help. It is during this session that an avoidance hierarchy is easy to introduce. The use of SUDS ratings, and how to record them for situations over the next week, is explained. We have used a 0–10 SUDS scale, where 0 = *no discomfort* and 10 = *great discomfort*. It is often helpful to begin this assignment using examples generated from the patient or earlier meetings to describe 3 to 5 situations. The patient is then instructed over the next week to continue developing the list until he or she has 10 to 15 scenes total.

It is also during this session that we try to formally meet with the significant other. In clinical practice, it is often important to meet with the significant other as part of the evaluation prior to treatment. This allows one to gain a fuller sense of the impact of the MVA on the person's behavior and to understand what resources exist or not to aid in the design of treatment.

The goals of meeting with the significant other are several: First, it is useful and often important to learn the spouse's (partner's) perception of the MVA's impact on his or her partner. This can range from drastic changes in sleep, driving, and mood to being surprised that their partner is in treatment at all. In fact, several patients did not tell their spouses that they were involved in treatment, and the spouses in turn expressed surprise that they met the criteria for a psychiatric disorder. This obviously reflects on a pattern of interaction and sharing between partners and raises questions of how the therapist may want to proceed with treatment.

Second, once the patient is willing to divulge information, the symptoms and overview of treatment can be provided. The goal is to try to enlist the significant other's support and understanding. He or she is given an explanation of our understanding of PTSD and the role conditioning and avoidance play in its presentation. At this time we begin to discuss how the significant other (i.e., spouse, partner, or friend) will be exposed to feared or anxiety-provoking situations and how they are to be mastered.

A plan is formulated as to how the partners may need to interact differently (i.e., to be encouraging and positive at best; at worst, to be neutral) when the patient is faced with the previously avoided situations. Partners play a large and often central role in the survivor's life. This often leads to "helpful behavior," such as driving the partner everywhere or doing the "extra" acts that limit possible exposure as a way of being understanding and helpful. At worst, they can be negative and hostile toward the changes that have occurred. Although we do not have data on the impact of this variable on treatment outcome, we believe the involvement of the spouse may have a large impact on treatment outcome. For example, a spouse can be very supportive and encouraging at times when the patient has become discouraged or his or her depression has worsened. Partners are invaluable when sharing descriptions of behavior, such as driving reactions, sleep and appetite changes, and interactions with friends and family members. Although they may have their own internal distortions of what is seen, when the couple is interviewed jointly, reasonable corroboration of details can often be found. In addition, when the situation is viewed differently, the subsequent dialogue has often been of great help in strengthening the relationship overall.

Finally, when the spouse has left the room, the patient is introduced to a shortened version of PMR, the eight-muscle-group relaxation. A description of the eight-muscle relaxation group relaxation exercise can be found in Appendix C. An audiotape of the exercise is provided, and homework is encouraged between sessions. Homework includes reading the MVA description aloud, relaxation practice, use of coping self-statements, and development of an avoidance hierarchy.

Session 4

As with each session, Session 4 begins with a review of how the homework assignments went. Homework assignments—which, as we mentioned, to this point included relaxation training, reading of the MVA description, use of coping self-statements, and development of the avoidance hierarchy—can now be expanded. As the MVA description is read it is now possible to use the coping statements before, during, and after the oral rendition. The same is true of the avoidance hierarchy, including the aspects of the exposure exercise that elicit higher SUDS ratings when the patient confronts those events.

The next major treatment intervention is the introduction of cognitive reappraisal. This is introduced as building on the coping statements learned earlier and on the way one thinks about a situation having a significant effect on what one experiences. The interpretation of a situation and automatic thoughts are then explained as patterns of appraisal that are learned (sometimes rapidly, as in the case of a traumatic event) and, subsequently, can be unlearned.

Ellis's A-B-C-D model (cited in Whalen et al., 1980) is then introduced, and distortions in thinking (Beck et al., 1979) are used as examples specific to the impact of MVAs. These distortions include premature conclusions, reality testing, all or nothing generalizations, and so forth. A handout of examples is provided.

Examples of activating events are numerous. These can include internal physiological states, emotions, thoughts about the event, news stories, comments from friends and family, and meetings with attorneys. Each of these scenes or stimuli is pointed out to the patients by the consequence of the act as it occurs (i.e., how it makes them feel). Most patients can very easily identify what happened to make them feel scared, anxious, or angry. The very process of analyzing the events in this cause –effect manner, even at times when patients argue there did not appear to be a clear stimulus, helps as the therapist explores with them the fact that the precipitating events of their discomfort are not random or without prediction. It is certainly true that precipitating events that trigger discomfort at times are not obvious or definite. However, the process of looking and the belief and direction the process provides can be extremely important for the patient's regaining control of emotional and behavioral responses.

Perhaps the most difficult process is helping the patients discern what types of beliefs or images drive their emotional and behavioral responses. Here patients will express ideas such as, "I've escaped being killed once, I won't be so lucky a second time!" "I'll never get better, I'm going to feel like this for the rest of my life!" "I can't stand feeling like this, and if anything bad happens, I'll lose my mind." "If I'm not totally better, I can't function at all." "It's unfair that this happened, and I'll never get over hating the man that did this to me!" "Something bad will happen again." "I should have been able to somehow make a difference, even leaving a few minutes earlier, or turning the wheel, might have saved me all this pain and upset." "I'm never safe when I'm behind the wheel or riding in a car because you never know what can happen." "I know what people are thinking, and they hold me responsible for what happened to . . . "

Each of these beliefs is challenged by the therapist in a fashion determined by the context of the therapeutic relationship. As Beck et al. (1979) pointed out, the cognitive therapist must first be a good psychotherapist who realizes the importance of the therapeutic alliance. Subsequently, an appreciation of the relationship determines how directly or in what fashion the faulty pattern of thinking is addressed. We have found that Beck's cognitive distortions have given a very efficient educational avenue for teaching the patient about the type of errors in thinking that might lead to powerful emotional consequences. Cognitive appraisal is introduced, primarily using an educational approach at first around the negative emotional or behavioral consequences and pointing out the potential impact of the faulty belief system. This is accomplished by using the patient's examples and by posing questions challenging the beliefs held. A hand-out of cognitive distortions is provided. Often, we add the examples used in the session at the bottom of the sheet to help the patient remember the process of challenging the faulty pattern of thinking.

Consistent with Beck et al.'s (1979) concern with the therapist's qualities and therapeutic relationship, we believe that a great deal more than technique takes place in the treatment sessions. There is a powerful element of human concern and empathy when individuals share a trauma they experienced and that continue to trouble them. This is as prevalent in MVA traumas as in other types of trauma (i.e., rape, physical injury, natural disasters, or war) that the authors have worked with. The importance of providing hope and an understanding of how past experiences, perhaps other traumas, have prepared them to arrive at this moment and to move on is an important therapeutic message. Four-muscle-group relaxation is then introduced, and a tape of their assigned exercise is provided for home practice. A great deal occurs in each session. The therapist may need to expand the lengths of the sessions or divide the sessions so that there is more than one meeting.

Discussion of the Driving Hierarchy

The negative impact of the accident on subsequent driving has been almost universally experienced among MVA survivors in our research and clinical experience. Some survivors experience fear and anxiety at the site of the MVA, whereas others cease all driving after the MVA. Some individuals make one or two efforts at driving and then become fearful, anxious, or experience a panic attack, resulting in a significant curtailing of driving (and riding) activities. The range of impact can vary dramatically. As a result, our intervention may also vary considerably. If necessary, one may begin the driving hierarchy by having the patient sit in an automobile and start the vehicle but not plan to drive. The next step is to apply relaxation and cognitive techniques until the patient feels calm.

Driving can then be added, starting with movement of the car in the driveway and local driving at times of little traffic (e.g., Saturday or Sunday morning). Increase the driving hierarchy as the patient can tolerate it and has demonstrated success. Because of the variability of driving impact, treatment length may vary as well. More than one session may be needed to adequately attend to all aspects of treatment outlined for a particular session.

Regular attention to the hierarchy-related driving behavior is important. Driving if possible should be performed on a daily basis, at whatever level the patient can tolerate.

If possible, the daily practice can be a functional activity (i.e., serves a legitimate purpose), such as completing an errand or doing shopping, that will serve as a reinforcer in its own right. If certain driving (e.g., a highway at rush hour) is avoided, one should see whether it is possible to tie in a reinforcing event at the completion of the driving homework (e.g., lunch with a friend).

If the patient seems "stuck" and is making little progress with the driving hierarchy, imaginal desensitization can be tried prior to in vivo exposure. It is also helpful at times for the therapist to accompany the patient in the vehicle in particularly fearful driving situations. In some circumstances significant others can assume the role of coach under the direction of the treating psychologist. During driving tasks it is important to be reassuring and positive and to model cognitive coping statements or reappraisal techniques.

In all likelihood the driving hierarchy tasks will elicit much in the way of negative self-talk and "catastrophic thoughts." Having the patients make notes on particular tasks and their subjective reactions is a way of bringing the thoughts more actively into the therapy session.

One should acknowledge to the patients that it is true that one cannot control the behavior of other drivers but that they can keep "good control" of their vehicle and operate it in a safe, prudent fashion. They are under no obligation to operate their vehicle at a speed they consider unsafe for the road conditions or when it is not safe in response to other vehicles crowding or blowing their horns. Some patients need to repeat these ideas to themselves as they drive in a "mantra-like" fashion.

For situations that occur infrequently (or, it is hoped, never), such as being cut off at high speeds or having another driver make rapid, unsignaled lane changes, imaginal exposure is often helpful. Here the practice can occur with provision of behavioral techniques (e.g., relaxation) or cognitive techniques (e.g., coping self-statements and cognitive reappraisal) until the anxiety or hyperarousal response is minimized or eliminated. The cognitive practice seems to help the confidence of the driver as well as provide the new manner by which they can imagine how they will react and deal with the situation.

Patients will usually become concerned about what they perceive as highly dangerous situations. For example, a patient kept imagining the accident that would occur if a driver changed lanes rapidly or cut him off. Imaginal exposure was used, wherein the patient imagined first mastery of the situation. Here patients can plan on the reaction from themselves that will "save them," deal with the rise of anxiety as it occurs, and imagine the anxiety's decline as the scene is managed well and passed successfully. However, it is equally important to address the fear wherein the cars actually crashed. Here, patients can repeatedly address the pain and horror they would experience. As they imaginally experience the feared event (i.e., the crash), continued exposure occurs until a minimal response or no arousal follows.

The scene is repeated as often as necessary until a sense of "boredom" follows. This can take several sessions to occur, but as with the repeated scene of patients' own MVA, with repeated imaginal exposure, the decline in anxiety and the provocation of emotional reaction is often extinguished or greatly improved.

Session 5

Following review of all homework assignments and the patient's reading of the MVA description (done at all sessions), cognitive techniques to deal with experiences are reviewed and improved or encouraged. Relaxation by recall is introduced after the patient is taken through a repetition of the last session's four-muscle-group relaxation.

If the patient is successful with relaxation by recall, he or she is then instructed to use this procedure at home. An audiotape of the exercise is provided for home use, and the patient is asked to continue at least once per day with the tape and once per day without the audiotape.

Patients performing relaxation by recall at home are instructed to supplement the exercise with the actual tension of the four muscle groups if they are not able to become relaxed with the recall alone. If they are unsuccessful or only partially successful with relaxation by recall, they are to continue with the relaxation exercises they are currently using, and relaxation by recall will be tried again in the next session. The largest portion of this session is spent challenging the patient's cognitive distortions or irrational beliefs and dealing therapeutically with the driving hierarchy and in vivo exposure that is taking place. This is continued over the next week.

Session 6

Again, begin the session with exposure to the MVA description as it is read by the patient. Use the patient's reaction as an introduction to the continued use of any negative statements and need for cognitive intervention. By this time many patients are no longer as upset as they read the MVA description. Some are, in fact, beginning to be bored by the assignment. If this seems to be the case, the reading exposure can be reduced to one time each day.

The driving hierarchy continues to be the focus for many patients, and cognitive–behavioral intervention is primarily the treatment provided. Some supportive counseling and encouragement is also helpful in aiding the patients' confidence as they challenge more difficult tasks from their personal hierarchy of feared events.

Cue-controlled relaxation is introduced by repeating the relaxation-by-recall method introduced in the last session. Cuing is explained to the patients as a method to help them relax quickly and efficiently in all of the situations they may encounter.

Cue-controlled relaxation is taught by first having the patient take a deep breath, pairing exhalation with subvocalizing the word *relax*. This is done with the patient's eyes both open and closed. The use of imagery is also encouraged. The notion of cuing as an automatic process is introduced, having the patient do the cue-controlled relaxation as many times per day as possible until it is automatic. The patient is given the homework task of using cue-controlled relaxation a minimum of 12 times per day. Ways to help the response become automatic include, for example, having the relaxation used (i.e., paired) whenever patients are stopped at a traffic light, hanging up or answering the telephone, or engaged in any other frequently occurring daily event.

Clinically, individuals often enjoy the process of cued relaxation. One woman in the treatment study expressed her enjoyment of pairing relaxation with traffic lights or stop signs and began to look forward to the moment as a "pause that refreshes."

Sessions 7 Through 9

The review of all relevant homework continues. As the patient makes progress, some tasks may diminish greatly in importance (e.g., driving or reading of the MVA description). These can then be tailored at the therapist's discretion.

The latter treatment sessions are now used to address the varied combination of symptom clusters that arise for this population. These major themes and symptom clusters fall into the following classifications: (a) psychic numbing; (b) existential issues; (c) estrangement, social isolation, and depression; and (d) anger. The transition is begun by reminding the patient of the symptom clusters or concerns that were present within the initial treatment session as the evaluation was reviewed.

Psychic Numbing

For those patients with psychic numbing, we begin by describing psychic numbing and estrangement as a symptom complex that can be thought of as a selective emotional-processing deficit (Litz, 1992). Numbing can then be viewed as an avoidance behavior, in this instance an effort to avoid the strong affect held in check because of its being viewed as dangerous and a reminder of the trauma. Feelings related to this are discussed as are any possible signs of current depression.

Over the course of treatment, patients often come to express how overwhelmed they have been by the enormity of the event. They do not know how to label the event but feel cut off or somehow different. The trauma uses all of their energy. It absorbs their thoughts, their dreams, and cuts them off from those parts of their life that used to hold such importance.

A woman in treatment shared how initially following her MVA she was euphoric. To have survived her MVA was exhilarating. Her van had caromed off a bridge, was sent off an embankment, and rolled two or three times until settling upside down, with her trapped inside. Rescue workers were able to extricate her within 30 to 40 minutes after the crash. She was taken to a local medical center and released with injuries to her neck and back. She was told several times that even with her air bag and seat belt, she was lucky to be alive.

The next day she went to the scene of the accident to see her vehicle. She had been driving a mini van. When she saw the crushed vehicle, she began to shake. All she could think was, "They're right, the way the van crumpled around me, I should have died."

Another MVA victim's car crashed into a telephone pole when forced off the road by a drunk driver. Although she escaped relatively unharmed, at the time of the accident she felt, as the car closed in on the pole, that she was going to die. She remembers thinking, "my daughter only works a block from here, and I'll never see her again." She wondered what would happen to her husband and mother. She sought treatment when the thoughts would not remit.

Many times the discussion of death and one's mortality will involve issues of spirituality and religion. As psychologists, we make it clear that we hold no answers in those areas, but ask about the meaning for patients. The effect of their life on others, what remains to be done, and why they survived are often topics the survivors bring up. When injury, or limitation of activities they once enjoyed such as a hobby or exercise, reminds them of the MVA with persistent pain, they look for a reason why and a way to draw meaning from the event. To help with this, one must know the patient by the history they reveal and by the personal views they share.

Existential Issues

One predominant theme frequently found among MVA survivors is the fear of death and graphic reminders of one's mortality. Rather than solely treating this as a cognition that generates anxiety, we have found it helpful to explore with patients questions regarding mortality and their underlying beliefs and fears. Inquiry into the meaning of mortality and possible internal cognitive dialogue are explored, but without any clear provision of a "correct answer." We have found it helpful to place their ideas in the context of a therapeutic relationship, allowing these areas to be explored in a safe and supportive atmosphere.

Patients have expressed the fear brought on by the near-death experience as that they had been but an instant from losing their lives. Some patients express the belief that there is no afterlife, and, subsequently, they focus on the fragility of their life and how instantaneously it can end. Others discuss the unfinished goals and plans they have and how these now have become more focused. Finally, many express the impact of their loss on others and how their relationships with family and friends are not as they would want them. They are all too aware of how they were not given a say in the matter, especially if they did not view themselves at fault for the MVA. Belief in an afterlife and God are often tested, and how these beliefs are held may also be offered to the therapist as important areas for discussion.

Estrangement, Social Isolation, and Depression

Estrangement can be conceptualized as being manifested through the acts of social isolation and a lack of positive events. These behaviors are described to the patient as contributors to the sense of isolation (and possibly depression). For patients who have become socially isolated and have been avoiding friends, family, and other previously pleasurable events, a formal program of reaching out to those social contacts is described and planned. This can include how to ask for help or contact as well as problem solving around these issues.

Patients are asked to describe previously enjoyed but now (possibly) avoided or limited activities. If they are unable to generate such a list themselves, they are assisted in this task. This is the provision of pleasant events scheduling (PES) as described by Lewinson (1972, 1976) as a treatment for depression. The technique is used here as a method of intervening within this psychic numbing symptom cluster.

Patients will often give us an excuse or explanation for why they have given up activities (e.g., they don't feel up to it or they are waiting until they feel better). We counter by assigning patients certain tasks (e.g., to call specific people without waiting for the impulse to arise). We also give a positive expectation to the outcome of the approach behavior. Patients' typical response to reengagement in previously enjoyed behaviors or to recontacting a friend is one of pleasure and surprise. We try to build on these positive reinforcements.

Clinically, patients who have been in an MVA are approached similarly to depressed patients. By this we mean that it is pointed out that many of the events that once gave them pleasure perhaps no longer accomplish this end. It is important to ascertain whether this is due to physical limitations (e.g., "I can't engage in sports because of my bad back") or psychological reasons. They are encouraged to generate a list of events that once held pleasure

Exhibit 16-3

Cognitive Reappraisal

A = Activating event (What happened?)

B = Belief (What were you thinking?)

C = Consequence (What emotional and behavioral reaction did you experience?)

D = Dispute (How to challenge your beliefs)

Distortions in Thinking (Examples)

1. Premature conclusions/jumping to conclusions

2. Reality testing (i.e., not assuming things to be true, when in fact, they may not be true)

3. All or none/black or white thinking

4. Sweeping generalization

5. Predicting the future

6. Mind reading

7. Overestimating/underestimating

8. _____

_____

_____

for them, or at least sounded as if they might be pleasurable. As shown in Exhibit 16-3, the symptom cluster for Criterion C showed significant improvement from the time of initial evaluation. The data do not allow us to discern what aspect of the treatment package may have been most helpful here, but our impression is that the increased activity and social contact was an important element of that improvement.

Anger

Cognitions related to fear of affect expression are also explored and addressed, with cognitive techniques introduced earlier in treatment. Related to this is a common theme of anger management. Many patients we see show increased hostility and irritability. The difficulty in managing anger is consistent with difficulty in the management of strong affect, but rather than suppress the emotion, leading to numbing, difficulty in modulating the expression of anger may occur. The anger may be directed at the other driver, "the system" of insurance companies, lawyers, or litigation doctors that may be treating them or providing mandated evaluations. Survivors often feel as if they are "on trial" while they perceive themselves as the injured party. Cognitive techniques can be tried to deal with assumptions of justice, fairness, and control, as well as behavioral techniques of relaxation to try to moderate the emotional reactivity as per earlier methods. A number of articles and books provide approaches to deal with anger (e.g., DiGiuseppe, Tafrate, & Eckhardt, 1994; Fein, 1993).

Anger often comes in the aftermath of an MVA trauma. A patient will angrily describe how "I didn't do anything wrong! I wasn't driving out of control! I did nothing to increase my risk while waiting at a stop sign! I don't even know who to feel most angry at, the other driver, the weather, or God."

It is of interest that in our study, and in practice, we did not often evaluate the drunk driver, the driver "clearly in the wrong," or the driver perceived as responsible for the MVA. We did see drivers who "contributed" to the accident scene by going too fast or not using caution when it may have helped. Survivors included drivers in cars wherein the passenger had suffered head injuries or may have died. But, again, they often had reasons as to why they should be angry at somebody or something else.

Our interventions with anger have followed the cognitive model of much of our treatment. One of the earliest interventions by Novaco (1975) appears based on the notion that individuals who are angry have a deficit in verbal mediation of behavior. Ellis (1977) proposed that the model of irrational beliefs leads to anger.

DiGiuseppe et al. (1994) more recently proposed a multiple-component treatment that assesses the patients' presence or absence of verbal mediating self-statements; presence of negative, positive, or vengeful automatic thoughts and irrational beliefs; and the patient's social skills for problem solving. They use exposure to anger-provoking situations and thoughts as a critical component of the intervention, coupled with cognitive coping statements and interventions for the automatic thoughts believed to drive the anger.

We found that encouraging the use of cognitive coping statements, such as, "Don't assume the worst." "You can react in ways other than anger." "How else might I react here?" can help in anger-provoking scenes. Identifying underlying beliefs using Ellis's (1962) A-B-C-D model can help clarify cognitions related to anger, such as "I'm being treated unfairly, and I can't stand it." Cognitions related to how they believe they've been treated, their stamina and endurance, and the fairness of life can be challenged and restructured within the therapeutic intervention.

Relaxation skills are also used. Brief relaxation can be suggested as a response to rising anger and followed by the use of the cognitive techniques. The guidelines of Deffenbacher (1995) point out that many angry individuals seem to hold the following cognitive biases and errors: overestimation and underestimation (i.e., overestimate the probability of a negative event and underestimate the personal or other coping resources), misattribution and single explanation (i.e., jump to highly personalized conclusions; act as if these conclusions are true), polarized conceptualization (i.e., good–bad, right–wrong), overgeneralization (i.e., broad sweeping conclusions such as everyone is dumb, worthless, always this way), inflammatory thinking (i.e., labeling events or people in highly negative ways such as *creep, bitch*), catastrophizing (casting events in highly negative extreme ways such as awful, terrible, can't stand it), and demanding and commanding (i.e., where they elevate their preferences and desires to moral edicts; commandments such as things ought to be, have to be, should be). When these distortions are present, anger responses become more likely. We have seen similar errors in thinking in our clinical experience. Some individuals will benefit from role playing or assertiveness training to better manage situations that provoke anger and related behavior. Exposure to anger-provoking situations and phrases might also be used and then managed within the treatment setting by developing a reaction other than a rapid response to angry feelings.

Concluding Treatment

Over the remaining sessions all of the active ingredients of treatment are used and adjusted as necessary. Patients may continue with driving and behavioral avoidance hierarchy work. Social contact and PES may be a necessary shift in focus, or it may have minimal usefulness. If depression is present, it requires intervention. Any method of treatment consistent with the needs of the patient may be provided. It is in these latter sessions that the individual needs of the patient are addressed in the manualized treatment. In clinical practice flexibility should be used and treatment length adjusted accordingly.

In actual clinical practice, the format provided above can be modified to suit each patient's needs. The length of treatment may also vary considerably. Burstein (1986) commented in his work on the considerable variability that exists in treatment. Treatment length of greater than a year is not uncommon.

One variable we believe may contribute to the persistence of PTSD is a chronic physical problem that does not improve. We believe that the pain or alteration of lifestyle adversely interacts with the subsequent emotional adjustment to the MVA. This is not to say that patients with permanent physical injury cannot improve emotionally; our work suggests they can. However, the interaction with physical and emotional factors can be very powerful. This may, in fact, turn out to be one of the potentiating variables for the more chronic PTSD victim that shows a slower rate of improvement. Our data (see Chapter 9) are suggestive but not definitive on this point. Even if this turns out to be true, it is believed to be only one of the potentially contributing variables, not the only one.

Earlier trauma has also shown itself as a variable adding to the occurrence of PTSD following an MVA. Treatment may need to deal with these issues as well and the expression this vulnerability or related issues manifest in psychological distress. This was noted in case examples in Chapter 15 and in one of the earliest reports of MVA-related PTSD (McCaffrey & Fairbank, 1985).

Medications, although not the focus of this book, also seem to have a role in the treatment of MVA-related PTSD. Whether to help with the co-morbid depression or the chronic pain, sleep disturbance, or symptoms of anxiety, a combined psychological and pharmacological intervention may, at times, be the treatment of choice. The decision for the provision of medications would, at this time, appear more based on clinical judgment than on any objective guideline.

Summary

This chapter provides a detailed description of the multifaceted treatment approaches developed to treat MVA survivors with PTSD. Although many of the interventions described are cognitive–behavioral in their theoretical base, the treatment acknowledges and plans for the provision of other diverse, related treatment areas and methods. Issues of one's mortality, dealing with past losses, and earlier traumas can often arise as a part of treatment.

Although the treatment manual was time limited, for many individuals additional treatment appears warranted. Again, we are encouraged that the outcome data from our focused, targeted treatment indicates that the treatment is a clinically useful method to guide the practicing clinician.

17

Summary and Conclusions

This book provides a comprehensive description of what is presently known about the psychological impact of MVAs on the survivor of the crash. We have tried to share summaries of the relevant literature and detailed results of our own work. Rather than rehash the body of the text, this section provides closing thoughts on our work to date and needed future work.

General Study Findings

The studies discussed in chapter 14, and our work as part of the Albany MVA Project, strongly support that PTSD following an MVA can be helped with psychological treatment. There is a crucial need now to conduct the necessary controlled studies to determine how well and for which patients these techniques work best.

It is very clear from our work that the symptoms measured by self-report, the CAPS, psychological tests, and psychosocial measures can all improve across targeted psychological intervention. Whether they improve more than a control group, or in one type of treatment over another, cannot be said.

Clinically, the patients in our pilot studies appeared to be largely indistinguishable from the type of patients seen in a private practice setting. We, in fact, selected this MVA population because we wanted to learn about the "real" patients who show up in a doctor's office. It is certainly arguable that patients willing to take part in a pilot study may be quite different from those who are unwilling to participate in a research project. It is also true that, whereas patients in our first study were provided psychological treatment similar to private patients not in the study, it could be argued that these individuals may be somewhat different just by being willing to take part in a rather lengthy assessment study.

Some people argue that clinical research tries to select only "pure" patients who manifest one diagnosis only and thereby do not look like the patients who arrive in clinics or private offices. Our studies were completed with patients who held several co-morbid diagnoses. And, although our protocol for the second study hoped to have some effect on depression, the generalization of cognitive–behavioral techniques sometimes helped and sometimes did not. The same was true for GAD.

One strong limitation of the second study was that it did not allow the clinician to attempt to treat all of the diagnosed conditions. Patients were referred for additional treatment if they still were depressed, were anxious, or had any symptoms that interfered with their functioning. This would obviously not be the case in a purely clinical setting.

The issue of symptom improvement is also important in considering treatment success. On the basis of the total CAPS and symptom clusters, the targeted psychological interventions worked well for treating PTSD. However, they did not eradicate the entire problem. Patients continued to have some symptoms, even if they remitted to the point of not being sufficiently symptomatic to merit a diagnosis of even subsyndromal PTSD. One could argue that even one symptom (e.g., nightmares, avoidance of a key part of one's life, or emotional functioning) would be cause enough to continue psychological treatment. Allowance of the patient's perception for point of termination would appear critical if placed in the context of how actual clinical decisions are made. The second study in particular would suggest that longer treatment might have been of benefit, particularly if co-morbid conditions or limited but significant symptoms of PTSD persisted.

Malatesta (1995) argued that manual-based treatment, in fact, creates an illusion whereby simple treatment can be effective for extremely complex problems. Although she wrote for another diagnostic group, that statement certainly appears true for this population. The concerns of MVA PTSD survivors are many and powerful. The fact that we can show improvement is very encouraging. Success, however, needs to be measured on a case-by-case basis.

Closing Thoughts

Although not the focus of this book, these techniques, assessment, and especially treatment have been found in clinical practice to serve equally well with trauma survivors of other populations. In clinical experiences with survivors of physical trauma (e.g., falls, physical injuries), railroad accidents, boating accidents, rape, and assault, treatment drawing from the same core of interventions (altered to be sensitive to the particular needs of each trauma population) has been (seemingly) equally useful. This leads one to discuss the paradigm of the MVA victim as a model for PTSD research and treatment. Although our knowledge of PTSD historically has come from survivors of war and the soldiers who fought, there are significant differences between those experiences from the traumas of "everyday life" that also seem to lead to significant psychological distress.

The occurrence of MVAs as a daily event reported in our newspapers and communities has unfortunately provided a population easily accessible to study and learn from. We do not need to wait for a natural disaster, large calamity, or war to study the phenomena of PTSD.

MVA survivors also require immediate attention for services. They need to resume a life free from anxiety and depression that includes driving and travel. A significant number of MVA survivors will require evaluation and treatment and ongoing studies to judge our effectiveness in providing that help. Furthermore, the survivors of the trauma in our experience are articulate and desirous of sharing the events of the trauma to the treating professional. One would guess that as our studies have approximated the real world of referrals in the United States, where physicians identify a problem and try to refer the patient to the appropriate provider. This is considerably different from sending out letters to people or offering a treatment not appearing to hold direct application for their distress.

We do know from epidemiological studies that MVAs are the most commonly occurring trauma within the United States. Millions of people each year are involved in MVAs, which can result in personal injury and, as we have shown, considerable psychological distress. Much remains to be learned in how we can understand and help these survivors. We can only hope that this book serves as a beginning for the considerable need that exists.

References

Allodi, F. A. (1974). Accident neurosis: Whatever happened to male hysteria? *Canadian Psychiatric Association Journal, 19,* 291–296.

American Association for Automotive Medicine. (1985). *The Abbreviated Injury Scale.* Des Plaines, IL: Author.

American Psychiatric Association. (1980). *Diagnostic and Statistical Manual of Mental Disorders* (3rd ed.). Washington, DC: Author.

American Psychiatric Association. (1987). *Diagnostic and Statistical Manual of Mental Disorders* (3rd ed., rev.). Washington, DC: Author.

American Psychiatric Association. (1994). *Diagnostic and Statistical Manual of Mental Disorders* (4th ed.). Washington, DC: Author.

Arindell, W. A., & Ettema, H. (1981). Dimensionele structuur, betrouwbaarheid en validiteit van de *Nederlandse bewerking van de Symptom Checklist (SCL-90). Nederlands Tijdschrift Voor de Psychologie, 36,* 77–108.

Barton, K. A., Blanchard, E. B., & Hickling, E. J. (1996). Antecedents and consequences of acute stress disorder among motor vehicle accident victims. *Behaviour Research and Therapy, 34,* 805–813.

Beck, A. T., Rush, A. J., Shaw, B. F., & Emery, G. (1979). *Cognitive therapy of depression.* New York: Guilford Press.

Beck, A. T., Steer, R. A., & Garbin, N. G. (1988). Psychometric properties of the Beck Depression Inventory: Twenty-five years of evaluation. *Clinical Psychology Review, 8,* 77–100.

Beck, A. T., Ward, C. H., Mendelson, M., Mock, J., & Erbaugh, J. (1961). An inventory for measuring depression. *Archives of General Psychiatry, 5,* 561–571.

Bernstein, D. A., & Borkovec, T. D. (1973). *Progressive relaxation training: A manual for the helping professions.* Chicago: Research Press.

Best, C. L., & Ribbe, D. P. (1995). Accidental injury: Approaches to assessment and treatment. In J. R. Freedy & S. E. Hobfoil (Eds.), *Traumatic stress: From theory to practice* (pp. 315–337). New York: Plenum Press.

Blake, D., Weathers, F., Nagy, L., Kaloupek, D., Klauminzer, G., Charney, D., & Keane, T. (1990a). *Clinician-Administered PTSD Scale (CAPS).* Boston, MA: National Center for Post-Traumatic Stress Disorder, Behavioral Science Division.

Blake, D., Weathers, F., Nagy, L., Kaloupek, D., Klauminzer, G., Charney, D., & Keane, T. (1990b). *Clinician-Administered PTSD Scale (CAPS), Form 2— One-Week Symptom Status Version.* Boston, MA: National Center for Posttraumatic Stress Disorder, Behavioral Science Division.

Blanchard, E. B., Hickling, E. J., Barton, K. A., Taylor, A. E., Loos, W. R., & Jones-Alexander, J. (1996). One-year prospective follow-up of motor vehicle accident victims. *Behaviour Research and Therapy, 34,* 775–786.

Blanchard, E. B., Hickling, E. J., Buckley, T. C., Taylor, A. E., Vollmer, A., & Loos, W. R. (1996). The psychophysiology of motor vehicle accident related post-traumatic stress disorder: Replication and extension. *Journal of Consulting and Clinical Psychology, 64,* 742–751.

Blanchard, E. B., Hickling, E. J., Forneris, C. A., Taylor, A. E., Buckley, T. C., Loos, W. R., & Jaccard, J. (1997). Prediction of remission of acute post-traumatic stress disorder in motor vehicle accident victims. *Journal of Traumatic Stress, 10,* 215–234.

Blanchard, E. B., Hickling, E. J., Mitnick, N., Taylor, A. E., Loos, W. R., & Buckley, T. C. (1995). The impact of severity of physical injury and perception of life threat in the development of post-traumatic stress disorder in motor vehicle accident victims. *Behaviour Research and Therapy, 33,* 529–534.

Blanchard, E. B., Hickling, E. J., & Taylor, A. E. (1991). The psychophysiology of motor vehicle accident related post-traumatic stress disorder. *Biofeedback and Self-Regulation, 16,* 449–458.

Blanchard, E. B., Hickling, E. J., Taylor, A. E., Forneris, C. A., Loos, W. R., & Jaccard, J. (1996). Effects of varying scoring rules of the Clinician-Administered PTSD Scale (CAPS) for the diagnosis of post-traumatic stress disorder in motor vehicle accident victims. *Behaviour Research and Therapy, 33,* 471–475.

Blanchard, E. B., Hickling, E. J., Taylor, A. E., & Loos, W. R. (1995). Psychiatric morbidity associated with motor vehicle accidents. *The Journal of Nervous and Mental Disease, 183,* 495–504.

Blanchard, E. B., Hickling, E. J., Taylor, A. E., Loos, W. R., & Forneris, C. A. (1996). Who develops PTSD from motor vehicle accidents? *Behaviour Research and Therapy, 34,* 1–10.

Blanchard, E. B., Hickling, E. J., Taylor, A. E., Loos, W. R., & Gerardi, R. J. (1994a). Psychological morbidity associated with motor vehicle accidents. *Behaviour Research and Therapy, 32,* 283–290.

Blanchard, E. B., Hickling, E. J., Taylor, A. E., Loos, W. R., & Gerardi, R. J. (1994b). The psychophysiology of motor vehicle accident related post-traumatic stress disorder. *Behavior Therapy, 25,* 453–467.

Blanchard, E. B., Hickling, E. J., Vollmer, A. J., Loos, W. R., Buckley, T. C., & Jaccard, J. (1995). Short-term follow-up of post-traumatic stress symptoms in motor vehicle accident victims. *Behaviour Research and Therapy, 33,* 369–377.

Blanchard, E. B., Kolb, L. C., Pallmeyer, T. P., & Gerardi, R. J. (1982). A psychophysiological post-traumatic stress disorder in Vietnam veterans. *Psychiatric Quarterly, 54,* 220–229.

Blonstein, C. H. (1988). Treatment of automobile driving phobia through imaginal and in vivo exposure plus response prevention. *The Behavior Therapist, 11,* 70–86.

Boudewyns, P. A., & Hyer, L. (1990). Physiological responses to combat memories and preliminary treatment outcome in Vietnam veteran PTSD patients treated with direct therapeutic exposure. *Behavior Therapy, 21,* 63–87.

Breslau, N., Davis, G. C., & Andreski, P. (1995). Risk factors for PTSD-related traumatic events: A prospective analysis. *American Journal of Psychiatry, 152,* 529–535.

Breslau, N., Davis, G. C., Andreski, P., & Peterson, E. (1991). Traumatic events and post-traumatic stress disorder in an urban population of young adults. *Archives of General Psychiatry, 48,* 216–222.

Brom, D., Kleber, R. J., & DeFares, P. B. (1989). Brief psychotherapy for post-traumatic stress disorder. *Journal of Consulting and Clinical Psychology, 57,* 607–612.

Brom, D., Kleber, R. J., & Hoffman, M. C. (1993). Victims of traffic accidents: Incidence and prevention of post-traumatic stress disorder. *Journal of Clinical Psychology, 49,* 131–140.

Bryant, R. A. (1996). Post-traumatic stress disorder, flashbacks, and pseudo-memories in closed head injury. *Journal of Traumatic Stress, 9,* 621–629.

Bryant, R. A., & Harvey, A. G. (1995a). Acute stress response: A comparison of head injured and non-head injured patients. *Psychological Medicine, 25,* 869–873.

Bryant, R. A., & Harvey, A. G. (1995b). Avoidant coping style and post-traumatic stress following motor vehicle accidents. *Behaviour Research and Therapy, 33,* 631–635.

Bryant, R. A., & Harvey, A. G. (1995c). Psychological impairment following motor vehicle accidents. *Australian Journal of Public Health, 19,* 185–188.

Bryant, R. A., & Harvey, A. G. (1995d). Processing threatening information in posttraumatic stress disorder. *Journal of Abnormal Psychology, 104,* 537–541.

Bryant, R. A., & Harvey, A. G. (1996). Initial posttraumatic stress responses following motor vehicle accidents. *Journal of Traumatic Stress, 9,* 223–234.

Bryant, R. A., Harvey, A. G., Gordon, E., & Barry, R. J. (1995). Eye movement and electrodermal responses to threat stimuli in post-traumatic stress disorder. *International Journal of Psychophysiology, 20,* 209–213.

Buckley, T. C., Blanchard, E. B., & Hickling, E. J. (1996). A prospective examination of delayed onset PTSD secondary to motor vehicle accidents. *Journal of Abnormal Psychology, 105,* 617–625.

Burstein, A. (1984). Treatment length in post-traumatic stress disorder. *Psychosomatics, 27,* 632–637.

Burstein, A. (1986). Can monetary compensation influence the course of a disorder? *American Journal of Psychiatry, 143,* 112.

Burstein, A. (1989). Post-traumatic stress disorder in victims of motor vehicle accidents. *Hospital and Community Psychiatry, 40,* 295–297.

Burstein, A., Ciccone, P. E., Greenstein, R. A., Daniels, N., Olsen, K., Mazarak, A., Decatur, R., & Johnson, N. (1988). Chronic Vietnam PTSD and acute civilian PTSD: A comparison of treatment experiences. *General Hospital Psychiatry, 10,* 245–249.

Cardena, E., & Spiegel, D. (1993). Dissociative reactions to the San Francisco Bay Area earthquake of 1989. *American Journal of Psychiatry, 150,* 474–478.

Cooper, N. A., & Clum, G. A. (1989). Imaginal flooding as a supplementary treatment of PTSD in combat veterans: A controlled study. *Behavior Therapy, 20,* 381–391.

Dalal, B., & Harrison, G. (1993). Psychiatric consequences of road traffic accidents. *British Medical Journal, 307,* 1282.

Derogatis, L. R. (1983). *SCL-90-R. Administration, scoring and procedures manual.* Towson, MD: Clinical Psychometric Research.

DiGiuseppe, R., Tafrate, R., & Eckhardt, C. (1994). Critical issues in the treatment of anger. *Cognitive and Behavioral Practice, 1,* 111–132.

Ehlers, A., Hofmann, S. G., Herda, C. A., & Roth, W. T. (1994). Clinical characteristics of driving phobia. *Journal of Anxiety Disorders, 8,* 323–339.

Ellis, A. (1962). *Reason and emotion in psychotherapy.* New York: Lyle Stuart.

Ellis, A. (1977). *How to live with and without anger.* New York: Readers' Digest Press.

Endicott, J., Spitzer, R. L., Fleiss, J. L., & Cohen, J. (1977). The Global Assessment Scale: A procedure for measuring overall severity of psychiatric disturbance. *Archives of General Psychiatry, 33,* 766–771.

Epstein, R. S. (1993). Avoidant symptoms cloaking the diagnosis of PTSD in patients with severe accidental injury. *Journal of Traumatic Stress, 6,* 451–458.

Fairbank, J. A., DeGood, D. E., & Jenkins, C. W. (1981). Behavioral treatment of a persistent post-traumatic startle response. *Journal of Behavior Therapy and Experimental Psychiatry, 12,* 321–324.

Fein, M. (1993). I.A.M. **A common sense guide to coping with anger* Integrated anger management.* Praeger: Westport, CT.

Feinstein, A., & Dolan, R. (1991). Predictors of post-traumatic stress disorder following physical trauma: An examination of the stressor criterion. *Psychological Medicine, 21,* 85–91.

Foa, E. B., & Kozak, N. J. (1986). Emotional processing of fear: Exposure to corrective information. *Psychological Bulletin, 99,* 20–35.

Foa, E. B., Rothbaum, B. O., Riggs, D. S., & Murdock, T. B. (1991). Treatment of post-traumatic stress disorder in rape victims: A comparison between cognitive–behavioral procedures and counseling. *Journal of Consulting and Clinical Psychology, 59,* 715–723.

Foa, E. B., Steketee, G., & Rothbaum, B. O. (1989). Behavioral/cognitive conceptualizations of post-traumatic stress disorder. *Behavior Therapy, 20,* 155–176.

Foeckler, M. M., Gerrard, F. H., Williams, C. C., Thomas, A. M., & Jones, T. J. (1978). Vehicle drivers and fatal accidents. *Suicide and Life-Threatening Behavior, 8,* 174–182.

Forneris, C. A., Blanchard, E. B., & Jonay, T. Y. (1996, March). Psychophysiological sequelae of sexual assault. *Proceedings of the 27th meeting of the Association for Applied Psychophysiology and Biofeedback* (pp. 38–39). Wheat Ridge, CO: Association for Applied Psychophysiology and Biofeedback.

Frederick, C. J. (1985). Selected foci in the spectrum of posttraumatic stress disorders. In J. Laube & S. A. Murphy (Eds.), *Perspectives on disaster recovery* (pp. 110–130). East Norwalk, CT: Appleton-Century-Crofts.

Gidron, Y., Peri, T., Connolly, J. F., & Shalev, A. Y. (1996). Written disclosure in post-traumatic stress disorder: Is it beneficial for the patient? *Journal of Nervous and Mental Disease, 184,* 505–507.

Gilliam, G., & Chesser, B. R. (1991). *Fatal moments: The tragedy of the accidental killer.* New York: Free Press.

Goldberg, D. P. (1972). The detection of psychiatric illness by questionnaire. *Institute of Psychiatry Maudsley Monographs* (No. 21). London: Oxford University Press.

Goldberg, L., & Gara, M. A. (1990). A typology of psychiatric reactions to motor vehicle accidents. *Psychopathology, 23,* 15–20.

Green, M. M., McFarlane, A. C., Hunter, C. E., & Griggs, W. M. (1993). Undiagnosed post-traumatic stress disorder following motor vehicle accidents. *The Medical Journal of Australia, 159,* 529–534.

Harber, K. D., & Pennebaker, J. W. (1992). Overcoming traumatic memories. In S. Christianson (Ed.), *The handbook of emotion and memory: Research and therapy* (pp. 359–387). Hillsdale, NJ: Erlbaum.

Harvey, A. G., & Bryant, R. A. (1996, August). *Incidence and diagnostic issues in acute stress disorder.* Paper presented at the 101st Annual Convention of the American Psychological Association, Toronto, Canada.

Helzer, J. E., Robins, L. N., & McEvoy, L. (1987). Post-traumatic stress disorder in the general population: Findings of the Epidemiologic Catchment Area Survey. *New England Journal of Medicine, 317,* 1630–1634.

Hickling, E. J., & Blanchard, E. B. (1992). Post-traumatic stress disorder and motor vehicle accidents. *Journal of Anxiety Disorders, 6,* 283–304.

Hickling, E. J., & Blanchard, E. B. (1997). The private practice psychologist and manual-based treatment: A case study in the treatment of post-traumatic stress disorder secondary to motor vehicle accidents. *Behavior Research and Therapy, 35,* 191–203.

Hickling, E. J., Blanchard, E. B., Schwarz, S. P., & Silverman, D. J. (1992). Headaches and motor vehicle accidents: Results of psychological treatment of post-traumatic headache. *Headache Quarterly, 3,* 285–289.

Hickling, E. J., Blanchard, E. B., Silverman, D. J., & Schwarz, S. P. (1992). Motor vehicle accidents, headaches, and post-traumatic stress disorder: Assessment findings in a consecutive series. *Headache, 32,* 147–151.

Hickling, E. J., Loos, W. R., Blanchard, E. B., & Taylor, A. E. (1997). Treatment of post-traumatic stress disorder (PTSD) after road accidents. In M. Mitchell (Ed.), *The aftermath of road accidents* (pp. 172–187). London: Routledge & Co.

Hickling, E. J., Sison, G. F. P., & Vanderploeg, K. D. (1986). The treatment of post-traumatic stress disorder with biofeedback and relaxation training. *Biofeedback and Self-Regulation, 11,* 125–134.

Hoffman, B. F. (1986). How to write a psychiatric report from litigation following a personal injury. *American Journal of Psychiatry, 143,* 164–169.

Holen, A. (1993). The North Sea oil rig disaster. In J. P. Wilson & B. Raphael (Eds.), *International handbook of traumatic stress syndromes.* New York: Plenum Press.

Horne, D. J. (1993). Traumatic stress reactions to motor vehicle accidents. In J. P. Wilson & B. Raphael (Eds.), *International handbook of traumatic stress syndromes* (pp. 499–506). New York: Plenum Press.

Horowitz, M. J., Wilmer, N., & Alvarez, N. (1979). Impact of Events Scale: A measure of subjective stress. *Psychosomatic Medicine, 41,* 209–218.

Horton, A. M. (1993). Post-traumatic stress disorder and mild head trauma: Follow-up of a case study. *Perceptual and Motor Skills, 76,* 243–246.

Jones, I. H., & Riley, W. T. (1987). A post-accident syndrome: Variations in the clinical picture. *Australian and New Zealand Journal of Psychiatry, 21,* 560–567.

Keane, T. M., Fairbank, J. A., Caddell, J. M., & Zimering, R. T. (1989). Implosive (flooding) therapy reduces symptoms of PTSD in Vietnam combat veterans. *Behavior Therapy, 20,* 245–260.

Keane, T. M., Malloy, P. F., & Fairbank, J. A. (1984). Empirical development of an MMPI subscale for the assessment of combat-related post-traumatic stress disorder. *Journal of Consulting and Clinical Psychology, 52,* 888–889.

Keane, T. M., Zimering, R. T., & Caddell, J. M. (1985). A behavioral formulation of post-traumatic stress disorder. *The Behavior Therapist, 8,* 9–12.

Keller, M. B., Lavori, P. W., Friedman, B., Nielsen, E., Endicott, J., McDonald-Scott, P., & Andreasen, N. C. (1987). A longitudinal interval follow-up evaluation: A comprehensive method for assessing outcome and prospective longitudinal studies. *Archives of General Psychiatry, 44,* 540–548.

Kelly, R., & Smith, B. (1981). Post-traumatic syndrome: Another myth discredited. *Journal of the Royal Society of Medicine, 74,* 275–277.

Kessler, R. C., McGonagle, K. A., Zhao, S., Nelson, C. B., Hughes, M., Eshleman, S., Wittchen, H-U., & Kendler, K. S. (1994). Lifetime and 12-month prevalence of *DSM–III–R* psychiatric disorders in the United States. *Archives of General Psychiatry, 51,* 8–19.

Kessler, R. C., Sonnega, A., Bromet, E., Hughes, M., & Nelson, C. B. (1995). Post-traumatic stress disorder in the national Comorbidity Survey. *Archives of General Psychiatry, 52,* 1048–1060.

Kilpatrick, D. G., Saunders, B. E., Amick-McMullan, A., Best, C. L., Veronen, L. J., & Resnick, H. S. (1989). Victim and crime factors associated with the development of crime-related post-traumatic stress disorder. *Behavior Therapy, 20,* 199–214.

Koch, W. J., & Taylor, S. (1995). Assessment and treatment of victims of motor vehicle accidents. *Cognitive and Behavioral Practice, 2,* 227–242.

Kolb, L. C., & Keane, T. (1988). *Physiology study of chronic post-traumatic stress disorder* (Cooperative Studies Program No. 334). Washington, DC: Veterans Administration.

Kraft, T., & Al-Issa, I. (1965). The application of learning theory to the treatment of traffic phobia. *British Journal of Psychiatry, 111,* 277–279.

Kuch, K. (1987). Treatment of PTSD following automobile accidents. *The Behavior Therapist, 10,* 224–242.

Kuch, K. (1989). Treatment of post-traumatic phobias and PTSD after car accidents. In P. A. Keller & S. R. Hayman (Eds.), *Innovations in clinical practice:*

A source book (Vol. 8, pp. 263–271). Sarasota, FL: Professional Resource Exchange.

Kuch, K., Cox, B. J., Evans, R. J., & Shulan, I. (1994). Phobias, panic and pain in 55 survivors of road accidents. *Journal of Anxiety Disorders, 8,* 181–187.

Kuch, K., Evans, R. J., Watson, P. C., Bubela, C., & Cox, B. J. (1991). Road vehicle accidents and phobias in 60 patients with fibromyalgia. *Journal of Anxiety Disorders, 5,* 273–280.

Kuch, K., Swinson, R. P., & Kirby, M. (1985). Post-traumatic stress disorder after car accidents. *Canadian Journal of Psychiatry, 30,* 426–427.

Kulka, R. A., Schlenger, W. E., Fairbank, J. A., Hough, R. L., Jordan, B. K., Marmar, C. R., & Weiss, D. S. (1988). *National Vietnam Veterans Readjustment Study Advanced Data Report:* Preliminary findings from the National Survey of the Vietnam Generation [Executive Summary]. Washington, DC: Veterans Administration.

Kulka, R., Schlenger, W., Fairbank, J., Hough, R., Jordan, B., Marmar, C., & Weiss, D. (1990). *Trauma in the Vietnam War generation.* New York: Brunner/Mazel.

Levine, B. A., & Wolpe, J. (1980). In vivo desensitization of a severe driving phobia through radio contact. *Journal of Behavior Therapy and Experiment Psychiatry, 11,* 281–282.

Lewinsohn, P. M., Biglan, A., & Zeiss, A. M. (1976). Behavioral treatment of depression. In P. O. Davidson (Ed.), *The behavioral management of anxiety, depression and pain.* New York: Brunner/Mazel.

Lewinsohn, P. M., & Libet, J. (1972). Pleasant Events Activity Schedule and depression. *Journal of Abnormal Psychology, 79,* 291–295.

Litz, B. T. (1992). Emotional numbing in combat-related post-traumatic stress disorder: A clinical review and reformulation. *Clinical Psychology Review, 12,* 417–432.

Lyons, J. A., & Scotti, J. R. (1995). Behavioral treatment of a motor vehicle accident survivor: An illustrative case of direct therapist exposure. *Cognitive and Behavioral Practice, 2,* 343–364.

Malatesta, V. J. (1995). Technological behavior therapy for obsessive compulsive disorder: The need for adequate case formulation. *The Behavior Therapist, 18,* 88–89.

Malloy, P. F., Fairbank, J. A., & Keane, T. M. (1983). Validation of a multimethod assessment of post-traumatic stress disorders in Vietnam veterans. *Journal of Consulting and Clinical Psychology, 51,* 488–494.

Malt, U. (1988). The long-term psychiatric consequences of accidental injury: A longitudinal study of 107 adults. *British Journal of Psychiatry, 153,* 810–818.

Malt, U. F., Blikra, G., & Hoivik, B. (1989). The three-year biopsychosocial outcome of 551 hospitalized accidentally injured adults. *Acta Psychiatrica Scandanavia, 80,* 84–93.

Malt, U. F., Hoivik, B., & Blikra, G. (1993). Psychosocial consequences of road accidents. *Eur Psychiatry, 8,* 227–228.

March, J. S. (1993). What constitutes a stressor? The "Criterion A" issue. In J. R. T. Davidson & E. B. Foa (Eds.), *Post-traumatic stress disorder: DSM–IV and beyond* (pp. 37–54). Washington, DC: American Psychiatric Press.

Marmar, C. R., Weiss, D S., Schlenger, W. E., Fairbank, J. A., Jordan, B. K., Kulka, R. A., & Hough, R. L. (1994). Peritraumatic dissociation and posttraumatic stress in male Vietnam theater veterans. *American Journal of Psychiatry, 151,* 902–907.

Mayou, R. (1995). Medico-legal aspects of road traffic accidents. Journal of *Psychosomatic Research, 39,* 789–798.

Mayou, R. (in press). Psychological quality of life and legal consequences of road traffic accident injury. *Medicine, Science and the Law.*

Mayou, R. A., & Bryant, B. M. (1994). Effects of road traffic accidents on travel. *International Journal of the Care of the Injured, 25,* 457–460.

Mayou, R., Bryant, B., & Duthie, R. (1993). Psychiatric consequences of road traffic accidents. *British Medical Journal, 307,* 647–651.

McCaffrey, R. J., & Fairbank, J. A. (1985). Behavioral assessment and treatment of accident-related post-traumatic stress disorder: Two case studies. *Behavior Therapy, 16,* 406–416.

McFarlane, A. C. (1988). The longitudinal course of posttraumatic morbidity: The range of outcomes and their predictors. *The Journal of Nervous and Mental Disease, 176,* 30–39.

McMillan, T. M. (1991). Post-traumatic stress disorder and severe head injury. *British Journal of Psychiatry, 159,* 431–433.

Meichenbaum, D. (1974). *Cognitive behavior modification.* Morristown, NJ: General Learning Press.

Meichenbaum, D. (1977). *Cognitive behavior modification: An integrative approach.* New York: Plenum Press.

Meichenbaum, D. (1985). *Stress inoculation training.* New York: Pergamon Press.

Meichenbaum, D. (1994). *A clinical handbook/practical therapist manual: For assessing and treating adults with post-traumatic stress disorder (PTSD).* Waterloo, Ontario, Canada: Institute Press.

Mendelson, G. (1981). Persistent work disability following settlement of compensation claims. *Law Institute Journal, 55,* 342–345.

Middleboe, T., Anderson, H. S., Birket-Smith, M., & Friis, M. L. (1992). Minor head injury: Impact on general health after 1 year. A prospective follow-up study. *Acta Neurologica Scandinavia, 85,* 5–9.

Miller, H. (1961). Accident neurosis. *British Medical Journal, 1,* 919–925, 992–998.

Modlin, H. C. (1967). The post-accident anxiety syndrome: Psychosocial aspects. *American Journal of Psychiatry, 123,* 1008–1012.

Mowrer, O. H. (1947). On the dual nature of learning: The reinterpretation of "conditioning" and "problem solving." *Harvard Educational Review, 17,* 102–148.

Munjack, D. J. (1984). The onset of driving phobias. *Behavior Therapy and Experimental Psychiatry, 15,* 305–308.

Muse, M. (1986). Stress-related post-traumatic chronic pain syndrome: Behavioral approach to treatment. *Pain, 25,* 389–394.

Napier, M. (1991). The medical and legal trauma of disasters. *Medico-Legal Journal, 59,* 157–179.

Nigl, A. (1984). *Biofeedback and behavioral strategies in pain treatment.* New York: SP Medical and Scientific Books.

Norris, F. H. (1992). Epidemiology of trauma: Frequency and impact of different potentially traumatic events on different demographic groups. *Journal of Consulting and Clinical Psychology, 60,* 409–418.

Novaco, R. W. (1975). *Anger control.* Lexington, MA: Lexington.

Ochberg, F. M. (1991). Post-traumatic therapy. *Psychotherapy, 28,* 5–15.

Parker, N. (1977). Accident litigants with neurotic symptoms. *Medical Journal of Australia, 2,* 318–322.

Peniston, E. G. (1986). EMG biofeedback-assisted desensitization treatment for Vietnam combat veterans' post-traumatic stress disorder. *Clinical Biofeedback and Health, 9,* 35–41.

Pitman, R. K., Altman, B., Greenwald, E., Longpre, R. E., Macklin M. L., Poire, R. E., & Steketee, G. (1991). Psychiatric complications during flooding therapy for post-traumatic stress disorder. *Journal of Clinical Psychiatry, 52,* 17–20.

Pitman, R. K., Orr, S. P., Forgue, D. F., deJong, J. B., & Claiborn, J. M. (1987). Psychophysiologic assessment of post-traumatic stress disorder imagery in Vietnam combat veterans. *Archives of General Psychiatry, 44,* 970–975.

Pitman, R. K., Sparr, L. F., Saunders, L. S., & McFarlane, A. C. (1996). In van der Kolk, B. A., McFarlane, A. C., & Weisaeth, L. (Eds.), *Traumatic stress: The effects of overwhelming experience on mind, body, and society* (pp. 378–397). New York: Guilford Press.

Platt, J. J., & Husband, S. D. (1986). Posttraumatic stress disorder and the motor vehicle accident victim. *American Journal of Forensic Psychology, 5,* 39–42.

Polter-Efron, R., & Polter-Efron, P. (1995). Letting go of anger: The 10 most common anger styles and what to do about them. Oakland, CA: New Horbinger Publications.

Quirk, D. A. (1985). Motor vehicle accidents and post-traumatic anxiety conditioning. *The Ontario Psychologist, 17,* 11–18.

Regier, D. A., Myers, J. K., Kramer, M., Robins, L. N., Blazer, D. G., Hough, R. L., Eaton, W. W., & Locke, B. Z. (1984). The NIMH Epidemiologic Catchment Area Program. *Archives of General Psychiatry, 41,* 934–941.

Robins, L. N., Helzer, J. E., Croughan, J., & Ratcliff, K. (1981). National Institutes of Mental Health Diagnostic Interview Schedule: Its history, characteristics, and validity. *Archives of General Psychiatry, 38,* 381–389.

Robins, L. N., Helzer, J. E., Croughan, J. L., Williams, J. B. W., & Spitzer, R. I. (1981). NIMH Diagnostic Interview Schedule, Version 3 (Publication No. ADM-T-42-3). Rockville, MD: NIMH, Public Health Service.

Rothbaum, B. O., & Foa, E. B. (1993). Subtypes of post-traumatic stress disorder and duration of symptoms. In J. R. T. Davidson & E. B. Foa (Eds.), *Posttraumatic stress disorder: DSM–IV and beyond* (pp. 23–35). Washington, DC: American Psychiatric Press.

Rothbaum, B. O., Foa, E. B., Riggs, D. S., Murdock, T., & Walsh, W. (1992). A prospective examination of post-traumatic stress disorder in rape victims. *Journal of Traumatic Stress, 5,* 455–475.

Rovetto, F. M. (1983). In vivo desensitization of a severe driving phobia through radio contact with telemonitoring of neurophysiological reactors. *Journal of Behavior Therapy and Experimental Psychiatry, 14,* 49–54.

Scotti, J. R., Wilhelm, K. L., Northrop, L. M. E., Price, G., Vittimberga, G. L., Ridley, J., Cornell, K., Stukey, G. C., Beach, B. K., Mickey, G. H., & Forsyth, J. P. (1992, November). *An investigation of post-traumatic stress disorder in vehicular accident survivors.* Paper presented at the 26th Annual Meeting of the Association for Advancement of Behavior Therapy, Boston, MA.

Shalev, A. Y., Orr, S. P., & Pitman, R. K. (1993). Psychophysiologic assessment of traumatic imagery in Israeli civilian patients with post-traumatic stress disorder. *American Journal of Psychiatry, 150,* 620–624.

Solomon, S. D., Gerrity, E. T., & Muff, A. M. (1992). Efficacy of treatment for post-traumatic stress disorder. *Journal of the American Medical Association, 268,* 633–638.

Spiegel, D., & Cardena, E. (1991). Disintegrated experience: The dissociative disorders revisited. *Journal of Abnormal Psychology, 100,* 366–378.

Spielberger, C. D., Gorsuch, R. L., & Lushene, R. E. (1970). *STAI manual for the State–Trait Anxiety Inventory.* Palo Alto, CA: Consulting Psychologists Press.

Spitzer, R. L., Williams, J. B. W., Gibbon, M., & First, M. B. (1990). *Structured Clinical Interview for DSM–III–R, non-patient edition* (SCID-NP; Version 1.0). Washington, DC: American Psychiatric Press.

Tarsh, M. J., & Royston, C. (1985). A follow-up study of accident neuroses. *British Journal of Psychiatry, 146,* 18–25.

Taylor, S., & Koch, W. T. (1995). Anxiety disorders due to motor vehicle accidents: Nature and treatment. *Clinical Psychology Review, 15,* 721–738.

Thompson, G. N. (1965). Post-traumatic psychoneurosis: A statistical survey. *The American Journal of Psychiatry, 121,* 1043–1048.

Traffic Safety Facts 1994: A Compilation of Motor Vehicle Crash Data From the Fatal Accident Reporting System and General Estimates Systems. (1995, August). National Highway Traffic Safety Administration, U.S. Department of Transportation.

Van der Kolk, B. A., McFarlane, A. C., & Hart, O. V. (1996). A general approach to treatment of post-traumatic stress disorder. In B. Van der Kolk, A. C. McFarlane, & L. Weisaeth (Eds.), *Traumatic stress: The effects of overwhelming experience on mind, body, and society.* New York: Guilford Press.

Veronen, L. J., & Kilpatrick, D. G. (1983). Stress management for rape victims. In D. Meichenbaum & M. E. Jaremko (Eds.), *Stress reduction and prevention* (pp. 341–374). New York: Plenum Press.

Walen, S. R., DiGiuseppe, R., & Wessler, R. L. (1980). A practitioner's guide to rational–emotive therapy. Oxford, England: Oxford University Press.

Watson, C. G., Juba, M. P., Manifold, V., Kucala, T., & Anderson, P. (1991). The PTSD interview: Rationale, description, reliability, and concurrent validity of a *DSM–III–R* based technique. *Journal of Clinical Psychology, 47,* 179–188.

Weathers, F. W., Blake, D. D., Krinsley, K. E., Haddad, W., Huska, J. A., & Keane, T. M. (1992, November). *The Clinician-Administered PTSD Scale: Reliability and construct validity.* Paper presented at the 26th annual meeting of the Association for the Advancement of Behavior Therapy, Boston, MA.

Weathers, F. W., & Litz, B. T. (1994). Psychometric properties of the Clinician-Administered PTSD Scale, CAPS-I. *PTSD Research Quarterly, 5,* 2–6.

Weathers, F. W., Litz, B. T., Herman, D. S., Huska, J. A., & Keane, T. M. (1993, October). *The PTSD Checklist: Reliability, validity and diagnostic utility.* Paper presented at the annual meeting of the International Society for Traumatic Stress Studies, San Antonio, TX.

Weathers, F., Litz, B., Huska, J. A., & Keane, T. M. (1994). *PCL-C for DSM–IV* (PTSD Checklist). Available from the National Center for PTSD, Behavioral Science Division, Boston VAMC, Boston, MA.

Weighill, V. E. (1983). Compensation neurosis: A review of the literature. *Journal of Psychosomatic Research, 27,* 97–104.

Wing, J. K., Cooper, J. E., & Sartorious, N. (1974). *Measurement and classification of psychiatric symptoms.* Cambridge, England: Cambridge University Press.

Wolpe, J. (1962). Isolation of a conditioning procedure as the crucial psychotherapeutic factor: A case study. *Journal of Nervous and Mental Disease, 134,* 316–329.

Wolpe, J. (1973). *The practice of behavior therapy* (2nd ed.). New York: Pergamon Press.

Motor Vehicle Accident Interview

Name _____

Subject No. _____

Date _____

I will now be asking you a number of different questions related to the accident.

1. Can you tell me the date of the accident? _____

2. Were you the driver or a passenger in the car? (1 = driver) (2 = passenger) (3 = pedestrian)

3. Can you describe for me what happened? _____

   _____

   _____

4. ‾‾‾ one vehicle ‾‾‾ number of vehicles
   ‾‾‾ pedestrians

5. Did you suffer any physical injuries from the accident? (1 = yes, 2 = no)

6. If yes, please describe _____

   _____

   _____

7. Were other people injured in the accident? (1 = yes, 2 = no) _____

8. If yes, please describe _____

_____

_____

9. Was anyone killed or seriously injured? (1 = yes, 2 = no). If yes, describe _____

_____

10. Did you miss any work/school because of the accident? (1 = yes, 2 = no)

11. If yes, (a) how much? _____ (days/weeks).

(b) Are you still out of work/school? (1 = yes, 2 = no)

12. Was there much damage to your vehicle? (1 = yes, 2 = no) _____ dollars or total loss.

13. If there was another vehicle, how much damage did it sustain? _____ dollars or total loss.

14. When did you first see a physician about your accident? Date _____ /_____
       Mo.   Yr.

15. What doctors have you seen? (List specialty) _____

_____

_____

16. Were you hospitalized? (1 = yes, 2 = no) If yes, for what and for how long? _____

Number of days _____

17. What have your physical symptoms been like since the accident occurred? _____

_____

_____

18. Are you continuing to have any pain or discomfort from the accident? _____

Describe _____

19. Are you taking any medication for the pain? (1 = yes, 2 = no)

20. What medicines have you been placed on? _____

_____

_____

21. Did you suffer any blow to your head? (1 = yes, 2 = no)

22. Did you suffer any loss of consciousness during the accident? (1 = yes, 2 = no) How long? _____

23. Have you noticed any drop in concentration? (1 = yes, 2 = no) How bad? (0 = not at all, 10 = totally unable to concentrate).

24. Do you have headaches as a result of/or since the accident? _____ If yes, give Headache Questionnaire after interview.

25. What is your estimate of present functioning? (0= not functioning, 100 = pre-accident functioning) _____

26. What do you think is your probability of returning to your pre-accident functioning?
(0%–100%) _____

27. Are you driving at the present time? (1 = yes, 2 = no) If no, why not? _____

_____

28. If you are, how has your driving/riding been affected by the accident? _____

29. In reference to your present travel, answer yes or no:
Restricted to local driving _____ , Avoidance of certain roads _____ , Avoid highway driving _____ , Avoid accident area only _____ , Reluctant to ride in a car _____ , Restrict speed _____ , Avoid pleasure trips, drive to work only _____ , Not drive at all _____ , Other (describe)

NOTE

At this point, switch to CAPS Interview, Form 1, Current and Lifetime.

Introduce by saying, "Now I want to ask you a series of questions about your ACCIDENT and your reactions to it, especially over the past month."

Continue With These MVA-Related Questions After the CAPS

During, or immediately after the accident, were you fearful or afraid? YES   NO

How fearful or afraid were you? (Rate: 0 = none, 100 = intensely afraid or terrified)

   Rating: _____

Did you have any feelings of helplessness during or immediately after the accident?

   YES   NO

How helpless did you feel? (Rate: 0 = no helplessness, 100 = extreme helplessness)

   Rating: _____

30. During the accident, how much danger did you feel that you were in?
   (Rate: 0 = none, 100 = extreme, life threatening)_____

31. Did you feel as if you might die? (Rate: 0 = no, 100 = certain I would die) _____

32. Have you ever had such feelings in the past? (1 = yes, 2 = no) If yes, describe _____

   _____

   _____

33. Have you ever had any auto accidents in the past? (1 = yes, 2 = no) _____

34. If yes, please describe, giving dates, severity, and circumstances. _____

_____

_____

35. How vulnerable do you feel now when you drive or are a passenger in a car?
(Rate: 0 = none, 100 = extremely) _____

36. How much control did you feel during the accident? (0 = none, 100 = complete) _____

37. If it was a two-car accident, how culpable do you feel the other driver was?
(Rate: 0 = none, 100 = totally) _____

38. Did you feel responsible for the accident? If yes, rate:
(0 = not at all, 100 = completely) _____

_____

39. Were there drugs or alcohol associated with the accident?
(1 = yes, 2 = no) If yes, list: _____

_____

_____

40. Had you been drinking or using any drug(s) prior to the accident? (1 = yes, 2 = no) If yes, were you at all impaired in performance by alcohol or drugs? _____

41. If others were involved, were any of the others drinking or using drugs? (1 = yes, 2 = no)

42. Were any traffic tickets issued? 1 = Yes, 2 = No. If yes, to whom _____

_____

43. Aside from accident related issues, are there any stressors effecting your life? (1 = yes, 2 = no)

Describe _____

_____

_____

44. Is there any litigation expected or under way as a result of
this car accident?

_____

_____

45. If yes, please describe _____

_____

_____

_____

46. Lawyers' names and addresses: _____

_____

_____

_____

_____

Now that we have talked about the accident in a variety of ways,
are there any last minute memories, or memories that seem more
vivid, such as things you saw, heard, felt, or smelled?

_____

_____

_____

_____

_____

_____

Go next to psychosocial data base

Previous Medical History

Have you had any previous serious illnesses?

(Describe) _____

_____

_____

_____

_____

_____

How would you rate your health before the accident? (Rate: 100 = "super healthy," 0 = chronic, interfering health problems)

_____

How do you rate your health since the accident? (Rate: 100 = "super healthy," 0 = chronic, interfering problems)

_____

How have you coped with earlier illnesses/injuries (if applicable)?_____

_____

_____

_____

Any previous psychiatric history? _____

_____

_____

Any family history of panic or anxiety? _____

Any family history of note, either medical or other pain and accident related histories? _____

_____

_____

Motor Vehicle Accident Follow-Up Interview

Subject's ID#: __ __ - __ __ __ __   Subject's Initials: __ __

Date of Intake: __ __ / __ __ / __ __   Rater: _____

Date of Follow-up: __ / __ / __   Status at time of
evaluation:

Follow-up Period: (Circle one)   0–Unknown N/A
   6 mo.   1–Not in treatment
  12 mo.   2–Outpatient
  18 mo.   3–Day treatment
  24 mo.   4–Inpatient
  30 mo.

If out of range, how long? (Circle one)
1–Not out of range   4–2 mo.
2–Less than 1 mo.   5–3 mo.
3–1 mo.   6–4 mo. or more

Reason for gap (Check any that apply):
____ No gap   ____ Could not schedule
____ Could not contact   ____ Other
____ Patient refused   _____

(Check all that apply):   Sources of information
____ Face to face with subject   ____ Hospital/clinic
     records

____ With relative/friend   ____ Mail questionnaire
____ Phone with subject   ____ Research
     notes/records

____ Letter from subject   ____ Other _____

____ Check if subject died   Date of death __ / __ / __

Longitudinal Course

This interview is designed to cover the subject's psychiatric course during the last 26 weeks. Recovery from previous episodes/conditions and/or the development of new episodes/conditions and their course are also to be determined. This information is to be recorded on the Longitudinal Picture of Psychiatric Status. The scales for these ratings are given in Appendixes A–M.

PRIOR TO CONDUCTING THE INTERVIEW THE INTERVIEWER SHOULD REVIEW PREVIOUS FOLLOW-UPS GIVING SPECIAL ATTENTION TO THE MOST RECENT ONE.

It may be helpful to fill in various items related to the subject's status at the time of the previous interview <u>on the pages of this form</u> (such as the kind of physical injuries, name of lawyers, etc.). In particular, <u>note on your interview forms</u> which PTSD symptoms were positive at the last interview, as well as which other psychiatric diagnoses were positive.

It will be of great benefit if you fill in the ratings for all PTSD symptoms and all psychiatric disorders for the first week of the follow-up with the values you obtained at your last interview.

On conducting the interview the interviewer may use clinical judgment as to the best way to elicit information regarding course. The following guidelines are offered to assist in this process.

Guidelines

1. Begin the interview by obtaining an overview of what has happened to the subject since the time of the last interview. This overview serves as a time to both reacquaint (or acquaint) the subject and interviewer while providing information on whether the subject has recovered, relapsed, and/or developed new conditions.

2. The interviewer should then return to questions about the subject's condition 26 weeks previously. For example, the interviewer might begin by saying;

> The last time we spoke together you were (descriptions of subject's condition at that time, e.g., "You were feeling very depressed and had trouble sleeping," "You were feeling well,"). HOW HAVE THINGS BEEN SINCE THEN?
>
> When did you begin to feel better? Worse?

3. The interviewer is to then trace the Psychiatric Status Ratings (PSR) for these episodes/conditions forward to the present, probing until the best level of recovery is determined. Although these ratings are made on a week-by-week basis, the subject does not have to be asked about how he or she was feeling during each week. Instead, *change points* that correspond to PSR ratings should be determined and the interviewer should make the weekly ratings on the basis of these *change points*. To help the subject date these *change points*, the interviewer should ask such questions as "Was that in November?" "Did that happen before or after Christmas?" and so forth.

4. If the occurrence of a new episode/condition is established, the interviewer should return to the probes to determine the development of other episodes of the same or different type.

Accident Related Issues

> When we last spoke it was about 1 month (or whatever is the appropriate interval) since your accident.

Physical Injury
(If previous physical injury)

> At that time you were recovering from (Fill in injuries)

1. _____

2. _____

3. _____ 4. _____

How has that been? Would you say you have fully recovered from?

1. _____ ? (yes, no) _____

(If "yes''') At what point would you say you had fully recovered? _____

_____

(Use LIFE methodology to try to pinpoint week of recovery and note on Rating Sheet 1)

(If "no") Have you improved at all? (yes, no) What are your problems with (1) now?

_____

_____

At what point did you notice improvement? _____

_____

(Use LIFE methodology to try to pinpoint time of noticeable improvement and note on Rating Sheet #1)

Now, would you say you have fully recovered from (2) _____

_____ ? (yes, no)

If "yes" at what point would you say you had fully recovered? _____

Use LIFE methodology to try to pinpoint week of recovery and note on Rating Sheet 1
(If "no")

Have you improved at all? (yes, no) What are your problems with (2) now?

_____

_____

At what point did you notice improvement? _____

'(Use LIFE methodology to try to pinpoint time of noticeable improvement and note on Rating Sheet 1)

3. _____ (yes, no)

Fully recovered _____

Noticeable improvement _____

4. _____ (yes, no)

Fully recovered _____

Noticeable improvement _____
(If no previous physical injury noted at initial interview)

Did you have any delayed physical consequences of accident?

_____

Obtain details and date physical symptoms began, current status, and when they ended.

Legal Issues

Were any traffic citations or arrests made as a result of the accident?   (yes, no)

Details _____

_____

_____

Has any legal action occurred over the accident? (yes, no)
Details _____

_____

_____

When did this first occur? _____

_____

(Use LIFE methodology to try to pinpoint time of first legal action related to MVA)

(If subject had seen a lawyer by first interview)

When we last spoke, you mentioned that you had contacted (name of lawyer)

_____

Are you filing any kind of civil suit related to the accident? (yes, no, maybe)

What is the status? _____

(Try to get date suit was filed and any other chronology)

Has someone else filed a civil suit against you as a result of the accident? (yes, no)

When did you first learn of it? _____

(Use LIFE methodology to pinpoint date)

What is its status? _____

Insurance Issues

Have you had any dealings with your insurance company over the accident? (yes, no) Details _____

Has there been any difficulty? (yes, no) _____

Details and chronology _____

Driving Status

Now when we last spoke, you told me (*Driving status—particularly impairment or discomfort*)

_____

_____

Are you driving now? (yes, no)

(If this is a *change* from last interview obtain details) _____

_____

When did the change occur?_____

(Use LIFE methodology to pinpoint time of change)

If subject was "driving reluctant" or "driving phobic" obtain details of current status, pinpoint when subject returned to

(a) driving to work _____

(b) driving alone _____

(c) driving for pleasure _____

(e) traveling on road where accident occurred _____

(f) or traveling at time of day of accident _____

Were any of these endured with moderate to severe discomfort?

_____

(Use LIFE methodology to pinpoint changes in driving status)

_____

_____

Have you had any additional accidents since we last talked? (yes, no)

(If "yes") Details, date, new symptoms

_____

Has anyone in your immediate family been involved in an accident since we last spoke? (yes, no)

(If "yes"") Details, date _____

Have you been involved in any other traumatic events since we last spoke?

(yes, no) Details, dates (Use LIFE methodology) _____

Has anyone in your family been involved in a traumatic event? (yes, no)

Details, dates: _____

Accident Related Follow-Up #1

Code	1	2	3	4	5	6	7	8	9	10	11	12	13	14	15	16	17	18	19	20	21	22	23	24	25	26
Physical injury																										
1.																										
2.																										
3.																										
4.																										
5.																										
New physical problems																										
1.																										
2.																										
3.																										
Legal issues*																										
First legal action*																										
Initiated suit*																										
Learning of being sued*																										

(continued)

331

Accident Related Follow-Up #1 (*continued*)

Code	1	2	3	4	5	6	7	8	9	10	11	12	13	14	15	16	17	18	19	20	21	22	23	24	25	26
Driving status																										
Driving to work																										
Driving for shopping																										
Driving for pleasure																										
Riding for shopping																										
Riding for pleasure																										
Traveling same road																										
Travel same time																										
New MVA*																										
Family MVA*																										
New trauma*																										
Family trauma*																										

Note: For Week 1, use ratings from previous interview for physical injury and driving status.

Physical injury

3 Noticeable impact on ADL from injury
2 Symptoms still present, but improved
1 Symptoms are barely noticeable
0 Symptom is absent

Driving status

3 Does not *perform* activity
2 Performs activity with noticeable difficulty
1 Performs activity with slight difficulty
0 No effect of MVA on activity

*Mark the week in which this occurred with an asterisk.

333

PTSD Symptoms Follow-Up

Code	1	2	3	4	5	6	7	8	9	10	11	12	13	14	15	16	17	18	19	20	21	22	23	24	25	26
1) Intrusive, recurrent recollections																										
2) Distress with symbolic exposure																										
3) Flashback, dissociate symptoms																										
4) Recurrent, distressing dreams																										
5) Avoid thoughts, feelings associated with MVA																										
6) Avoid activities remindful of MVA																										
7) Inability to recall aspects of MVA																										
8) Diminished interest in activities																										

Code	1	2	3	4	5	6	7	8	9	10	11	12	13	14	15	16	17	18	19	20	21	22	23	24	25	26
9) Detachment/ estrangement																										
10) Restricted range of affect																										
11) Foreshortened future																										
12) Difficulty with sleep																										
13) Irritability, anger																										
14) Difficulty concentrating																										
15) Hypervigilance																										
16) Exag. startle																										
17) Physical reactivity to symbolic event																										

Note: For Week, 1 use rating from previous CAPS. Fill in dates before the follow-up interview.

Rating scale:

0 = Symptom was absent at last interview
1 = Symptom was previously present but is now absent
2 = Symptom abated but still present at clinical level
3 = Symptom present at clinical level–no abatement
4 = Symptom has become *worse* since last interview

Home Practice Relaxation Tape

This is the tape to assist you with your home practice of relaxation. You will be going through the same exercises we practiced in the clinic. You should be comfortably seated in a recliner or upholstered chair or laying on a bed. Be sure to remove your glasses if you wear them. Also, loosen any tight or restrictive clothing that you have on.

Now, begin to let yourself relax. Close your eyes, and we will go through the relaxation exercises.

I want you to begin by tensing the muscles in your right lower arm and right hand. Study the tensions in the back of your hand and your right lower arm. Study those tensions and now relax the muscles. Study the difference between the tension and the relaxation. Just let yourself become more and more relaxed. You feel yourself becoming drowsy, that will be fine too. If you think of relaxation and of letting go of your muscles they will become more loose and heavy and relaxed. Just let your muscles go as you become more and more deeply relaxed.

Next, I want you to tense the muscles in your left hand and left lower arm. Tense those muscles and study the tensions in the back of your left hand and in your left lower arm. Study those tensions and now relax the muscles. Study the difference between the tension and the relaxation.

This time I want you to tense both hands and both lower arms by making fists, tensing the muscles in both hands and both lower arms. Study those tensions and now relax them. Study the difference between the tension and the relaxation. You are becoming more and more relaxed. Drowsy and relaxed. As you become more relaxed you feel yourself settling deep into the chair. All your muscles are becoming more and more comfortably relaxed. Loose and heavy and relaxed.

This time I want you to tense the muscles in your upper arm by bringing your right hand up toward your shoulder and tensing the biceps muscle. Study the tensions there in your right upper arm, study those tensions and now relax your arm. Study the difference between the tension and the relaxation.

This time I want you to tense the muscles in your left upper arm by bringing your left hand up to your shoulder, tensing the muscle in your left biceps area. Study those tensions in your left biceps; study those tensions and now relax the arm. Study the difference between the tension and the relaxation. The relaxation in going deeper and still deeper. You are relaxed, drowsy, and relaxed. Your breathing is regular and relaxed. With each breath you take in, your relaxation increases. Each time you exhale, you spread the relaxation throughout your body.

This time I want you to tense both upper arms together by bringing both hands up to your shoulders, tense the muscles in both upper arms, both biceps areas. Study those tensions and now relax the muscles. Study the difference between the tension and the relaxation. Just continue to let your muscles relax.

Next, I want you to tense the muscles in your right lower leg. Tense the muscles in your right lower leg, particularly in your calf and study the tensions there in your right lower leg. Study those tensions and now relax the muscles. Study the difference between the tension and the relaxation. Note the pleasant feelings of warmth and heaviness that are coming into your body as your muscles relax completely. You will always be clearly aware of what you are doing and what I am saying as you become more deeply relaxed.

Next, I want you to tense the muscles in your left lower leg, in the left calf area. Study the tensions in your left lower leg. Study those tensions, now relax the muscles. Study the difference between the tension and the relaxation. Just continue to let your leg relax.

Now, this time I want you to tense both lower legs together. Tense the muscles in both lower legs, both calf muscles. Study those tensions and now relax your legs. Study the difference between the tension and the relaxation. Just continue to let those muscles relax. Let them relax.

Now, the very deep state of relaxation is moving through all the areas of your body. You are becoming more and more comfortably relaxed, drowsy and relaxed. You can feel the comfortable sensations of relaxation as you go into a deeper and deeper state of relaxation.

Next, I want you to tense the muscles in your thighs by pressing your legs together from the knees upward. Press your upper legs against each other and study the tensions throughout your thighs. Study those tensions; now relax the muscles. Study the difference between the tension and the relaxation. Just let those muscles continue to relax.

This time I want you to tense the muscles in the abdominal area by drawing your abdominal muscles in tightly. Draw them in tightly and study the tensions across the entire abdominal region. Study those tensions and now relax the muscles. Just let them relax and study the difference between the tension and the relaxation. Just let yourself become more and more relaxed. As you think of relaxation, you are letting go of your muscles; they will become more loose and heavy and relaxed. Just let your muscles go as you become more and more deeply relaxed.

This time I want you to tense the muscles in your chest by taking a deep breath and holding it. Hold it; hold it and now relax. Study the difference between the tension and the relaxation. The relaxation is growing deeper and still deeper. You are relaxed; your breathing is regular and relaxed. With each breath you take in, your relaxation increases. Each time you exhale you spread the relaxation throughout your body.

Next, I want you to tense the muscles in your shoulders and upper back by hunching your shoulders and drawing your shoulders upward toward your ears. Study those tensions across your upper back; study those tensions and now relax your muscles. Study the difference between the tension and the relaxation. Note the pleasant feelings of warmth and heaviness that are coming into your body as your muscles relax completely. You will always be clearly aware of what you are doing and what I am saying as you become more deeply relaxed.

Next, I want you to tense the muscles in the back of your neck by pressing your head backward against the rest or against the bed. Study the tensions in the back of your neck, across your shoulders, and the base of your scalp. Study those tensions, and now relax the muscles. Study the difference between the tension and the relaxation.

Next, I want you to tense the muscles in the region around your mouth by pressing your lips together tightly. Press your lips together tightly without biting down and study the tensions in the region around your mouth. Study those tensions and now relax the muscles. Study the difference between the tension and the relaxation. You are becoming more and more relaxed, drowsy and relaxed. As you become more relaxed, feel yourself settling deep into the chair. All your muscles are becoming more and more comfortably relaxed, loose and heavy and relaxed.

This time I want you to tense the muscles in the region around your eyes by closing your eyes tightly. Just close your eyes tightly and study the tensions all around your eyes and upper face. Study those tensions, and now relax the muscles. Just continue to let them relax, and study the difference between the tension and the relaxation. The very deep state of relaxation is moving through all of the areas of your body. You are becoming more and more comfortably relaxed, drowsy and relaxed. You can feel the comfortable sensations of relaxation as you go into a deeper and deeper state of relaxation.

This time I want you to tense the muscles in your lower forehead by frowning and lowering your eyebrows downward. Study the tensions there in your lower forehead and the region between your eyes. Study those tensions and now relax the muscles. Study the difference between the tension and the relaxation.

This time I want you to tense the muscles in your upper forehead by raising your eyebrows upward and wrinkling your forehead. Raise them up and wrinkle your forehead. Study the tension in the upper part of your forehead. Study those tensions; now relax the muscles. Study the difference between the tension and the relaxation.

Now, I want you to relax all the muscles of your body. Just let them become more and more relaxed. I am going to help you to achieve a deeper state of relaxation by counting from 1 to 5, and as I count you feel yourself becoming more and more deeply relaxed, further and further down into a deep restful state of deep relaxation. 1. You are going to become more deeply relaxed. 2. Down, down into a very relaxed state. 3. . . . 4. More and more relaxed. 5. Deeply relaxed.

Now, I want you to remain in your very relaxed state. I want you to begin to attend just to your breathing. Breath through your nose. Notice the cool air as you breath in and the warm moist air as you exhale. Just continue to attend to your breathing. Each time you exhale mentally repeat the word *relax.* Inhale . . . exhale . . . relax.

Now, I am going to help you to return to your normal state of alertfulness. In a little while I shall begin counting backward from 5 to 1. You will gradually become alert. When I reach 2, I want you to open your eyes. When I get to 1, you will be entirely aroused and in your normal state of alertfulness.

Ready? 5, 4 . . . You are becoming more and more alert; you feel very refreshed. 3, 2 . . . Now, your eyes are open and you are beginning to feel very alert, returning to your normal state of alertfulness . . . 1

This is the end of your relaxation tape.

Index

About the Authors

EDWARD B. BLANCHARD, PhD, received his doctoral degree in clinical psychology from Stanford University in 1969. After holding faculty positions at the University of Georgia, the University Mississippi Medical Center, and the University of Tennessee Center for Health Sciences, Dr. Blanchard went to the University at Albany, State University of New York, in 1977 and has remained there ever since. In 1990, Dr. Blanchard was named Distinguished Professor of Psychology by the American Psychological Association. He is currently director of the Center for Stress and Anxiety Disorders at the University at Albany.

Dr. Blanchard began work on PTSD in collaboration with Larry Kolb, MD, at the Albany Veteran's Administration in 1981, focusing primarily on assessment research with Vietnam veterans. In 1990, he began collaborative research on motor vehicle accident survivors with Edward J. Hickling, PsyD. The present volume is the product of that research collaboration, which was sponsored by a grant from the National Institute of Mental Health (NIMH).

EDWARD J. HICKLING, PsyD, received his doctor of psychology degree in clinical psychology from the University of Denver's School of Professional Psychology in 1982. Dr. Hickling was director of training and a consultation liaison psychologist at the Veteran's Administration Medical Center in Albany, NY, until 1987 when he left to enter full-time private practice. In addition to his practice in clinical psychology, Dr. Hickling is an assistant professor in the Department of Health and Rehabilitation Sciences at Russell Sage College in Troy, NY, and is part of the clinical faculty for the Department of Psychiatry at Albany Medical College.

Dr. Hickling's earlier research on PTSD included the assessment and treatment of Vietnam veterans. He has collaborated with Dr. Blanchard on psychological assessment and treatment of motor vehicle accident survivors since 1990, serving as co-principal investigator on the NIMH-sponsored research that resulted in the major portion of this volume.